The Complete Guide to
Selling Your Business
For the Most Money
(Without letting anyone know it's for sale)

**Based upon experience gained in
selling more than two thousand private businesses**

A three step program of instruction and software designed especially for
Independent Business Owners, their
Advisors and Business Brokers

Step One (READY) — *Identify best buyer and optimum value, ratify timeliness of selling*

Step Two (AIM) — *Develop marketing strategies and materials for type buyer targeted, prepare for Due Diligence and arrange financing*

Step Three (FIRE) — *Begin the selling process*

The Complete Guide to

Selling Your Business
For the Most Money
(Without letting anyone know it's for sale)

©Copyright MMVIII Theodore P Burbank

17 Causeway Street

Millis, MA 02054

Website: http://www.buysellbiz.com

Printed in the United States of America

ISBN: 978-09645237-3-9

Table of Content

Step One - Ready

Step Two - Aim

Step Three- Fire

Appendix

Step One - **Ready**

Before you decide to sell you need straight answers to some very important questions i.e.:

- *What's the business worth?*

    With seller financing or

    Without seller financing

- *How do I identify the buyer:*

    Willing to pay the best price and

    Able to take the business to the next level

- *How do I avoid exposure to the all the rest?*

- *How can I aggressively sell and still maintain utmost confidentiality?*

Before You Start

Selling, or buying, a Private business does not present a pretty picture. Most all who attempt it fail, even the professionals! First, you need to know why this is so and; secondly, how make sure you are successful in selling your business. You need to know how to avoid the mistakes and traps that lay ahead ready to catch and destroy the uninformed business seller.

Important

Your "Business Selling System" is designed to walk you through the process one step at a time. "Inch by inch it's a cinch." Avoid the temptation to skip what may appear mundane and uninteresting segments. Each piece is a link in the chain of events that must be completed if a successful sale is to be consummated.

The Lay of the Land

If you are considering the sale of your business you should know what lies in store for you if you choose to attempt a sale using usual selling methods.

Success in attempted sales by those doing the selling:

- **Business Owners**   **2%**
- **Real estate brokers**   **5%**
- **Business brokers**   **14% to 25%**
- **Investment bankers**   **90+%**

Why are the results so dismal?

Family and private businesses are sold under very unique conditions. In fact, the environment and rules differ from the disciplines of selling anything else you can imagine! Attempting to sell a business the way you would sell a house can result in the destruction of the business.

Don't most small businesses eventually sell?

No - A survey of more than 5,000 franchised businesses indicates and our survey of 150 business owners who, over a period of several years, had told us they intended to sell their business by themselves reveal the following.

Franchises 76% closed - 24% Sold How many simply sold assets is unknown as is whether the franchisor or broker assisted in the sale. Why would a franchise simply close when the franchise document itself costs thousands?

FSBOs or For Sale By Owner - 70% the telephone was disconnected, 28% had given up thoughts of EVER selling and, only 2% had been sold

Can results be improved?

Yes , results can and have improved dramatically for those who follow the principals outlined in the **"Business Selling System" (BSS)**. We perfected the BSS over a period of years while selling more than 2,000 businesses. Business brokers who follow the BSS enjoy an effectiveness rate of 90+% and business owners selling on their own following BSS principals will dramatically improve their success rate as well. That is, once you understand why selling a business differs from selling anything else you can imagine.

How successful are buyers in finding a business to buy?

One has to interpolate this answer from the records of business brokers to estimate the answer as no other record of buyer activity currently exists. Based upon business broker records, one in twenty buyers in the hands of a rookie broker could be predicted to make an offer to buy a business. A rookie usually needs three offers to have one sale. Wow, sixty exposures before the average rookie would make a sale!

Success rates improved when experience brokers were involved to one sale for every twenty buyers. Intermediaries, dealing with individuals as buyers rather than corporate or strategic acquirers, usually place one of six buyers into a business. The ratio of individual buyers to sale could be as high as one of two, if in the hands of an exceptional broker/intermediary. Buyers who engage a professional to conduct a pro active acquisition campaign on their behalf are successful ninety plus percent of the time (based upon our experience). A summary of the success of buyers by options available:

	Success Rate
Buyers on their own	estimate 2%
With a rookie broker	2%
Experience broker/Intermediary	5 - 15%
Broker/Intermediary using BSS	50%
Professional pro-active campaign	90+%

Get Help!

Do not hesitate to engage the help of your spouse, a trusted friend or relative as you work with your BSS, especially the Profiling section. We found that it was a rare individual who was proficient in all aspects of first preparing a business for sale and then selling it. Therefore, we developed teams of persons with complimentary talents to assure the best and most comprehensive job possible for our business owner clients.

For example: If your spouse has better writing skills while you are comfortable with the analytical and financial aspects of the process you should consider assigning the writing portion of the process to your spouse while you tackle the number crunching.

Reasons Why
Selling a Business is Unique

Businesses must be sold in secret
Sell it but don't let anyone know it's for sale. In other words, maintain utmost confidentiality. Therefore, generally accepted methods of advertising and targeting the right market must be modified.

No one really knows what a business is worth
Ask twelve people and you will get twelve different answers. Unlike virtually every other commodity sold there is no "Blue Book of Values" for either buyers or sellers to reference in determining a business's value.

Future value of the purchase is dependent upon who buys it
We all have witnessed a down at the heels business come alive and prosper under new management. Regrettably, we have also witnessed the opposite.   What made the difference? -- Right buyer—Wrong buyer.   What else is sold where the viability of the item purchased and its future value is so dependent upon who buys it?

Financing is complicated by "Goodwill"
Financing the purchase of a business would be straight forward if the value of a business and the value of its assets were the same. Goodwill generally is a major component of a business's value and it does not represent a tangible asset banks can use as collateral. Therefore lenders typically ask for outside collateral from the buyer, perhaps a lien on their home, and/or that a seller's note is part of the lending package.

Three legged stool
Lenders prefer a "three legged" approach to financing a business acquisition: 1) a meaningful down payment from the buyer, 2)some level of seller financing subordinate to the lender's loan and 3) lender's loan.

Lenders will review the "five Cs" when deciding to make a commercial loan.

- **_Capacity_** - The borrower's _capacity_ is a measure of their qualification to receive the loan requested. Business experience and track record, financial strength of the business, the outlook for its industry are all a part of the mix
- **Capital** - Lenders require that the borrower also have a meaningful amount of _capital_ at risk, thereby insuring the borrower's commitment to the deal as well as reducing the lender's exposure to loss.
- **_Collateral_** - Sufficient _collateral_ shows the borrower's ability to guarantee the loan with tangible assets as a secondary source of repayment. Goodwill is generally a significant portion of the sale price. This presents an issue the lender must overcome before a loan can be authorized.
- **_Credit_** - A borrower's _credit_ history provides a picture of how the applicant has handled previous financial dealings.
- **_Character_** – Although the least quantifiable, _character_ may well be the most important assessment that the lender can make about the prospective borrower. If a borrower does not demonstrate integrity and trustworthiness, the loan proposal will be declined.

Buyers don't know what they want to buy

A majority of buyers profess to be in search of either a Light Manufacturing opportunity or perhaps a Distribution company. This actually is code for "I really don't know what I want to buy but I would feel dumb telling you that." Eventually virtually all buyers admitted to us that they really did not know what they wanted to buy. They knew what they did not want and, as with art, would recognize the right opportunity when they saw it.

The odds of a person buying the business that attracts them to our office are 1 in 500! The odds of buying a company within the industry for which the buyer initially stated a preference is 1 in 50.

As evidence: We reviewed fifty-five of our Quick Print sales to determine how many were sold as a result of advertisements placed offering a printing company for sale. We were not surprised to find only one. Those who purchased the other fifty-four had come to us in search of something else, perhaps light manufacturing or distribution. How do you sell something to someone who does not know they want to buy it?

Major asset hidden and/or disguised

Private business owners, and their accountants, work hard at minimizing profits in order to lessen taxes. Profits are important to possible business buyers. Unlike public companies where maximizing profits makes for happy shareholders and big bonuses for CEOs, small businesses do not keep their books to show maximum profits.

One must be able to look between the lines to determine the real earnings of a private business. This complicates the business buying process considerably as most people are "Financial Illiterates" and don't even do their own tax returns.

"Some of the world's greatest feats were accomplished by people not smart enough to know they were impossible."

Sale of a business is a life changing event for both buyer and seller
"Selling a business is a life-style or personal decision and not purely a financial matter"
Financial considerations are important but do not drive the decision to sell. Business owners generally are motivated to sell their businesses to gain a lifestyle change. They want to sell so that they and their businesses can each move on to different levels. The decision to sell is made from a combination of personal and financial considerations.
At some point in this balancing act it boils down to "it's only money." Only you, the business owner, are capable of making the determination where that point is. What other transaction can you imagine that involves such a high degree of personal involvement and financial uncertainty?

Too many buyers
Owners of what type business complains they have too many customers? - Business brokers! Yes, those who sell businesses for a living will tell you that buyers drive them to distraction. It seems everyone either says they are a buyer or knows one. Buyers are a dime a dozen. Finding the right buyer, now that's another story.

It's always a seller's market for viable businesses. Less than five percent of the population are business owners. Estimates regarding how many people want a business of their own range from 40% to a high of 70%. If we assume 20% of the 5% are considering selling their businesses, 1% of the population owns what 40% to 70% of the population wants to have.

Regardless of the accuracy of the estimates, it is safe to say that it is always a seller's market. An economic down turn intensifies buyer activity as layoffs and downswing brings more than the usual numbers of buyers into the market. Can you think of any other situation where a person who has something to sell complains of having too many customers?

Conflict of personal and financial motivations
A business is to its owner what a child is to its parents. Your business is an extension and a reflection of you. It's your baby and you do not really have to sell. You have sacrificed yourself, and your family life. There have been times when you did not take a paycheck; rather you put the money back into the business -- all those long hours, your hopes, your dreams. Now you are thinking of selling? Isn't that like putting your baby up for adoption for the money?

So far we have dealt with some of the factors and conditions that combine to make the process of buying or selling a business unique. We next will be addressing how the basic and constant principles of human nature are woven into the BSS to produce win-win transactions.

You may go through the motion to sell but,
unless this inner conflict is resolved,
your subconscious will not allow your business to be sold.

Secretive and Unique Selling Environment

The Business Selling System's (BSS) approach to selling businesses combines the secretive and unique environment in which private businesses are bought and sold with basic selling techniques and human nature.

Unique selling environment summarized
*"Don't let anyone know it's for sale but sell it for the best price
to a person who doesn't know they want to buy it and do it quickly."*

Perhaps this is why more than 75% of all private businesses simply sell their assets and close the doors. How do you sell a business without anyone knowing it is for sale?

A successful system or process must be built upon truth and reality. It cannot be constructed upon myths or negatives. The first step is to identify and acknowledge the truths, realities and unique environment that surround the selling/buying of a private company. Let's call this foundation **Realities.**

Two Groups of Realities

Realities surrounding selling a business can be divided into two groups:

➢ Unique to selling a Private Business and
➢ Principles and Realities of Human Nature

Realities Unique to Selling a Private Business

- Business Owners typically do not want anyone to realize they are even considering a sale, never mind actually selling their business.
- Buyers don't know what they want to buy
- Neither Buyer, Seller or their advisors really know what a business is worth but all have an opinion
- Only a buyer with proper credentials will succeed in operating your business – all others will drive it into the ground
- Transaction structure and financial requirements will vary depending upon the size and type of company and/or buyer involved
- Buyers really want to buy a business with "all the right things to be wrong" and not a perfect business
- Motivations to buy or sell a business are personal or emotional and issues regarding lifestyle are usually more important than money
- Owners of Private companies have to "wear all the hats" in operating their businesses
- Buyers would rather start a business of their own than buy yours
- Maintaining Confidentiality is crucial when selling a private company
- It is difficult to find competent advice and counsel when buying a business

Principles and Realities
of Human Nature

- Different buyers pay different prices
- Only the right buyer will pay the right price
- No one pays more for anything than they believe it is worth – no matter who is doing the selling
- Motivation trumps logic
- Perception of utility affects value i.e.: "Highest and Best Use" principle in real estate
- Individuals differ in level of skill, interests, education, and talents – no one is equally talented in all directions (No one is a "Round Ball")
- You do not know what you don't know
- Value increases as one's perception of risk decreases

Basic principles of sales

Apply two basic principles: *highest and best use* and *motivation.*

Highest and Best Use

Which has more value, a glass of water or a glass of diamonds? "The diamonds" you say? Obviously correct unless you are six days in the desert without water, then certainly, the water will have much greater value.

With regard to a business, the person who recognizes the *most opportunity* will voluntarily pay the highest price as he sees the most value and perceives the least risk.

Motivation

The decision to sell a business is generally motivated by personal or lifestyle considerations. Business owners do not usually decide to sell their business based purely upon financial considerations.

The motivations to buy a business usually revolve around issues of control and personal expression and not money. Yes, financial considerations are important but are not the driving force or motivation behind the desire to own a business.

Both the business buyer and seller are to become involved in a milestone and lifestyle changing event, one that could have very important financial implications. Suffice it to say that both will be making important decisions in a very emotionally charged atmosphere. After a sale has been consummated, their lives will not be the same.

Competent Advice

Advisors will be able to assist with the financial and legal aspects of a transaction and yet be totally unaware of the important personal factors involved. If one analyzes a transaction from the financial side only, it usually will not make total sense. A business is sold only when personal and financial gains are in balance. Only the seller and buyer know where that balance lies.

Placing Your Business up for Adoption

Let's use an adoption analogy. Why is it that adoptive parents do not choose to adopt a mature child (you have a mature business)? From a purely logical or analytical (financial) stance, adopting a mature child makes good sense. You could choose the type of child you prefer. Perhaps a girl who enjoys hiking, fishing and camping as do you. Why not a child who has graduated from college with highest honors? Perhaps she graduated from Harvard with an

MBA degree. Why not? Makes good sense doesn't it? It certainly makes good sense from a financial viewpoint. Obviously it doesn't happen that way because basic motivations for adoption are not addressed.

Motivation Trumps Logic
Adoptive parents want the opportunity to give to the child, to sacrifice for it. They want the opportunity to shape and mold the child in their own image. The logic of adopting an older child is overridden. Even one capable of caring for you financially in your old age is seldom ever considered.

Buyers real motivation is to start a business of their own More people start new businesses from scratch than acquire existing ones. What are their chances for success? Would it not make more sense to buy an established survivor?

An ever growing number of buyers are considering franchises. Franchises are very popular because the buyers gain a business they started from scratch, but they are not alone. They have help and ongoing backup. Motivation is addressed as is fear of failure.

Important to note: New franchises can be sold in the open just like anything else as Confidentiality is not an issue, that is, not until the franchise is to be re-sold. Franchisors seldom, if ever, make earnings claims to prospective franchisees. They can get into trouble with the FTC if they do. Franchisees understand that it will take time to reach break-even and even longer before they are profitable. The buyer's prime motivation is independence - making money is secondary.

Combining "Highest and Best Use" and Motivation
We have discussed two seemingly unrelated ideas: First, highest and best use; Second, personal or emotional desire to mold and shape. How can you put these dynamics to work to your advantage when attempting the sale of your business? The answer is very straight forward and key to the success of our Business Selling System.
First, what does the business need? What is not being done that should and can be done? What might be done better, added, changed or eliminated?
Owners of a small business essentially wear all the hats. Business owners are in charge of everything from strategic planning to taking out the rubbish. They are responsible for it all. However, no one is equally talented in every direction. People are not "Round Balls." We are very good at some things, good at others and possibly not so good at the rest. Some things we just do not know about. Unfortunately, very often we don't know what it is that we don't know.

There are no perfect people just as there are no perfect businesses. Every business contains elements that represent an opportunity for someone to capitalize upon.

Not the Money Alone
We have indicated that business opportunity seekers are not interested in solely making money! Instead, they seek opportunities to use their skills, talents and resources. They want to satisfy the desire to "show their stuff" and to be in control. If they can find the "Right

Business" they want to be able to improve and make it grow. Put their mark on it. Make it theirs, and, oh yes, make money doing it.

Important First Step

As the business owners, you know your business from the inside-out better than anyone. However, it's the view from the outside-in that is most important in your ability to sell your business. It is also the first step in determining what your business might be worth and who should buy it.

The view of your business from the outside in is the first step in the process of determining what your business might be worth and who should buy it

---

Apply "Round Ball Theory"

View your business from the Outside-In. You need to complete a profile of the business, (more detail on this later). Outline the strengths, weaknesses, uniqueness and areas of opportunity represented. The reverse or negative of this profile will represent the profile of the optimum or best buyer.

For example, a company makes a great widget, or provides a wonderful service. The owner is a genius in design and a stickler for quality and service. The company has grown quite nicely over the years and its product, or service, is widely used in your region.

The firm's strong suits are manufacturing and design and the weak suits are sales and marketing, administration and finance. Reverse this profile and you discover the buyer should have strengths in sales and marketing, plus a solid background in administration and finance.

All the right things are wrong!

When buyers possessing the required skills view the business, they will recognize the opportunities you have presented them. They also become very excited because all the right things are wrong! They can fix them. They can inject what is needed into the business. They can make it theirs. Following the adoptive child analogy, they will have the ability to send the child (your business) to college.

The person who sees the most opportunity will pay the highest price. What is more important is that they *can* and *will* capitalize on the opportunity you have created. Your company, your employees, their families and yours - all will win with the "Right Buyer!"

Conversely, if the business is sold or otherwise transferred to someone who fails to recognize the full opportunity:
a) You not only fail to receive the best price, but
b) The buyer is not able to capitalize upon the opportunities the business represents
No one knows what they don't know. If your business is sold to someone who doesn't know what to do with it the future of the company and all that it serves is in jeopardy. Your ability to obtain maximum value for your business as well as its future depends entirely upon your finding the "Right Buyer." Obviously this is equally important to the buyer.

A Business Valuation Primer

Before You Begin

As you are well aware, you and your accountant work diligently at minimizing earnings in order to limit taxation. That is the way it is with Private companies. Before you begin you should know and understand how the three buyer types determine earnings.

The first type, the Industry buyer, is reluctant to assess any value to your earnings and focuses primarily upon the value of your assets. Industry buyers do not want to pay for "Goodwill." Goodwill represents the portion of the price in excess of the value of your business's asset value.

The primary difference between the Financial and the Sophisticated buyers is that the Sophisticated buyer will take projections of future earnings into account and the Financial buyer will not.

Sophisticated buyers and their advisors determine value based upon their expectation of future earnings and their valuation methods reflect this thinking. Financial buyers pay for the present earnings and assume that future increases in earnings will be as result of their efforts and therefore resist paying you for what they will do.

Recasting or Normalizing Earnings

Your efforts in minimizing taxes have to be undone. Hopefully you have not disguised or hidden income in such a way that it cannot be found or it will not be credited or added back to earnings.

Review Chapter 12 of "In & Out of Business. . . Happily" entitled *Bottom Line or Between the Lines* addresses this subject in detail. To summary the exercise—to estimate earnings that will be available to a new owner for their: debt service, owner compensation and actual depreciation reserves after all necessary business expenses have been paid.

Income Statement or Profit and Loss (P&L) adjustments fall into three general categories:
- Non Cash
- Non Recurring
- Discretionary expenses

Expenses falling into these three broad categories may be added back to Earnings and are referred to as adjustments. Buyers do not pay for stolen goods, a/k/a skim.

Success is going from failure to failure without a loss of enthusiasm.
Winston Churchill

Financial Buyer Earnings Calculations

Discretionary Earnings is the calculation typically used by Financial buyers. You will notice it includes the present owner's compensation.

The only two adjustments, non – recurring professional fees and excess salaries were added back in this example. It is usual to have many others expenses such as: automobile related expenses, personal insurance of the owner, travel or entertainment expenses a new owner need not have etc. added back. This exhibit develops two earnings numbers, Pre Tax Earnings also referred to as Income Before Taxes and Discretionary Earnings (DE).

Adjusted Income and Expense

Year	2007	2006	2005	2004	2003
Revenue	2,606,287	2,784,517	2,641,288	2,508,939	2,361,616
Cost of Sales:					
Beginning Inventories	593,068	556,837	422,644	362,361	266,276
Purchases	1,873,689	2,085,779	2,078,676	1,883,787	1,782,720
Labor		-			
less Ending Inventories	(639,032)	(593,068)	(556,837)	(422,644)	(362,361)
Cost of Sales Total	1,827,725	2,049,548	1,944,483	1,823,504	1,686,635
Gross Profit	778,562	734,969	696,805	685,435	674,981
Total Expenses	667,639	650,988	605,159	554,813	574,867
Income Before Taxes	**110,923**	**83,981**	**91,646**	**130,622**	**100,114**
Adjustments:					
Officer's Compensation	65,000	65,000	60,000	60,000	57,000
Depreciation	19,713	17,426	7,200	18,101	21,478
Amortization					
Interest	4,879	5,614	4,794	5,029	4,058
Professional Fees	30,000			30,000	
Excess Salaries	100,000	100,000	100,000	100,000	100,000
Total Adjustments	219,592	188,040	171,994	213,130	182,536
Net Expenses	448,047	462,948	433,165	341,683	392,331
Discretionary Earnings	**330,515**	**272,021**	**263,640**	**343,752**	**282,650**

The exhibit above is produced by the Business Selling System's software.

Caution

Buyers and their advisors will only add back items clearly identified on the tax return or financial statement. If you and or your accountant have not clearly label discretionary expenses or otherwise allowed them to be easily identified, buyers will be reluctant to add them back to earnings. Neither unrecorded income nor unidentifiable discretionary expenses will be recognized or applied by buyers, their advisors or bankers.

How Financial Buyers
Choose an Earnings Number

Which of all the earnings numbers we have calculated will a Financial buyer choose to use when calculating Value? Some Financial buyers will use only the most current year's earnings. Others will calculate average earnings both weighted and straight to make their decision as the exhibit below illustrates.

	Discretionary Earnings	Weight	Extension
2007	330,515	5	1,652,575
2006	272,021	4	1,088,084
2005	263,640	3	790,920
2004	343,752	2	687,504
2003	282,650	1	282,650
Totals	1,492,578	15	4,501,733

Most recent year	330,515	
Straight Average	298,516	
Weighted Average		300,116
Estimate of earnings that a Financial Buyer will perceive as available for acquisition	$	300,000

The exhibit above is produced by the Business Selling System's software.

The outlook for the business, its industry, the trading area, the competitive environment and other considerations all combine to flavor your buyer's opinion. In the example above earnings have been somewhat erratic. Earnings have ranged from a high four years ago of $343,752 to a low of $272,021 two years ago. Straight and weighted averages both produce a similar earnings number of essentially $300,000 but again, earnings two years ago were $272K.

The Story Behind the Story

What caused profits to increase by $58,000 in 2006? Does the company's business fluctuate depending upon good weather bringing tourists and 2006 was a good year? If so $300,000 would be a prudent figure to use. If in 2006 the company's business increased because of events that could be expected to continue, such as a ten year contract with a new customer, then $330,000 *or more* might be more applicable.

Risk: You cannot discover new oceans unless you have the courage to lose sight of the shore.

Sophisticated Buyer
Earnings Calculations

Earnings Before Taxes is the number Sophisticated buyers and their advisors use to begin calculating Reconstructed or Adjusted Earnings. This number is the adjusted by deducting a reasonable compensation package for an owner or manager of a business of its size and complexity. A compensation package includes: compensation, cost of medical insurance, FICA and other taxes, automobile and other perks as may be usual to the position.

Before this type buyer can be comfortable with an Earnings number, analysis and projections have to be prepared and a clear understanding of company operations and the outlook for the future must be understood.

You will notice in the projections below that Cost of Sales % and Net Expenses are based upon the company's recent experience. It is also apparent that the outlook for future revenues is modestly optimistic with annual increases in Revenues of $200,000.

	Projected Current Yr.	Case 1	Case 2	Case 3	Case 4	Case 5
Target Revenues	2,800,000	3,000,000	3,200,000	3,400,000	3,600,000	3,800,000
Target % Cost of Sales *	65.6%	65.6%	65.6%	65.6%	65.6%	65.6%
Target $ Cost of Sales	1,836,800	1,968,000	2,099,200	2,230,400	2,361,600	2,492,800
Gross Profit	963,200	1,032,000	1,100,800	1,169,600	1,238,400	1,307,200
Target Net Expenses *	450,000	480,000	510,000	540,000	570,000	600,000
Discretionary Earnings	513,200	552,000	590,800	629,600	668,400	707,200
Target Manager's Salary	123,500	123,500	123,500	123,500	123,500	123,500
Adjusted EBIT	389,700	428,500	467,300	506,100	544,900	583,700
Target Ratios:						
Gross Profit	34.4%	34.4%	34.4%	34.4%	34.4%	34.4%
Net Expenses	16.1%	16.0%	15.9%	15.0%	15.0%	15.0%
Adjusted EBIT	13.9%	14.3%	14.6%	14.9%	15.1%	15.4%

*Recent experience used in projections

The exhibit above is produced by the Business Selling System's software.

If exciting prospects for dramatically increasing revenues and profits can be documented then this type buyer is prepared to pay you **"Tomorrow's Price Today."**

---

*"Only when the tide goes out do you discover
who's been swimming naked"*

Warren Buffett

Usual EBT Calculations (Earnings Before Taxes)

You will notice the EBIT calculation begins using Income Before Taxes and is adjusted by, in this case, deducting "Appropriate Owner's Compensation." Buyers will calculate what they consider an appropriate compensation package and replace yours with it. In this exhibit the owner's compensation package was lower than what an acquirer or industry norms would expect as reasonable. The EBIT value was therefore reduced by the difference. The EBIT value will be increased in cases where an owner's compensation exceeds industry norms

Various EBT (Earnings Before Taxes) Calculations

	Discretionary Earnings	330,515	272,021	263,640	343,752	282,650
Less:	Appropriate owner's compensation and	123,500	123,500	123,500	123,500	123,500
	Replacement reserves	5,000	5,000	5,000	5,000	5,000
	Adjusted EBIT	202,015	143,521	135,140	215,252	154,150
	Income Before Taxes	110,923	83,981	91,646	130,622	100,114
Plus:	Interest	4,879	5,614	4,794	5,029	4,058
	Depreciation	19,713	17,426	7,200	18,101	21,478
	Amortization	0	0	0	0	0
	EBIT-DA	135,515	107,021	103,640	153,752	125,650
Less:	Depreciation	19,713	17,426	7,200	18,101	21,478
	Amortization	0	0	0	0	0
	EBIT	115,802	89,595	96,440	135,651	104,172
Less:	Interest	4,879	5,614	4,794	5,029	4,058
	EBT	110,923	83,981	91,646	130,622	100,114

The exhibit above is produced by the Business Selling System's software.

Which EBT Earnings is Appropriate for Use?

The appropriateness depends upon your company's size and level of earnings. Businesses can be placed into one of four groups.

Group	Revenue	Earnings	Appropriate EBT
Main Street	up to $1 million	up to $250K	Adjusted EBIT
Upper Main Street	under $5 million	up to $1 million	Adjusted EBIT - EBITDA
Middle Market	under $20 million	$1 million +	EBITD - EBIT
Wall Street	$20 million +	$1 million +	EBIT - EBT

It is estimated that 90% Private businesses fall into our Main Street and Upper Main Street categories. We therefore will primarily be using Adjusted EBIT earnings as the next exhibit indicates.

How Sophisticated Buyers
Choose an Earnings Number

This Exhibit arrays Company earnings both past and projected. The earnings this buyer settles upon is directly tied to the quality of your documentation of the basis for these projections.

In this hypothetical example it might well be that sales and profitability were the result of: (take your pick) new product line, introduction of a sales force, new residential construction in the area, expansion of facility, new multi year contracts and so forth.

Year	Adjusted EBIT	Wgt	Extension	Wgt	Extension
2011	544,900			1	544,900
2010	506,100			2	1,012,200
2009	467,300			3	1,401,900
2008	428,500			4	1,714,000
Est. Current Yr.	389,700	3	1,169,100	5	1,948,500
2006	207,015	5	1,035,075	5	1,035,075
2005	148,521	4	594,084	4	594,084
2004	140,140	3	420,420	3	420,420
2003	220,252	2	440,504	2	440,504
2002	159,150	1	159,150	1	159,150
	875,078	18	3,818,333	30	9,270,733

Most recent yr.   207,015

5 Year Straight average   175,016

Weighted average   212,130

Weighted historic and future average   309,024

Estimated Current Year   389,700

Estimated First Year   428,500

Estimate of earnings that a Sophisticated Buyer will perceive as available for acquisition $ **380,000**

The exhibit above is produced by the Business Selling System's software.

The choice of $380,000 could be increased as might the weight given to it the further into the year you were. Increased sales by month compared to same period the year before that were tracking the projections would give added comfort to this buyer in choosing an earnings based upon projections.

About Weighting

Weighting is a method of measuring relative importance and probability.

For Example: More weight or credit will be given to recent performance than will be assigned to performance in the more distant past. As time progresses, less and less weight will generally be assigned to historic financial performance. Therefore, when assessing earnings over a period of years, the highest weight will be assigned to the most recent year and less to prior years. Three years of earnings might be weighted 3, 2, 1 -- four years 4, 3, 2, 1.

Unusual or unrepresentative distant years might be discounted entirely. For example: If, four years ago, a bridge affording access to the business was under repair for 6 months (causing the enterprise to lose money that year), the weighting might be 5, 4, 3, 0, 1.

The example above weights estimated current year results at 1. More weight can be given to an estimate of current year results at the end of November than in January. Therefore an estimate based on results through November could be afforded a weight of five.

Measuring Probability – In the previous exhibit we made an educated guess at what earnings a buyer would be comfortable using. We could have also weighted the several methods as to the probability of use to develop an answer. This is what we do when comparing valuation results however; we use a fraction of one or a percentage instead. In the exhibit below you will notice that the user has given zero weight to Multiple of EBIT valuation methods and essentially equal weight to the remaining methods.

Method	Value	Weight	Extension
Excess Earnings	1,189,961	0.35	416,486
Discounted Cash Flow	1,089,691	0.32	348,701
Capitalization of Earnings	1,100,000	0.33	363,000
Multiple of EBIT	1,250,000	0.00	-
	4,629,652	1.00	1,128,187
Straight Average Value	1,126,551		
Weighted Average Value	1,128,187		
Target Value	**$ 1,125,000**		

The exhibit above is produced by the Business Selling System's software

The weighted average is compared with a straight average before a Target Value is chosen.

Begin Step One

Now is the time to start using Business Selling System's unique software. Now is the time to get out your tax returns and financial statements. If you have five years worth you should use them. Fewer years are ok but the protocol is five years. The next step is to assess the value of your company through the eyes of the three buyer types we have previously identified.

The Objectives:

- **Buyer Identification** - Identify the type buyer who will pay you the most money for your business
- **Value and Transaction Structure** - Calculate both the a) Cash Price and, b) Probable Price and, c) Transaction Structure under which your business might sell
- **Value Enhancement** – What can be done both long and short term to increase the value of the company and enhance probability of a sale
- **Analyze** - Perform the review and analysis that buyers and their advisors will conduct when reviewing your business

Begin Data Entry

The very first screen of the Business Selling System asks for Balance Sheet data. Chances are good that you do not have a Balance Sheet, especially if your business is unincorporated. If this is the case simply construct one for the most recent year only as the sample below illustrates.

Comparative Balance Sheets

Assets						
Year	2007	2006	2005	2004	2003	2002
Current Assets:						
Cash	15,325	27,852	15,265	21,557	5,143	17,458
Marketable Securities	27,500					
Accounts Receivable	222,437	230,121	210,045	194,552	187,889	191,237
Inventories	63,903	59,306	61,127	58,871	51,244	49,577
Loan's to Shareholders	16,354	19,954	19,954	10,000	5,000	5,000
Prepaid Expenses	5,214	6,483	5,744	6,145	4,988	3,751
Total Current Assets	**350,733**	**343,716**	**312,135**	**291,125**	**254,264**	**267,023**
Fixed Assets						
Leasehold Improvements	85,173	105,246	127,500	-	-	-
Equipment and Machinery	87,429	71,887	73,258	88,547	92,554	93,750
Vehicles	32,145	34,552	46,223	34,557	36,558	41,259
Office Equipment	10,258	11,457	12,444	9,541	7,554	6,500
less Accumulated Depreciation	(53,558)	(51,658)	(50,147)	(43,225)	(41,225)	(37,500)
Total Fixed Assets	**161,447**	**171,484**	**209,278**	**89,420**	**95,441**	**104,009**
Other Assets						
CSV Life Insurance	27,500	24,230	20,457	17,236	14,558	12,457
Annuities	57,500	57,500	57,500	57,500	57,500	57,500
Other	-	-	-	-	-	-
Total Other Assets	**85,000**	**81,730**	**77,957**	**74,736**	**72,058**	**69,957**
Total Assets	**597,180**	**596,930**	**599,370**	**455,281**	**421,763**	**440,989**

The format of your Balance Sheet may vary from the format found here. If so, combine values into an appropriate heading. For example, your statement may include Cash, Savings Account and Certificates of Deposit as separate headings. You could combine these values and enter under Cash.

Tax returns for Corporations contain a Balance Sheet whereas the sole proprietor's Schedule C and partnership returns do not.

If your company is not a Corporation or LLC and you have accountant's Financial Statements you can choose to use them instead of your tax returns. Balance Sheet data will enable your *Business Selling System* software to perform extensive Financial Ratio Analysis for your firm.

CAUTION

Do not mix tax return and financial statement data. Use either tax returns or financial statements when entering data into your BSS software but NOT FROM BOTH – Do not mix the numbers.

What's being sold and what will you keep

Objective:
- Separate Assets and Liabilities into those being sold and those you will keep.
- Convert Values to Fair Market Value (FMV)
- Calculate a Residual Value which is separate from the sale value of your company

Adjusting the Balance Sheet

Assets	Book Value	Adjustment	FMV Transferable Assets	FMV Retained Assets
Cash	27,852			27,852
Marketable Securities	27,500			27,500
Accounts Receivable	230,121			230,121
Inventories	59,306		85,000	
Prepaid Expenses	6,483			6,483
Leasehold Improvements	105,246	(105,246)	0	
Equipment and Machinery	71,887	(21,887)	50,000	
Vehicles	34,552	(9,552)	25,000	
Office Equipment	11,457	(6,457)	5,000	
CV of Officer Life Ins.	81,730			81,730
FMV of Transferable Assets			165,000	
FMV Value of Retained Assets				373,686

Use your best estimate of the Fair Market Value (FMV) of your assets.
Review Chapter 12 of "In and Out of Business . . . *Happily*" for additional insight into Balance Sheet Adjustments.

Liabilities	Book Value	Adjustment	Transferable Liabilities	Retained Liabilities
Accounts Payable	247,552			247,552
Accrued Taxes	14,241			14,241
Current Portion LT Debt	10,972			10,972
Line of Credit	20,000			20,000
Notes to Shareholders	15,000			15,000
Notes payable - Banks	130,470			130,470
Noted payable - Other	-			-
Deferred Income Taxes	-			-
Capital Leases	-			-
Other	-			-
Book Value of Liabilities	438,235			
Value of Transferable Liabilities			0	
FMV Value of Retained Assets				373,686
Value of Retained Liabilities				438,235
Residual Value				**-64,549**

ALERT

In this example you see a negative Residual Value (retained Assets less retained Liabilities) of $64,549. The cash at closing will have to cover this amount plus other closing costs such as attorney and accountants fees and broker commissions if a broker is employed to sell the business. If elements of debt can be assumed by the buyer the cash required at closing could be reduced. Therefore, keep this number in mind as you decide whether selling is practical, appropriate or timely.

Three types of Sale

Asset Sale - Essentially all Private companies are sold debt free as "Asset" sales. Therefore, Cash and Accounts Receivable as well as Accounts Payable and essentially all company debts are retained by the business owner.

Stock Sale - Public companies and many larger Private companies are sold as "Stock" sales. In this type sale all company Assets and Liabilities are assumed by the acquirer. Everything stays the same, only the shareholders are changed.

Hybrid Stock/Asset - Larger Private and smaller Public companies often are sold under hybrid conditions. The sale is typically an Asset sale however; Cash, Accounts Payable and Receivable plus Notes, Leases and other select elements of debt are assumed by the buyer as part of the transaction structure.

Estimate Asset Values

The following three screens ask you to estimate the Replacement, Liquidation and Collateral Values of your assets. This exercise is fairly straight forward however; you may want to check with a lender and auctioneer to ratify the appropriateness the default percentages.
Answer these questions before moving on to the Income Statement

Estimated Cost to Replace

Purchasers routinely estimated the costs of creating a similar enterprise when considering the purchase of an existing business. This exhibit estimates the results of such an exercise.

	Book Value	Estimated Cost to Replace
Inventories	593,068	600,000
Prepaid Expenses	6,483	5,000
Leasehold Improvements	-	20,000
Equipment and Machinery	71,887	75,000
Vehicles	-	40,000
Office Equipment	-	
Organizational Expenses	-	
Other	-	
Estimated Cost to Replace	**$**	**740,000**

Estimated Liquidation Value

Lenders routinely use this value when calculating collateral values for lending purposes.

	Fair Market Value	Liquidation Factor	Liquidation Value
Cash	27,852	1.00	27,852
Marketable Securities	-	1.00	-
Accounts Receivable	230,121	0.95	218,615
Inventories	600,000	0.85	510,000
Prepaid Expenses	6,483	0.90	5,835
Leasehold Improvements	-	-	-
Equipment and Machinery	50,000	0.70	35,000
Vehicles	-	0.90	-
Office Equipment	-	0.25	-
CV of Officer Life Ins.	-	0.50	-
Estimated Liquidation Value			**797,302**

Imagination: A mind stretched by new ideas never regains its original dimensions.

Collateral Value of Transferable Assets

	Liquidation Value	Usual % Loan to Value	Collateral Value	
Accounts Receivable	218,615	0.00	-	*
Inventories	510,000	0.50	255,000	
Prepaid Expenses	5,835	0.00	-	*
Leasehold Improvements	-	0.70	-	
Equipment and Machinery	35,000	0.50	17,500	
Vehicles	-	0.90	-	
Office Equipment	-	0.50	-	
CV of Officer Life Ins.	-	0.80	-	
Estimated Collateral Value			$ 272,500	

* Assets being retained, not part of sale

Calculating Earnings and Adjusting the Profit and Loss Statement (P&L)

You will hear folks refer to using multiples of earnings to determine a company's value. The question is which earnings computation is being referred to? With Public companies it's after tax earnings but it's not as straight forward with Private Firms. The worksheet below calculates the six different earnings numbers used by acquirers of Private companies and their advisors.

The format of this worksheet may not mirror your Tax Return or Income Statements (P&L). The major difference may be that labor expended in production of your product or service may not have been included in calculating your Cost of Sales. To gain the most benefit from this program we suggest you enter your Direct Labor costs under Cost of Sales. Direct labor does not generally include sales or office salaries which are typically recorded as an overhead expense.

Once you have entered the major income and expense items this screen asks you to "add back" to profit those expenses that are discretionary, unnecessary, or not likely to reoccur as Expense Adjustments.

Review Chapters 12 and 15 of "In and Out of Business. . . *Happily*" for more information on Adjusting the P&L also referred to as "Normalizing Income Statements" and "Recasting Income Statements."

Effort: Life does not require us to be the biggest or the best. It only asks that we try.

The data entered down to Income Before Taxes is simply the values found on your tax returns or financial statements.

Year	2007	2006	2005	2004	2003
Adjusted Income and Expense					
Revenue	3,106,287	2,984,517	2,841,288	2,508,939	2,361,616
Other	1,200	1,200	1,200	1,200	1,200
Total Revenue	3,107,487	2,985,717	2,842,488	2,510,139	2,362,816
Cost of Sales:					
Beginning Inventories	593,068	556,837	422,644	362,361	266,276
Purchases	2,122,350	2,000,820	1,995,661	1,683,766	1,582,766
Labor	100,000	100,000	100,000	100,000	100,000
less Ending Inventories	(639,032)	(593,068)	(556,837)	(422,644)	(362,361)
Cost of Sales Total	2,176,386	2,064,589	1,961,468	1,723,483	1,586,681
Gross Profit	929,901	919,928	879,820	785,456	774,935
Total Expenses	667,639	650,988	605,159	554,813	574,867
Income Before Taxes	**262,262**	**268,940**	**274,661**	**230,643**	**200,068**

Add Backs

Enter values for Officer's compensation, Depreciation, Amortization, Interest and any other amount that can be identified and recognized as either Discretionary or non-recurring. In other words, expenses a new owner will not have.

Your ability to document add-backs will increase a buyer's comfort level and have a positive impact on your company's value.

Teamwork: There is no exercise better for the heart than reaching out and lifting people up.

Adjustments:					
Officer's Compensation	65,000	65,000	60,000	60,000	57,000
Depreciation	19,713	17,426	17,200	18,101	21,478
Amortization	5,555	5,555	5,555	5,555	5,555
Interest	4,879	5,614	4,794	5,029	4,058
Owner's club dues	2,000	2,000	1,800	1,800	1,800
Personal Auto and Insurance	18,500	17,985	19,875	17,985	18,125
Total Adjustments	115,647	113,580	109,224	108,470	108,016
Discretionary Earnings	**377,909**	**382,520**	**383,885**	**339,113**	**308,084**
Less Appropriate Officer Compensation	(123,500)	(123,500)	(123,500)	(123,500)	(123,500)
Adjusted EBIT	**254,409**	**259,020**	**260,385**	**215,613**	**184,584**
Earnings Before Taxes	262,262	268,940	274,661	230,643	200,068
Interest	4,879	5,614	4,794	5,029	4,058
Depreciation	19,713	17,426	17,200	18,101	21,478
Amortization	5,555	5,555	5,555	5,555	5,555
EBIT DA	**292,409**	**291,921**	**297,416**	**254,299**	**227,101**
less Depreciation/Amortization	25,268	22,981	22,755	23,656	27,033
EBIT	**267,141**	**268,940**	**274,661**	**230,643**	**200,068**
less Interest	4,879	5,614	4,794	5,029	4,058
EBT	**262,262**	**263,326**	**269,867**	**225,614**	**196,010**
Net Expenses	551,992	537,408	495,935	446,343	466,851

E = Earnings   B = Before   I = Interest   T = Taxes   D = Depreciation
A = Amortization

CAUTION

Add backs sometimes are difficult to discern as they may have been lumped in with other expenses or not recorded at all. Expenses that are not readily identifiable or recognizable as discretionary or non-recurring should not be added back. Also, unless the expense can be identified on the tax return, it cannot be added back.

Example: A non-working family member is paid a few hundred dollars a week from the cash register – no adjustment.

This information is used by Sophisticated buyers when calculating earnings available for acquisition debt service and return on their invested capital.

Other Information

What would you have to pay a person to manage/operate this business?

Yearly salary/wage	100,000
Health/life insurance	5,000
Federal/state employment taxes	15,000
Vehicle	3,500
Other	-
Total Cost of Manager	$ 123,500

How much should be spent annually to keep the facility and equipment in suitable condition to remain competitive? $ 5,000

Bankability and Risk Analysis

The outlook for your business, your industry and the market or area you serve has an impact on how outsiders view your opportunity and the value they will place upon it. The next two questionnaires should reflect the perception of your business from the outside in. The first represents a lender's view and the second that of acquirers and their advisors.

The questions require you provide an answer in the form of a number between 0 and 6.

Environmental

  0 - Produces or uses a highly hazardous material(s)

  3 - Moderate but controllable amounts of material
     representing possible environmental risk   **6.0**

  6 - No process or material(s) representing environmental
     risk present

Record Keeping

  0 - Minimal records prepared by management

  3 - Financial statements prepared by respected CPA   **4.0**
     or accountant

  6 - Audited statements prepared by major accounting firm

                      Company Score   **3.6**

    Definition of Score

   0 to 2.5 Financing unlikely

  2.6 to 3.5 Limited financing possible

  3.6 to 4.5 Financing probable

  4.6 to 6.0 Financing likely

        Collateral Value from Worksheet $ 272,500

Estimated amount of outside financing to fund a transaction $ 270,000

The exhibit below is a partial view of the worksheet

Ideally you have obtained the estimated amount of outside financing from an actual lender.

ALERT

Value is diminished greatly when third party financing is restricted or unavailable. With a score of 3.1 financing in a tight market may not be available leaving seller financing as the only financing option left on the table. Possible buyers of this hypothetical company could be frightened off by banks or other lenders refusal to consider acquisition funding or, providing funding only if buyer agrees to onerous conditions.

Action Items

In order to enhance the value of your business and the probability of its sale:

- Address all areas where you have a low score to enhance the probability of your buyer obtaining acquisition funding
- Contact possible lenders for: a)credentials they will require of your buyer and, b)the amount they would be willing to lend using company assets as collateral

Valuable Resources - A list of lenders comfortable with providing acquisition financing is to be found in the Appendix section.

Risk Analysis

This exhibit converts the probable subjective view of the Risk, Stability and other factors into a numeral that should represent an appropriate Capitalization Rate (Risk/Reward Ratio) for your business. It must be noted that a low rating (Zero or One) may prevent a sale from occurring unless the buyer is able to perceive the low rating as opportunity.

Note - This exhibit can assist you in developing your Buyer Profile in that areas where

you have a low score must be seen as areas of opportunity or areas of little concern to your ideal buyer.

The exhibit below is a partial view of the worksheet

Environmental Rating	
0 - Produces or uses a large amount of hazardous materials, strict licensing	
3 - Minimal amounts of hazardous materials used, no licensing required	**4.0**
6 - No hazardous materials used or produced	
Union Rating	
0 - Union shop	
3 - No union, some unionization in the industry	**3.0**
6 - No union, no history of unions in the industry	
Occupancy Rating	
0 - No lease available, business is location sensitive	
3 - Lease, with options, extends for eight years - rents predetermined	**2.0**
6 - Real estate included or long lease (15 years +) with predetermined rents	
Total of Ratings	**47.5**
Divide by the number of ratings	**16.0**
Produces a Multiple of	**3.0**
or a Capitalization Rate of	**33.7%**

You will notice that the Cap Rate of 33.7% in the above chart is the same as a multiple of 3.

"A true measure of your worth includes all the benefits others have
gained from your success."

--- *Cullen Hightower*

MORE ON CAPITALIZATION RATES

The rate of capitalization ("Cap Rate"), also known as the risk reward ratio, is commonly used in valuing businesses by the more sophisticated investor. As noted below, capitalization rates vary depending upon the business venture's risk as perceived by the buyer. Most Private companies develop Cap Rates in the Medium High to Medium Low Ranges, typically in the mid 30% band.

RISK and business characteristics by band	CAP RATE
High Risk	
Venture Capital	60 - 100%
Start-Up Companies	50 - 60%
Medium High Risk	
Existing Company, Mature Products, Company, Industry, Owner Leaving, Easy Market Entry	35 - 50%
Medium Low Risk	
Established Company, Existing Markets, Normal Competition, Owner May Remain, Somewhat Ease of Market Entry	20 - 35%
Low Risk	
Established Company, Established Market, Little or No Competition, Profitable, Low-Risk Markets, Owner Remaining, Difficult Entry into Market	10 - 20%
Risk Free	
Money Market Rate	3 - 10%

"The road to happiness lies in two simple principles: find what it is that interests you and that you can do well, and when you find it, put your whole soul into it ---every bit of energy and ambition and natural ability you have."

--- John D. Rockefeller III

Determine the Values of Your Business

In this hypothetical example values vary dramatically depending upon the class of buyer that can be attracted i.e.:

- ✓ Asset or Industry Buyer only saw value in the assets or $160,000
- ✓ Financial or Lifestyle Buyers might pay $750,000
- ✓ Sophisticated or Corporate Buyers would see a value of $1,125,000

In the above case, possible serious damage to the company will be avoided and confidentiality maintained by eliminating competitors and other Industry players as potential buyers. The remaining question, will a Sophisticated buyer find this company attractive? If not, what can be done so that the Sophisticated buyer will see the company as an exciting opportunity?

Review - For more information on buyer types refer to "In and Out of Business. . . *Happily*".

Industry or Asset Buyer Methods

Values are imported into this worksheet and arrayed, totaled and weighted. A straight and weighted average is computed and you then decide the value most likely to be used by this buyer.

	Book Value	Book Value Adj to FMV	Liquidation Value
Inventories	59,306	85,000	72,250
Equipment and Machinery	87,429	50,000	35,000
Vehicles	32,145	25,000	22,500
Office Equipment	10,258	5,000	2,864
Other	-	-	40,865
Less Depreciation	(51,658)		
Book Value $	**137,480**		
Adjusted Book Value		**$ 165,000**	
Liquidation Value			**$ 173,479**

		Summary	
Methods	**Values**	**Weight**	**Extension**
Book Value	137,480	0.10	13,748
Adjusted Book Value	165,000	0.80	132,000
Liquidation Value	173,479	0.10	17,348
	475,959	1.00	163,096
Straight Average	158,653		
Weighted Average		163,096	
Probable Industry Buyer Value			**$ 160,000**

The exhibit above is produced by the Business Selling System's software

Financial or Lifestyle Buyer

The Lifestyle buyer is the most abundant buyer and is easier to attract than the Sophisticated buyer. This buyer does not consider projections of future profitability when calculating value.

Company earnings have to cover:

- New owner's wage,
- Acquisition debt service and,
- Replacement reserves.

Financial Buyer's Earnings Computation

	Discretionary Earnings	Weight	Extension	
2006	377,909	5	1,889,545	
2005	382,520	4	1,530,080	
2004	383,885	3	1,151,655	
2003	339,113	2	678,226	
2002	308,084	1	308,084	
Totals	1,791,511	15	5,557,590	
Most recent year	377,909			
Straight Average			358,302	
Weighted Average				370,506
Estimate of earnings that a Financial Buyer will perceive as available for acquisition			$	**380,000**

The exhibit above is produced by the Business Selling System's software

Summary of Financial Buyer's Valuation Calculations

Methods	Values	Weight	Extension
Basic	735,000	0.25	183,750
Discretionary Earnings	777,273	0.30	233,182
Comparable Sales	789,855	0.30	236,957
Cost to Replace	225,000	0.05	11,250
Debt Capacity	1,009,634	0.10	100,963
	3,536,761	1.00	766,102
Straight Average Value	707,352		
Weighted Average Value		766,102	
Target Value		$	**750,000**

The exhibit above is produced by the Business Selling System's software

Note – The Debt Capacity method produces a "spike" value of more than one million dollars dramatically illustrating the positive impact financing can have on a business's value.

You can capitalize upon this phenomenon by:

- Doing a bit of groundwork locating favorable acquisition financing,
- Obtaining lender's "profile" criteria and
- Being willing to participate in the financing package.

This information should also be made part of the Profile of your ideal buyer. You want a person willing, qualified and capable of handling significant acquisition debt.

Other methods will produce spike or optimum values as well. This valuation information should then be incorporated into your Buyer Profile as well as your marketing materials..

Example: In cases when the Basic Method (Asset value + Earnings) produces the optimum value because the company is asset rich, buyer benefits include:

- Minimal Goodwill or higher percentage of purchase price available from lenders
- Fall back security the value of assets represents

Review Chapter 18 of "In & Out of Business. . . *Happily*" for detailed information regarding methods used by Financial and Lifestyle buyers.

Transaction Structure – Is it a fair deal?

This exhibit calculates the fairness and predicts the most probable deal structure.

Assumptions:	Seller's Note	Bank Note
Interest Rate	9.0%	9.0%
# Years Note	8.0	8.0
# Years Covenant not to Compete	5.0	
# Years Consulting Agreement	5.0	
The Ratios under this scenario equal:	**77.4%**	
Possible Structure:	**Terms**	
Target Purchase Price	750,000	
Down Payment	350,000	
Covenant not to Compete	50,000	
Consulting Agreement	50,000	
Bank Note	270,000	
Seller's Note	30,000	
Total Purchase Price	750,000	
Annual Debt Service:		
Covenant not to Compete	10,000	
Consulting Agreement	10,000	
Bank Note	48,782	
Seller's Note	5,420	
Total Debt Service	74,202	
Discretionary Earnings	380,000	
less Debt Service	(74,202)	
less Return on Buyer's on Cash Down	(35,000)	
Earnings available for Owner's		
Compensation and Depreciation reserves	$ 270,798	

The exhibit above is produced by the Business Selling System's software

NOTE

Financial and Lifestyle Buyers generally expect the ratio of living wage to down payment to range between 70% and 90%. When the ratio drops below 70% our database of actual sales indicates that a transaction is unlikely to occur.

Example: The Financial Buyer with a down payment of $100K will typically expect a living wage of between $70K and $90K is available after debt service and replacement reserves. You will notice in the Comparable Sales method that the ratio of down payment to Discretionary earnings was 1.02 – essentially dollar for dollar.

Calculate an All Cash Price

This exhibit calculates the negative impact restricted financing has upon price by measuring the increase in perception of risk as financing diminishes. In this example value decreases more than $150,000 if seller financing is refused.

Target Purchase Price	$	750,000	
Usual Down Payment		200,000	
Probable Bank Loan		270,000	
Possible Cash at Transfer		470,000	
Usual Seller's Note		280,000	
Total Price (FMV)		750,000	

1) Unfinanced portion of Transaction — 37.3%
2) Divide by 2, add result to CAP rate as
   an adder for lack of financing — 18.7%
3) CAP Rate for this business — 33.7%
4) Discount Rate — 52.4%
5) Apply Discount Rate to usual Seller's Note to calculate Present Value

	Annual note payments:	Present Value Factor	Present Value of Payments
1st year	73,863	0.656380	48,482
2nd year	73,863	0.430834	31,823
3rd year	73,863	0.282791	20,888
4th year	73,863	0.185618	13,710
5th year	73,863	0.121836	8,999

6) Present Value of usual Seller's Note — 123,903
7) Add Cash at Transfer — 470,000

Estimated Fair Cash Value — **593,903**

ALERT - The lack of or restricted financing will have a diminishing and negative impact on a company's value. In fact, refusal to provide financing, especially the seller's refusal may prevent a company from ever being sold. Additionally, most lenders will walk away from funding if the seller refuses to participate in the financing package.

Sophisticated or Corporate Buyer

Can you attract a Sophisticated Buyer or is the Financial Buyer your only realistic choice? We have sold many Main Street businesses to Sophisticated buyers who, frankly, were quite pleased and surprised at the opportunities the smaller companies represented. You may have to do some work before you can successfully attract this high paying buyer.

Review - To obtain an overview of what you may have to do before you can attract a Sophisticated or Corporate buyer we suggest you review Chapter 11 in "In & Out of Business. . . *Happily*".

Sophisticated buyers and their advisors perform detailed financial analysis of your company and review the outlook of not only your industry but the outlook for the market(s) you serve. The *Business Selling System, (*BSS) software automatically produces the Financial Analysis this buyer and their advisors will routinely perform.

Comparative Ratio Review

The exhibit below represents a portion of the several pages of analysis BSS produces. The analyst will be looking for consistency and patterns and primarily a basis upon which to base projections of future performance.

Year	2007	2006	2005	2004	2003
Sales	3,107,487	2,985,717	2,842,488	2,510,139	2,362,816
Cost of Sales	2,176,386	2,064,589	1,961,468	1,723,483	1,586,681
Ratio	70.0%	69.1%	69.0%	68.7%	67.2%
Period Average	68.9%				
Cost of Goods	2,076,386	1,964,589	1,861,468	1,623,483	1,486,681
Ratio	66.8%	65.8%	65.5%	64.7%	62.9%
Period Average	65.3%				
Labor Cost	100,000	100,000	100,000	100,000	100,000
Ratio	3.2%	3.3%	3.5%	4.0%	4.2%
Period Average	3.6%				
Expenses	667,639	650,988	605,159	554,813	574,867
Ratio	21.5%	21.8%	21.3%	22.1%	24.3%
Period Average	22.1%				
Net Expenses	551,992	537,408	495,935	446,343	466,851
Ratio	17.8%	18.0%	17.4%	17.8%	19.8%
Period Average	18.1%				

The   exhibit above is produced by the Business Selling System's software

A review of the above ratios indicates reasonably consistent results and modestly increasing sales. Projecting future results should be fairly straight forward for this company.

Projections

The table below represents BSS's simplified projection worksheet.

	Projected Current Yr.	Case 1	Case 2	Case 3	Case 4	Case 5
Target Revenues	3,200,000	3,400,000	3,600,000	3,800,000	4,000,000	4,200,000
Target % Cost of Sales	69.0%	69.0%	69.0%	69.0%	69.0%	69.0%
Target $ Cost of Sales	2,208,000	2,346,000	2,484,000	2,622,000	2,760,000	2,898,000
Gross Profit	992,000	1,054,000	1,116,000	1,178,000	1,240,000	1,302,000
Target Net Expenses *	496,000	525,000	555,000	580,000	620,000	630,000
Discretionary Earnings	496,000	529,000	561,000	598,000	620,000	672,000
Target Manager's Salary	123,500	123,500	123,500	123,500	123,500	123,500
Adjusted EBIT	372,500	405,500	437,500	474,500	496,500	548,500
Target Ratios:						
Gross Profit	31.0%	31.0%	31.0%	31.0%	31.0%	31.0%
Net Expenses	15.5%	15.4%	15.4%	14.6%	14.5%	14.8%
Adjusted EBIT	11.6%	11.9%	12.2%	12.5%	12.4%	13.1%

*Recent experience used in projections

The next exhibit illustrates how this information is used by this buyer.

Sophisticated Buyer's Earnings Computation

Year	Adjusted EBIT	Wgt	Extension	Wgt	Extension
2011	496,500			1	496,500
2010	474,500			2	949,000
2009	437,500			3	1,312,500
2008	405,500			4	1,622,000
Est. Current Yr.	372,500	1	372,500	1	372,500
2006	254,409	5	1,272,045	5	1,272,045
2005	259,020	4	1,036,080	4	1,036,080
2004	260,385	3	781,155	3	781,155
2003	215,613	2	431,226	2	431,226
2002	184,584	1	184,584	1	184,584
	1,174,011	16	4,077,590	26	8,457,590

Most recent yr.   254,409

5 Year Straight average   234,802

Weighted average   254,849

Weighted historic and future average   325,292

You will recall that we have normalized Owner Compensation and that this earnings figure, unlike the Financial buyer's calculation, is net of a new owner's compensation package.

CAUTION - Providing buyers with projections can be risky especially when they are not supported with factual data. Too many business brokers and intermediaries develop "hockey stick" projections or projections of exceedingly increasing profitability. The result - essentially all rosy projections are considered insulting and are routinely ignored by the audience they were intended to impress.

Projections can also prove dangerous in our litigious environment, especially when the projections are unsupported by factual data or third party experts or authorities. However, providing data and information required to make projections is an entirely different matter. Providing the required information with which this buyer will make their own rosy projections positions you as a savvy businessperson. Your BSS software provides you this data.

Summary of Sophisticated Buyer's Valuation Methods

Method	Value	Weight	Extension
Excess Earnings	1,189,961	0.35	416,486
Discounted Cash Flow	1,089,691	0.25	272,423
Capitalization of Earnings	1,100,000	0.15	165,000
Multiple of EBIT	1,250,000	0.25	312,500
	4,629,652	1.00	1,166,409
Straight Average Value	1,157,413		
Weighted Average Value	1,166,409		
Target Value			$ 1,160,000

Transaction Structure

Whereas Lifestyle buyers feel a fair down payment should approximate the present earnings of the company the Sophisticated buyer has a different view. Sophisticated buyers use the Capitalization Rate (Risk/Reward Ratio) they established to measure the fairness of the amount of capital investment required.

Transaction Structure continued

Example: Discretionary Earnings of $350K less an appropriate owner/manager salary divided by the initial investment will produce an ROI percentage.

	$350K	Discretionary Earnings
less	250K	Salary, Debt service and Depreciation Reserves
equals	$100K	$ Return on Investment (ROI)
divided by	400K	Down Payment
equals	25%	% Return on Investment (ROI)

This exhibit measures the fairness of a transaction through the prism of a Sophisticated buyer.

Assumptions:	Seller's Note	Bank Note
Interest Rate	8.0%	8.0%
# Years Note	10.0	10.0
# Years Covenant not to Compete	5.0	
# Years Consulting Agreement	5.0	
The Capitalization Rate developed for this company is:		33.7%
The Ratio under this scenario equal:	43.3%	
Possible Structure:	Terms	
Target Purchase Price	1,160,000	
Down Payment	500,000	
Bank Loan	270,000	
Covenant not to Compete	50,000	
Consulting Agreement	50,000	
Seller's Note	290,000	
Total Purchase Price	1,160,000	
Annual Debt Service:		
Covenant not to Compete	10,000	
Consulting Agreement	10,000	
Seller's Note	43,219	
Bank Note	40,238	
Total Debt Service	103,457	
Adjusted EBIT	370,000	
less Debt Service	(103,457)	
less Return on Buyer's on Cash Down	(50,000)	
Buyer's Return on invested capital	$ 216,543	

Corporate or Sophisticated Acquirers will deduct an appropriate manager's salary, debt service and reserves for depreciation from Discretionary Earnings and then calculate the return on their initial investment (ROI). The ROI should approximate the capitalization rate developed as a measure of risk appropriate to the opportunity (plus or minus 10%).

Convert Fair Market Value
to Fair Cash Value

Fair Market Value (FMV) is universally defined as a price received in "cash or equivalent." However, because financing for the acquisition of small and mid size businesses is restricted, the American Society of Appraisers (ASA) has redefined FMV for business transfers as "the price received under terms usual in the marketplace" i.e. Seller Financing. This exhibit measures the impact of restrictive financing and demands for a cash transaction and converts the Sophisticated Buyer's terms price to Fair Cash Value.

NOTE - The down payment typically is limited to $500,000 if the buyer is an individual.

Target Purchase Price	$	1,160,000
Usual Down Payment		500,000
Probable Bank Loan		270,000
Possible Cash at Transfer		770,000
Usual Seller's Note		390,000
Total Price (FMV)		1,160,000

1) Unfinanced portion of Transaction — 33.6%
2) Divide by 2, add result to CAP rate as
   an adder for lack of financing — 16.8%
3) CAP Rate for this business — 33.7%
4) Discount Rate — 50.5%
5) Apply Discount Rate to usual Seller's Note to calculate Present Value

Annual note payments:		Present Value Factor	Present Value of Payments
1st year	102,881	0.664476	68,362
2nd year	102,881	0.441528	45,425
3rd year	102,881	0.293385	30,184
4th year	102,881	0.194947	20,056
5th year	102,881	0.129538	13,327

6) Present Value of usual Seller's Note — 177,354
7) Add Cash at Transfer — 770,000

Estimated Fair Cash Value $ 947,354

ALERT - In this example the reduction in value is close to the amount of seller financing required obtaining full value. It would be particularly foolhardy for this business owner to refuse participation in financing considering the difficulty in selling a private company without seller's participation in the financing package.

More on Seller Financing

The need for seller participation in financing a transaction is one of the items that make selling a business different from selling essentially anything else you can imagine.

A summary of the reasons why:

- Lenders require a degree of seller participation
- Buyer's confidence in the deal increases making a deal more likely
- Increase confidence of buyer and lender equates to higher value
- Business is more likely to actually sell with seller financing than without
- Fair Market Value (with seller financing) is higher than Fair Cash Value

It is normal for a business owner to resist the concept of seller financing for a significant number of good reasons primary of which are:

- How do you know you will get paid?
- What if the buyer doesn't make it?
- Would rather have all the money now

These fears diminish and your willingness increases as the *Business Selling System* helps you identify the profile of your ideal buyer. Do not close the door on seller financing in the beginning. You do not have to agree to provide financing until after you have met and approved of your buyer.

Impact of Demand for a Cash Deal

You also have probably noticed the negative impact a demand for an all cash price has upon a company's value. In this example the lender requested the seller of the business participate in the acquisition funding (as essentially all lenders will).

They required 10% or a $120,000 seller note, the balance of the purchase price would be cash at closing provided by the bank and buyer in the amount of $1,080,000. More than the predicted all cash price without seller financing. Perhaps more important than extra dollars at closing is that without some measure of seller financing there may not be a closing at all.

There is strong evidence that firm refusals to participate in providing some measure of acquisition funding scares away most buyers, especially Financial or Lifestyle buyers, and most all lenders. The practical question such firm refusals raise is "What does the seller know that we don't?" When perception of risk goes up, value goes down or vanishes entirely.

The graduate with a Science degree asks, "*Why does it work?*"
The graduate with an Engineering degree asks, "*How does it work?*"
The graduate with an Accounting degree asks, "*How much will it cost?*"
The graduate with a Liberal Arts degree asks, "*Do you want fries with that?*"

Summary of all Values

This summary indicates that a Financial or Lifestyle buyer willing to finance the acquisition to the max or a Sophisticated or Corporate buyer, if the company is prepared to attract one, are the buyers of choice.

Industry or Asset Buyer Methods	Values	Weight	Extension
Book Value	137,480	0.10	13,748
Adjusted Book Value	165,000	0.80	132,000
Liquidation Value	173,479	0.10	17,348
		1.00	
Probable Industry Buyer Value		$	160,000
Financial or Lifestyle Buyer Methods			
Basic	735,000	0.25	183,750
Discretionary Earnings	777,273	0.30	233,182
Comparable Sales	789,855	0.30	236,957
Cost to Replace	225,000	0.05	11,250
Debt Capacity	1,009,634	0.10	100,963
		1.00	
Probable Financial Buyer Value		$	750,000
Estimated Cash Value	$ 593,903		
Sophisticated or Corporate Buyer Methods			
Excess Earnings	1,189,961	0.35	416,486
Discounted Cash Flow	1,089,691	0.25	272,423
Capitalization of Earnings	1,100,000	0.15	165,000
Multiple of EBIT	1,250,000	0.25	312,500
		1.00	
Probable Sophisticated Buyer Value		$	1,160,000
Estimated Cash Value	$ 947,354		
Target Value		$	1,160,000

The general who wins the battle makes many calculations in his temple
before the battle is fought.
The general who loses makes but few calculations beforehand.

Sun Tzu

Step Two - *AIM*

In Step One you confirmed that a sale of your business is timely and have decided to proceed.

The next steps are to:

Identify the characteristics of your ideal buyer,
Arrange for acquisition financing for your buyer,
Review taxation consequences,
Prepare marketing materials that fully describe your opportunity,
Compile a complete Due Diligence package

2008 Parker Nelson Publishing

How to Identify and Find the "Right Buyer"

Attracting business opportunity buyers is a relatively easy task. All you have to do is spend money on advertising and wait for the telephone to start ringing. Finding motivated and realistic buyers capable of operating your business is another story. You probably do not want to start traipsing a hoard of possible buyers through your business in the hope that one will turn out to be qualified to both purchase and operate your business.

More Stats - 60 to 1

In our first years of business brokerage my records show that it took twenty buyer interviews to get one offer and it took three offers to close one sale. Sixty buyer interviews resulted in one sale! Wow, that's a lot of people and a whole lot of work. You certainly don't want to have anywhere near sixty people poking around your business just because they think they might want to buy it. Do you want to give sixty people copies of your tax returns?

We found a better way

We eventually realized that our real role was more similar to that of a Career Counselor (on the buy side) and Head Hunter or Recruiter (on the sell side) rather than that of a Real Estate Broker. We were, after all, interviewing future presidents and CEOs for our business owner clients and placing candidates into new careers. What tools did recruiters employ in recruiting executives?

I contacted an acquaintance who was a career counselor and explained what I did and asked for direction. He agreed that we both were doing essentially the same job i.e. placing people in new careers. The first step he took, he explained, was to inventory the candidate's skills, resources, training and interests. Next was to suggest careers matching the skill sets of the candidate.

We developed a tool, with the career counselor's aid, to assist us in helping our buyers find the business that would be right for them. We named the tool our "Buyer Profile and Business Identification Workbook." Buyers visiting us for the first time would now leave our offices with homework. We included a copy of this workbook in the appendix of this book for reference only. We do not expect you will be comfortable asking candidates to complete and return it to you although it would help you considerably in understanding them and their personality.

3 to 1 - Our effectiveness improved dramatically once we began "Profiling" buyers as well as businesses. Eventually my top producers would interview two buyers for every sale or one sale for every two buyers interviewed. Wc became up to thirty times more effective using the deliberate three step process of what is now our Business Selling System.

You only have one business to sell so we have developed a tool similar to our "Buyer Profile and Business Identification Workbook" for you to use to identify the traits and characteristics of your ideal buyer.

Profiling allowed us sell our client's businesses
with exposure to three or less buyers

Recruiting a New President and CEO

Because we are actually in the process of recruiting a new president for your company we can look to the process successful recruiting firms employ for guidance. We modified the methods they use into four separate elements.

Develop a Profile The goal is to develop a comprehensive profile of your ideal candidate. The question is how? The answer - Start by profiling yourself and your business.

Profile yourself and your business - We operate our businesses, not only for financial reasons but also personal and lifestyle reasons and, a business is generally a reflection of the owner. Those areas of interest to the owner were pursued; other items go wanting or are ignored.

By profiling yourself and your business you are actually developing a profile of your ideal buyer. He need not be your clone. Actually, he should have skills and interests in those areas where you are lacking or weak. He should be able to appreciate and maintain what has allowed the company to get where it is today, plus have the necessary skills to bring the firm to the next level of profitability.

Visualize a bell curve rating the levels of proficiencies and shortcomings of your business. The high points might well represent the company's facility, employees, products or service, equipment and the low points: sales and marketing, and systems and controls. The negative or reverse of this curve will represent the skills the new owner should possess.

Your Areas of Strength
Buyer Able to Maintain

Need Improvement   **Need Improvement**
Buyer's Strengths   *Buyer's Strengths*

Example:

Present Management	Successor
Needs sales/marketing	Strong sales/marketing
Strong systems/controls	Maintain system and controls
Strong product development	Appreciate product
Weak finance	Strong finance
Average manager	Above average manager
Worn out	Energetic

NOTE

Here is where business owners typically can use some help. We often are too close to our business and our self to be totally objective in this process.

Motivation - Remember, buyers are looking for a business upon which they can imprint their image, one that they can make their own. They really want a business that has "All the right things wrong with it". You are searching for the candidate who will recognize the opportunity your business represents and will be able to take it to the next level. In order to do that, the buyer should be able to maintain what you have created and posses the skills, resources, interests and abilities you lack.

You can now identify your ideal acquirer by the skills, interests and resources required of a new president in order that the company may flourish. Those candidates failing to fit this profile need not be considered further.

Essentials Profile Elements

In order to attract the right buyer for your business, you need a crystal-clear picture of the type of person you're looking for. The description should go beyond just experience and education to include work and character traits that will impact a person's ability to grow your company.

The profile you create will serve multiple purposes; help identify where your candidate might be found, how to write the ads and other marketing materials. It becomes a key element in your screening process, helping you develop the right questions to ask of candidates you attract.

The five profile elements are:

- **Job description** - What should be their primary responsibility?
- **Work experience** - What background experience will help get the job done?
- **Skills** - What unique skills must the person bring to the company?
- **Style** - How will the person get the job done?
- **Personality** - What kind of personality will match your company culture?
  We will address each of these pieces below.

Job Description

Develop a summary of the responsibilities as well as a list of the key duties that will be performed by the new president. Think this through thoroughly. A hazy or incorrect description will make it harder for you to match a candidate and a job because you're not sure what the job actually entails. What primary skills are required to move your business up to the next level?

In a very small business, say an auto body shop, one might assume the new owner should be an experienced auto body mechanic. That is, someone who knows the business and can take over from the existing mechanic owner. We however, have a different view. Does the company really want a "Clone" of the present owner as the new leader? Will a clone have the skills required to take the business to a higher level? Will the "Clone" see the most opportunity or will he just look at the business simply as *a job with a lot more responsibility and risk?*

Why not try and attract a "Clone"?

It is quite easy to find a clone, perhaps one of the present employees would be interested in buying the company. The problem is generally that an employee typically will view your company's value through the eyes of an Industry or Asset buyer.

The candidate need not be an auto body mechanic but must be mechanically savvy and understand what is involved in operating an auto body repair shop. A person lacking *Mechanical* ability would be held hostage by employees who realized the boss had no clue as to what was going on.

The present owner is a great mechanic but lacks *Sales* and *Marketing* prowess. A new president with these skills could certainly increase sales and bring the company to a new level. The new president should not be the "doer" but rather the "getter." This person perhaps lacks the skills that were needed to create the company but has all the qualifications to move it forward.

Increased business means increased staff therefore skills in managing people are required so we add *Management* skills to the profile. Essentially we are seeking a candidate who wants to run a company rather than do the job. Our candidate's profile dictates we find an enterprising company builder rather than a task oriented craftsman.

Much of the work this business gets comes from referrals. Insurance agents and auto dealers can become major sources of new and repeat business. The new president ideally will have networking skills or perhaps connections in these or other appropriate areas. We will therefore add *Networking* to our Profile.

You may find yourself too close to your business to be effective in developing a Profile and find a third party's input of significant value. None of us know what we don't know and a trusted outsider's view often proves invaluable.

The writer does not have at lot of experience or knowledge of the auto body business and therefore may have missed additional Profile elements. Conversely, someone from another industry, say marine hull repair, might have invaluable suggestions based upon their industry that should be applicable to auto body repair.

Is a special niche or type of business being overlooked or avoided? Can an additional product or service be added? Is fiberglass repair being avoided and does adding it require a skill or interest that could be added to our Profile?

We developed a matrix to help you in your efforts to identify and rate the level of skill and ability your business requires of its new president. There is a copy in the Exhibit section for your use.

The example on the following page is an example of how our hypothetical Auto Body Shop owner might complete the worksheet.

Skills and Knowledge desired of the New President

Listed below are specific areas where you can rate levels of skill and comfort on a scale of 1 – 10 with 10 being the highest. Use this matrix first to measure your levels and then, do it again with the new president in mind. We provide you with a blank matrix in the Exhibit section.

	Low				Medium				High	
Accounting	1	2	3	4	5	6	7	8	9	10
Finance	1	2	3	4	5	6	7	8	9	10
Artistic	1	2	3	4	5	6	7	8	9	10
Taxes	1	2	3	4	5	6	7	8	9	10
Selling	1	2	3	4	5	6	**7**	**8**	**9**	10
Marketing	1	2	3	4	5	6	**7**	**8**	**9**	10
Sales Mgmt	1	2	3	4	5	**6**	**7**	**8**	9	10
Managerial	1	2	3	4	5	**6**	**7**	**8**	9	10
Motivational	1	2	3	4	5	6	7	8	9	10
Analytical	1	2	3	4	5	6	7	8	9	10
Verbal	1	2	3	4	5	6	7	8	9	10
Writing	1	2	3	4	5	6	7	8	9	10
Mechanical	1	2	3	4	5	6	**7**	**8**	**9**	10
Design	1	2	3	4	5	6	7	8	9	10
Computer	1	2	3	4	5	6	7	8	9	10
Programming	1	2	3	4	5	6	7	8	9	10
Systems	1	2	3	4	5	6	7	8	9	10
Controls	1	2	3	4	5	6	7	8	9	10
Concepts	1	2	3	4	5	6	7	8	9	10
Manual	1	2	3	4	**5**	**6**	**7**	8	9	10
Athletic	1	2	3	4	5	6	7	8	9	10
Task Oriented	1	2	3	4	5	6	7	8	9	10
Social	1	2	3	4	5	6	7	8	9	10
Investigative	1	2	3	4	5	6	7	8	9	10

| **Enterprising** | 1 | 2 | 3 | 4 | 5 | 6 | **7** | **8** | **9** | 10 |

Other:

Networking	1	2	3	4	5	**6**	**7**	**8**	9	10
	1	2	3	4	5	6	7	8	9	10
	1	2	3	4	5	6	7	8	9	10

Work experience/education

Industry familiarity, educational background and, professional certification may all be crucial to helping you screen candidates. Will experience in your industry be essential or will skills from other industry experience be of benefit? What education background will have a bearing on the candidate ability to perform the job? Will industry or job-specific certification be required?

List work experiences and education that would be either required or helpful.

Required	**Helpful**
Selling	Automobile related connections
Business development	Developed sales team
Manage a staff	

46

Skills

What unique skills must your candidate possess? Review the duties the person will perform and assess what skills are required to complete those tasks. Your list should include hard skills (what the person knows) and soft skills (how the person applies that knowledge). "Hard" skills are those will appear on your resume -- your education, experience and level of expertise in different arenas. Soft Skills are generally considered "people skills".

Example of Soft Skills

Curiosity, Agreeable, Conscientious, Effective Communicator, Problem Solving, Winner's Attitude, Listening Skills, Negotiator, Conflict Mediator. Core Values, Team Player, Loner, Task Orientated, Creativity, Handle Criticism, Motivate Others, Multi Tasking all are examples of Soft Skills.

List the hard and soft skills your ideal candidate should possess.

Hard Skills	Soft Skills
Management experience	Positive attitude
Sales Training/Experience	Good customer relations
	Multi Tasking

Style

In a small business, how a person does their work can be as important as what they do. For example, a person who works best on their own might not fit well in a culture that encourages team work.

Some typical work styles:

- Works best in a team
- Works best alone
- Needs direction
- Generates solutions independently
- Tackles problems head on
- Thinks problems through
- Finds creative solutions
- Highly organized

List the preferred work style of your ideal candidate.

Work Style

Well organized
Finds creative solutions
Delegates effectively

Personality

What kind of personality works best in your organization? Take work style a step further to consider the attitudes and manners you want in your successor. Your goal will be to find the type of person that is most productive in the work environment you've created, and can complement your current workforce. Develop a list of the character traits you most value. The list will include things like sense of humor, honesty, compassion, driven, laid back.

Personality Traits

Honesty
Diplomatic

IMPORTANT

The larger and more complex the business, the more comprehensive and detailed the Profile will be. Developing a proper Profile is more difficult and time consuming than one might initially believe. The quality of the effort spent on this foundational element of selling your business to the right party, quickly and quietly is directly proportional to the level of success you will obtain.

Develop
Marketing Materials

Marketing materials generally consist of two items:

- One page profile of the business
- Comprehensive Business Review or Prospectus

One Page Business Profile

This is developed for a business of any size and may be all that is required of the smallest businesses with simple operations.

The One Page Profile is designed to provide a good overview of the opportunity and is often sent to prospective buyers along with a Confidentiality Agreement in exchange for Financial Statement, Resume and other background information. It may be all that is required in the case of the smallest businesses.

A typical One Page Profile will briefly cover:

Type Business
Short History
Market Served and Marketing Area
Customer Concentrations
Sales Segmentation
Operations
Facilities/Equipment
Financial Overview
Staff
The Opportunity

The intent is to provide an overview of the size and scope of the company and the opportunity your business represents. Some of the above items might be inappropriate for your business and other headings inserted instead.

The purpose is to convey a concise overview of the company and the opportunity it represents.

NOTE

One should not be able to specifically identify the business from information contained in the One Page Profile, especially if confidentiality is to be maintained.

Sample

This is provided to candidates in response to their initial inquiry and to begin the screening and qualification process.

New England Distributor	
Financial: 2007	Revenue $5,300,000 Discretionary Earnings $650,000+ Strong balance sheet and operating ratios.
Services multiple industries	Including: construction, manufacturing & distribution, public order and safety, transportation, public safety and healthcare; Servicing multiple industries allows it to best weather economic swings.
Company's Competitive Advantage	Low price point, strong 50+ year reputation, long standing relationships with its customers and suppliers
Customer base	Over 90% of its core product line customers have been with the company for more than 10 years. The company enjoys similar relationships with its suppliers.
Customer Concentrations	Average customer represents less than 1% of the total sales and no one customer represents more than 3% of sales.
Cumulative growth rate	124% since 2001
Facility	Operates out of Company owned 7,000 square foot office/warehouse with a total of 7 employees (including owner). Room for expansion on five acre lot. Real Estate available for lease or purchase.
Financing	Financing is in place for the person or company with a suitable down payment and qualifications to operate a company of this size and type.
The Opportunity Reason for Sale	Company needs a sales force to service its large customer base. Thirty year owner wants to retire. Will stay on for suitable transition period to assure smooth transfer.
In order that we may proceed, please send your Financial Statement, Résumé, Confidentiality Agreement and any other information you deem appropriate to: **Opportunity** PO Box 123 Sunnyvale, XZ 00000	

This One Page Profile for a Breakfast and Lunch business is a bit simpler as is the business.

Breakfast and Lunch

History	This Coffee Shop/Breakfast and Lunch was established in 1980 and completely renovated in 2002
Location/Facility	Located in the center of an historic New England seaport town. Seats 66, - 10 at the counter, 36 in booths and 20 at tables. Parking in lot for 25 cars plus on street and municipal lot across the street.
Staff	5 full time and 10 part time employees – All need the job and will remain after a sale.
Hours of Operation	Open six days – Mon - Saturday, 5 am to 2pm Closed on Sunday

Financial:

Year	2007	2006	2005	2004	2003
Volume	330K	350K	380K	365K	370K
Earnings*	81K	97K	124K	118K	122K

*Discretionary Earnings = pre-tax earnings, interest, amortization, discretionary and non recurring expenses plus owner's compensation

The Opportunity	Expand hours and menu. Restaurant should be re-opened Sunday mornings to service parishioners of the three churches within a half mile of the shop.
Financing	Financing is in place for the person with a suitable down payment and qualifications to operate this business.
Reason for Sale	Owner's poor health forces sale. Will stay on for suitable transition period to assure smooth transfer.

In order that we may proceed, please send your Financial Statement, Résumé or summary of your work experience, Confidentiality Agreement and any other information to:

Opportunity
PO Box 123
Sunnyvale, XZ 00000

NOTE

NOTE Confidentiality as to the identity of this business may have been compromised by the description "*Parking in lot for 25 cars plus on street and municipal lot across the street.*" Writing a concise one page description the company represents is not as easy as it might first appear.

Do not be surprised if it takes you several hours to complete the task. As Benjamin Franklin is reported to have said; "I apologize for writing you such a long letter but I had not the time to write a shorter one."

Comprehensive Business Review (CBR)

A CBR is provided to a candidate only after you are convinced they are:

1) Financially able and

2) Their education, background and experience qualify them to operate your business.

A CBR should not be given out to just anyone requesting one. Candidates must pass through your screening process before you give them your CBR. We typically would only have to **use two or three CBRs before the business was under contract**. We will be discussing the screening process in depth in subsequent chapters. Fortunately, a significant portion of the CBR is automatically generated by your *Business Selling System* software.

Purpose of a CBR:

To provide a track for your candidate and their advisors to follow as they review and later investigate your opportunity.

We have included a *Business Profile* data gathering sheets in the Appendix for you to use as a guide when developing your CBR. The subjects itemized below will give you an idea of what your CBR should cover. They represent the information most requested and questions most often asked by business buyers.

Business:

- Name and Form of Ownership
- Year business was established and, if applicable, the year present owner acquired
- Description of the Business
- Square footage Business occupies, Number of Seats etc.
- Special licenses required, vending contracts, franchise or license contracts

Industry:

- What is the social status, visual appeal, desirability of this Business or Industry?
- Have liability insurance rates gone up?
- What is the trend for this Industry?
- What is the status of local labor pool for this Business?

Lease:

- How many months remaining with option to renew for an additional period of years?
- Does lease contain option to buy Real Estate?
- Is Lease assignable or a new Lease available?

Staff:

- How many family members active in Business?
- Number of non-family employees: Full-time, Part-time – Will they stay or leave?

Operations

- Hours Open: # days open
- How much training is required to perform and understand this company's operations?
- New business is obtained by: (Owners influence, walk in, direct mail, etc
- What special license, degree or skills would a new owner need
- Present marketing strategy?

Customers:

- How many Customers does the Business serve?
- What number of Customers account for 25% of Volume?

Financial:

- How accurately can you predict Revenues?
- How important is the Owner to the Revenues of this Business?
- Over last three years, how have Gross Sales been trending?

Overview:

- What are the businesses strong points?
- What are the opportunities?
- How could the Business be improved?

Competition:

- How many Competitors in marketing area? How many have failed in last two years ? How many are new (within last two years)?

Impending Changes:

- Are traffic flow, government regulations, zoning and competition etc. pending? If yes, would the Business be affected positively and/or negatively?

CBRs usually contain between15 to 50 pages. As you would imagine, the larger and more complex the business, the more pages required to describe it.   We are including two sample CBRs, for your review.

CAUTION

Do not leave anything that might be construed as negative out of your CBR. Surprises kill deals and if the surprise is found after the deal is done – the only winners generally are the attorneys.

NOTE - Every business has areas of neglect or issues that need attention.
Your ideal candidate will be the person who will recognize
these matters as opportunities.

What to do? Either:

1) Deal with the problem and fix it or,

2) Highlight the issue as an opportunity a new owner can capitalize upon.

Remember - Buyers get excited when "All the right things are wrong!"

POINTS TO REMEMBER

- Everything included in the CBR should be able to be documented.
- Avoid hyperbole and flowery descriptions; stick to the facts.
- Credibility is enhanced with third party ratification of CBR positions.
- Keep the candidate and level of advisor input you can expect in mind as you write the CBR
- Be sure the numbers and opportunity are supported by the story i.e.: declining sales, opportunity to re-open on Sundays and owner in poor health

Sample CBR

Confidential Business Profile

This memorandum contains certain confidential and proprietary information concerning the business affairs of ████████████, Inc. (Company) and is to be used solely for the purpose of evaluation the possible acquisition of this company.

This memorandum and any other related material are intended solely for the confidential use of those persons to whom it is transmitted and returned to YOUR COMPANY upon completion of the review and without copies having been made.

By accepting this memorandum the recipient acknowledges and reaffirms the Confidentiality and Non Disclosure Agreement executed _____ and that all information contained in the is memorandum is subject to said agreement.

Presented to:_____

Presented by:_____

Accepted by: _____

Print Name: _____

Return upon completion of review to:

Name

Street address

City, State Zip Code

Table of Contents

The Company

████████████ (the Company) is located in the ████████ Industrial Park, on █ ████████ Road, ████████, ██ The Company provides Welding service and precision Metal Fabrications for area machine shops. The company also fabricates marine fuel tanks. The Company has the capability to weld and fabricate using essentially any metal.

History

The company was formed by the present owner in 1968 and moved to the present location in 1986. The company was formed as a C Corporation with a fiscal year end of September 30. Starting in a small barn in 1968 it now is located in a 10,000 s/f clear span building close to all major highways.

Market Served

The company serves two different markets.
- Marine, both commercial and pleasure - builds fuel tanks for both commercial and pleasure crafts. The fuel tanks are considerable in size and are not to be confused with the small portable tanks used with outboard engines.
- Job shop serving the needs of area machine shops and major corporations in the area

Market Area

The marine fuel tank business serves many marinas and fishing vessels in the area from Boston to Cape Cod and Providence, RI. Tanks can be built and shipped anywhere however, present management is comfortable with things as is and has no plans to expand outside this market.

The welding and fabrication is localized with the Company serving several major corporations in the area.

Outlook for the Market Served

The outlook for the pleasure craft segment of the business is positive. According to the National Sporting Goods Association (NSGA) "Power Boating is the Highest Gaining Outdoor Activity in 20██; up 6.2%..."

-

Customer Concentrations

The company does have two major customers on the welding and fabrication side of the business that at the present time consists of about 30% of the business. The marine fuel tank business does not experience a customer concentration issues.

Sales Segmentation

The marine fuel tank business is about 70% of the overall business. The marine fuel tank business is priced on a time and material basis, while the job fabrication is done on an hourly shop rate basis.

Operations

The company's normal work week is Monday through Friday from 7:30 to 5pm. During the summer they are open a half day on Saturday.

Facilities

The company leases from the ██████████████ the premises in the amount of about 10,000 square feet. The rent is competitive for a like type of building, about $5.00 a square foot.

Equipment

The equipment is maintained and in operating order for the types of work that is being completed. The suitability matches the type of work being completed and the condition is good. The fair market value of the equipment is appraised at **$350,000.** Complete Equipment list can be found in the Exhibit section.

Financial

Revenues and earnings are summarized below. Additional Ratios and Comparative Income Statements and Balance Sheets are included in Exhibits.

Year End 9/30	2007	2006	2005	2004	2003
Revenue	701,475	730,905	890,952	648,188	654,398
Cost of Goods	57,080	49,238	216,837	80,124	64,935
Ratio	8.1%	6.7%	24.3%	12.4%	9.9%
Period Average	12.9%				
Net Expenses	568,148	614,270	585,248	509,119	507,614
Ratio	81.0%	84.0%	65.7%	78.5%	77.6%
Period Average	76.8%				
Discretionary. Earnings *	**91,320**	**80,051**	**97,833**	**73,397**	**101,812**
Ratio	13.0%	11.0%	11.0%	11.3%	15.6%

Period Average	12.3%			
Labor Cost	331,245	365,973	347,304	295,650	282,440
Ratio	47.2%	50.1%	39.0%	45.6%	43.2%
Period Average	44.8%			

- Dollars available for new owner's compensation, acquisition debt service, actual depreciation reserves and return on invested capital.

NOTE

This Company enjoys moderate profitability compared with the value of the assets employed. The highest valuation for was the Basic Method (Value of Assets plus Cash Flow). Following this thinking, the information on this page suggests a valuation approximating $450,000. To support this value we had the assets appraised by a respected appraiser and included this information in the CBR.

Staff

The staff of the Company consists of four employees as welders and the owner and his wife who would be leaving the company upon the sale after a transition phase. All four of the employees are proficient in all Company operations.

The employment rooster as of January 2007:

Name	Position	Rate	Tenure	Stay/ Leave	Hours w/k	Age
Mark	Welder	15.75	12 yrs	Stay	40	35
Sheldon	Welder	14.00	8 yrs	Stay	40	43
Alice (owner)	Office	12.50		Leave	20	
Ronald	Welder	13.50	5 yrs	Stay	40	33
Roy (owner)	Welder	10.50		Leave	20	
Edwin	Welder	11.00	3 yrs	Stay	40	48

Financing

Financing is in place in the amount of **$400,000** for the candidate with a down payment of 20% and qualifications to operate the Company.

The Opportunity

The company presents a great opportunity for an acquirer with sales and marketing expertise to grow the business by adding products and expanding services in the markets it already serves:

- Add marine water tanks, fish holds to the tank product line
- Expand the fuel tank business further into the northeast and Mid-Atlantic area.
- Branding of the marine fuel tanks to foster brand awareness
- Add fabrication of boat towers, T-Tops and radar arches to compliment the fuel tank business

Additional growth can be achieved by adding a sales force. Yellow pages are the only advertising used by the company and most of its business comes from word of mouth and referrals.

The company is presently at 50% of its operating capacity providing the opportunity for growth without incurring major capital expense.

Reason for Sale

The owner founded the Company almost forty years ago and now wants to retire to the home they recently purchased in Florida.

NOTE

Lender(s) have pre-approved loaning up to $400,000 to a qualified candidate further supporting an unspoken valuation in this range.

Exhibits

Comparative Balance Sheet

From Federal 1120

Assets

Year End 12/31	2007	2006	2005	2004	2003
Current Assets:					
Cash	116,698	184,077	132,130	102,610	151,758
Marketable Securities					
Accounts Receivable	51,447	45,221	37,894	41,225	27,541
Inventories	45,777	38,995	27,588	15,999	21,875
Prepaid Expenses	3,719	3,719	3,719	3,719	3,719
Total Current Assets	**217,641**	**272,012**	**201,331**	**163,553**	**204,893**
Fixed Assets					
Leasehold Improvements					
Equipment and Machinery	598,282	584,505	576,625	576,315	573,648
Vehicles	85,418	85,418	85,418	85,418	65,221
Office Equipment	35,778	30,456	30,456	27,554	25,446
less Accumulated Depreciation	(564,331)	(548,510)	(537,391)	(523,466)	(509,773)
Total Fixed Assets	**155,147**	**151,869**	**155,108**	**165,821**	**154,542**
Other Assets					
Other	0	0	0	0	0
Total Other Assets	0	0	0	0	0
Total Assets	**372,788**	**423,881**	**356,439**	**329,374**	**359,435**
Liabilities					
Current Liabilities					
Accounts Payable	12,444	17,588	11,457	8,512	6,522
Accrued Profit Sharing					
Accrued Taxes	1,245	1,452	1,733	975	855
Current Portion LT Debt					
Line of Credit					
Notes to Shareholders					
Total Current Liabilities	**13,689**	**19,040**	**13,190**	**9,487**	**7,377**
Long Term Liabilities					
Notes payable - Banks					
Noted payable - Other					
Capital Leases					
Other	1,286	2,424	2,801	6,522	5222
Total Long Term Liabilities	**1,286**	**2,424**	**2,801**	**6,522**	**5,222**
Total Liabilities	**14,975**	**21,464**	**15,991**	**16,009**	**12,599**
Stockholder's Equity	**357,813**	**402,417**	**340,448**	**313,365**	**346,836**
Total Assets and Liabilities	**372,788**	**423,881**	**356,439**	**329,374**	**359,435**

Information obtained from Company tax returns

Adjusted Income and Expense

Year End 12/31	2007	2006	2005	2004	2003
Revenue	701,475	730,905	890,952	648,188	654,398
Cost of Sales:					
Beginning Inventories					
Purchases	57,080	49,238	216,837	80,124	64,935
Labor					
less Ending Inventories					
Cost of Sales Total	57,080	49,238	216,837	80,124	64,935
Interest Income	15,073	12,654	12,318	14,452	13,701
Schedule D Capital Gain					5,400
Gain/Loss from 4797			(3,352)		862
Gross Profit	659,468	694,321	683,081	582,516	609,426
Total Expenses	647,419	686,668	675,310	578,804	569,777
Income Before Taxes	**12,049**	**7,653**	**7,771**	**3,712**	**39,649**
Adjustments:					
Officer's Compensation	63,415	61,259	59,352	55,987	44,813
Depreciation	15,821	11,119	30,710	13,693	17,350
Interest	35	20	0	5	0
Total Adjustments	79,271	72,398	90,062	69,685	62,163
Net Expenses	568,148	614,270	585,248	509,119	507,614
Discretionary Earnings *	**91,320**	**80,051**	**97,833**	**73,397**	**101,812**

NOTE

Detailed expense data has been intentionally omitted. Providing this detail is unnecessary at this point and, if included, simply invites the candidate and his advisors to get off the main issue and to drift off into trivia instead.

Main Issues at this Point:

- Can this business' earnings support a reasonable living wage and debt service?
- Is this an opportunity that "fits" the candidate and therefore should be pursued?

Examples of Trivia: (if detailed expenses data is included)
 Why is the rubbish removal expense so high? Etc.

Equipment List

Arco Welding Machine

2004 GMC Flatbed Truck

2001 Ford F250 PU

Acme Fork Lift

Welding Machine

Assembly Tables

More equipment

More equipment

More equipment

More equipment

More equipment

More equipment

More equipment

More equipment

More equipment

More equipment

More equipment

More equipment

More equipment

More equipment

More equipment

More equipment

More equipment

More equipment

More equipment

NOTE

An equipment or facilities list is appropriate for inclusion in your CBR when the assets can illustrate the operating capacity of your company.

Manufacturing firms, such as Machine Shops and Injection Molding companies, routinely include a list of their equipment as part of their marketing effort for this very reason.

Comparative Ratio Analysis

Year	2007	2006	2005	2004
Sales	730,905	890,952	648,188	654,398
Cost of Sales	57,080	49,238	216,837	80,124
Ratio	7.8%	5.5%	33.5%	12.2%
Period Average	16.0%			
Cost of Goods	57,080	49,238	216,837	80,124
Ratio	7.8%	5.5%	33.5%	12.2%
Period Average	16.0%			
Labor Cost	-	-	-	-
Ratio	0.0%	0.0%	0.0%	0.0%
Period Average	0.0%			
Net Expenses	568,148	614,270	585,248	509,119
Ratio	77.7%	68.9%	90.3%	77.8%
Period Average	95.2%			
Income Before Taxes	**12,049**	**7,653**	**7,771**	**3,712**
Ratio	1.6%	0.9%	1.2%	0.6%
Period Average	2.4%			
Discretionary. Earnings	**91,320**	**80,051**	**97,833**	**73,397**
Ratio	12.5%	9.0%	15.1%	11.2%
Period Average	15.2%			

NOTE

Additional ratio analysis was left out of this CBR as the candidate targeted is a Lifestyle Buyer. One who's profile suggests strong sales and marketing skills and reasonable mechanical ability. An additional two pages of numbers is overkill with this group of buyers.

Sample CBR #2

Introduction

This Confidential Business Review (Report) of the Company was prepared for the Reader of this document, a sincere and qualified buyer interested in pursuing an acquisition of this business (You). It has been submitted to you with the understanding that you have previously signed a confidentiality agreement with the Company and have been authorized to review this confidential information about the Company.

If a confidentiality agreement has not been signed, you are not authorized to review this document and might be held liable for damages as a result of knowledge gained from this report. Copies of any segment of this report are strictly prohibited unless previously authorized by the Company.

This report has been structured to help You evaluate this opportunity. We anticipate the information contained within this report will provide you with sufficient knowledge to evaluate information about the business to determine whether you find the business suitable and attractive for a potential acquisition.

Information about the Company was provided by Owner(s) and/or Management, and from books, records & financial statements and operating data, to assist with an evaluation of the Company. Data regarding the industry, marketplace, and other relevant information within which the Company operates, has been obtained from a number of sources including proprietary databases, trade journals, etc. Results and conclusions can be no more accurate than this data and information allow. Management has indicated any estimates made were based on good faith, intended to provide You further information to represent the business in a fair and reasonable manner, and were based on Management's knowledge, expertise or information that may or may not be tracked within its information systems.

Information contained within this Report is to be used as tools to better understand:
- A general overview of the Industry, its future outlook, general competition and trends
- Government regulations impacting the industry.
- The Company's Financial Performance and Position.
- Information about the Customers, Suppliers, Employees and Operations
- The Company's Uniqueness, and the Opportunity it represents.
- Whether the information contained within warrants an investment by You.

It must be clear that the validity of all of the information within this report is limited in time. Market conditions and input data can cause information in this report to change. The duration over which this kind of information is valid depends heavily upon this business, its industry, and general economic conditions. This report has been developed solely for You and will not be presented to unauthorized parties who have not been appropriately informed about this opportunity and the clauses incorporated into the confidentiality agreement you have previously signed.

Table of Contents

The Company

████████████████████████. (CEI) is a C Corporation with its president as the only shareholder. CEI was founded in 1992 in ████████, ██ as an authorized distributor of ████████ Communication Equipment and provides sales, rental, engineering and support services for the integration of wireless voice and data communication systems.

Products Provided and Serviced

Portable, mobile and base station radios in VHF, UHF and 900 MHz frequencies, repeaters, batteries, parts and accessories.

Markets Served

Government entities, fire and safety, private/public sector security, mobile fleets, construction companies, warehousing, hospitality industry, property management all are prime candidates for CEI's products and services.

Two-way radios are used in a variety of applications including:
- Coordination of efforts between teams, departments and organizations
- Maintenance, construction and other wide ranging activities
- Public safety, emergency response or disaster relief
- Enhancement to existing communications
- Special events, promotions

Location

CEI moved from ████████, ██ to larger quarters at its present 2,200 square foot location in July of 2000. This is a leased location near the intersection of Interstate ███ and route ███ in an office/industrial park. The current lease is assignable and has options to renew to June 30, 2018 at predetermined rents.

Staff

There are four non family employees in addition to the president.

Position	Salary	Tenure	Benefits
Office Manager	$44,200	4 years	HMO, Vested SEP/IRA
Technical Sales Rep	34,320	5 years	HMO, Vested SEP/IRA, Car
Technician	29,120	1 year	HMO
Service	40,000	2 years	HMO

Benefits

All employees, past and present, have signed a Non-compete agreement with CEI. Aetna HMO Health Insurance costs $250 per employee per month.

Owners Background

The President was a sales representative of two way communication equipment for five years prior to founding CEI. He currently spends approximately five hours a week on sales and marketing with the balance of his time spent equally between Administrative duties and Personnel/Financial management.

Operations

CEI operates five days a week from 8:30 A.M. to 5 P.M. Most sales and service activity is generated by incoming telephone calls. The source of the calls can be segregated as follows:

- 50% -. Existing customers (batteries, new equipment, service etc.)
- 30% -. Yellow Page advertising
- 20% -. Internet

Sales/Marketing

As noted above CEI does not have an outside sales force. Most sales activity is in reaction to incoming calls from existing customers and advertising efforts. CEI mails (How many) newsletters periodically to (How many) customers and possible customers The Company also will "FAX Blast" (How many) customers with announcements of specials and sales.

The Internet web site www.████████.com is generating an increasing amount of activity with an estimate of 800 visitors a month.

Segmentation of Sales

Details of sales and target gross profit by segment:

Segment	Estimate Volume	Target Gross Profit
2-way equipment sales	1,000,000	40%
2-way repairs	125,000	75%
2-way rentals	40,000	90%

Customer Concentrations

The top ten customers by percentage of sales

Year	2002	2001	2000
17.9	7.8	6.9	
12.1	6.5	4.9	
4.5	4.7	4.6	
3.3	3.8	3.4	
2.4	2.8	3.0	
2.3	2.7	2.9	
2.3	2.2	2.5	
2.0	2.0	2.4	
1.7	1.9	2.2	
1.5	1.9	2.1	
Remainder	50.0	63.7	64.9

Customers by Industry

Year	2002	2001	2000
	Police	School	Construction
	Federal	Construction	PA
	School	Retailer	Business Services
	Construction	Business Services	Property Management
	PA	Government	Hospitality
	College	Hospitality	Property Management
	Construction	Property Mgmt	School
	Business Services	Contractor	Contractor
	Contractor	School	Contractor
	School	Janitorial	Property Management

The Industry

Several factors have combined to enhance the outlook for the 2-way communications industry:

- Increased security concerns and
- Government spending on Homeland Security
- New FCC rules mandate equipment upgrades

Two way systems are not subject to congestion shutdowns such as those experienced during 9-11 by Nextel and cellular telephones. In view of this, Federal, State and local governments as well as private sector entities are updating their communications equipment as part of their disaster preparedness planning.

The FCC has mandated upgrades of equipment capable of operating in "Narrow Band" frequencies, (See Exhibit 1). It is these frequencies within which 2-way radios operate. Most existing equipment will therefore have to be replaced with equipment conforming with the new rules.

Financial

Year	2002	2001	2000
Revenue	1,233,466	1,089,269	1,108,687
Cost of Sales Total	722,395	591,104	610,708
Gross Profit	511,071	498,165	497,979
Net Expenses	298,183	283,505	299,335
Discretionary Earnings	*212,888	214,660	198,644

* Dollars available for new owner's compensation, acquisition debt service, actual depreciation reserves and return on invested capital

CEI appears to be a well run company as the ratio analysis data in the Exhibit section of this report illustrates.

- Exhibit 2 - Comparative Operating Ratios
- Exhibit 3 - Ratios to Measure Safety and Liquidity
- Exhibit 4 - Ratios Measuring Operating Efficiency

Acquisition Financing

Pre-approvals for financing of amounts to $1,000,000 (including working capital) have been obtained and are in place. The candidate must have prior sales and management experience to qualify for this funding.

Assets

Assets to be included in the sale include all inventory, furniture, equipment, telephone numbers, goodwill, trademarks, trade-names and other intangible assets. See Exhibit 5 for balance sheet data.

Advantages this Business Represents

- Operates five days, Monday thru Friday 8:30 to 5:00 leaving weekends and evenings free for the rest of ones life.
- The Two-way radio business enjoys healthy profit margins.
- Repeat business from existing customers
- Increased security concerns elevate the need for CEI's products and services
- FCC has mandated replacement of existing two way telephone systems over the next several years
- CEI represents the premier supplier in the industry

Marketplace Economy

If employment rates are an indicator of economy trends, the economy in the marketplace served by CEI appears to be strong. Unemployment rates for the region are declining and are lower than the national average. Currently the national unemployment rate is 5.6 while VA and MD stand at 3.8 and 4.3 respectively.

Source: U. S. Bureau of Labor Statistics

State and Local Government Spending

Homeland Security Funding is becoming available. CEI's products and services will be needed by Schools, Hospitals, Universities, Police and Fire Departments and others. Below are the NIGP Code and Description of Products listed on the Commonwealth of Virginia's web-site.

NIGP Code	Description
72500	RADIO COMMUNICATION, TELEPHONE, AND TELECOMMUNICATION EQUIPMENT, ACCESSORIES, AND SUPPLIES
72595	Recycled Communications Equipment (Including Batteries, Radios, Telephones, Telecommunication Equipment, etc.)

Opportunity

Develop an outside sales force to capitalize on the unique opportunities available for growth in sales and profits i.e.:

- New FCC rules mandate equipment upgrades
- Increased security concerns
- Government spending on Homeland Security.

Register as a vendor with Virginia and Maryland's Cities, Counties, Schools, Hospitals, Fire and Police. The city of Alexandria alone reports spending $400 million a year with registered vendors.

For information on becoming a registered Vendor in Virginia go to:
http://evaregishelp.dgs.state.va.us/

Maryland's Procurement Web sites:
http://www.emarylandmarketplace.com/emm/index.cfm
http://compnet.comp.state.md.us/procurement/default.asp

Industry Information Resources:

FCC Website http://www.fcc.gov/
Proposed Rules http://hraunfoss.fcc.gov/edocs_public/attachmatch/FCC-03-34A1.doc
American Mobile Telecommunication Association http://www.amtausa.org/
Canadian Wireless Telecommunication Association http://www.cwta.ca/

Exhibit 1

Federal Communications Commission (FCC) regulations

In 1995, the Federal Communications Commission (FCC) adopted regulations that will ultimately split each existing radio channel into four channels.

The rules adopted by the FCC envisioned that most people would transition to the 12.5 kHz bandwidth channels from the current 25 kHz bandwidth channels, and later transition to the 6.25 kHz bandwidth channels, as such equipment became available.

Rather than requiring licensees and new applicants to meet the narrower bandwidth channeling by specific target dates, the FCC decided to encourage the transition to narrowband operations by requiring that new radio equipment submitted to the FCC for certification on or after February 14, 1997 must be capable of operation within a bandwidth of 12.5 kHz, and equipment submitted for certification on or after January 1, 2005 must be capable of operation with a bandwidth of 6.25 kHz.

However, the FCC allowed previously-certificated 25 kHz bandwidth equipment to be sold indefinitely, allowing existing licensees of wideband equipment to continue purchasing such equipment to expand their radio systems and to license new systems.

The FCC reasoned that market forces would drive the transition to narrowband operations when it was in the interest of licensees to do so. As channels became increasingly congested or interference increased, licensees would have the incentive to buy more spectrally efficient, i.e. narrowband, equipment. The FCC believed that licensees operating in or near the major metropolitan areas would have the incentive to convert to narrow band equipment sooner because interference in those areas was greater, while licensees operating in remote areas, may be able to delay the conversion to narrow band for many years.

In 1998, the American Mobile Telecommunications Association (AMTA) filed a petition with the FCC stating that the transition to narrow band equipment was proceeding too slowly and asking the FCC to establish specific dates by which licensees would have to start using narrow band equipment or lose their primary status. The FCC has agreed that the conversion to narrow band equipment is proceeding too slowly, and has asked the public to comment on whether a mandatory transition date is necessary, and if so, what those dates should be.

Exhibit 1 continued

FCC Releases Second Report and Order (R&O) and Second Further Notice of Proposed Rule Making (FNPRM)

Decisions made mandating the transition to narrowband technologies in the VHF and UHF Re-farming bands include:

1) Beginning six months after publication of this 2nd R&O in the Federal Register, prohibit any applications for new operations using 25kHz channels, for any system operating in the 150-174mHz or 421-512mHz re-farming bands.

2) Beginning six months after publication of this 2nd R&O in the Federal Register, prohibit incumbent 25kHz Part 90 licenses in the 150-174mHz and 421-512mHz bands from making modifications to their systems that expand their respective authorized interference contours as a result thereof.

3) Beginning January 1, 2005, prohibit the certification of any equipment capable of operating at one voice path per 25kHz of spectrum, i,e., multi-mode equipment that includes a 25kHz mode.

4) Beginning January 1, 2008, prohibit the manufacture and importation of any 25 kHz equipment (including multi-mode equipment that can operate on a 25 kHz bandwidth).

5) Beginning January 1, 2013, require non-public safety licensees using channels in these bands to deploy technology that achieves the equivalent of one voice path per 12.5kHz of spectrum.

6) Beginning January 1, 2018, require public safety licensees using channels in these bands to deploy technology that achieves the equivalent of one voice path per 12.5kHz of spectrum.

The 2nd FNPRM seeks comment on additional issues related to promoting spectrum efficiency in the private land mobile radio services (PLMRS). The 2nd FNPRM seeks comment on whether the equipment certification provision in the current rules is sufficient to promote migration to one voice path per 6.25kHz bandwidth, or equivalent technology, or whether migration to 6.25kHz bandwidth or equivalent technology should be mandatory.

These rules are certain to be challenged by the filing of Petitions for reconsideration. We recommend regular viewing of the FCC website for further updates. To view the complete Report & Order and Further Notice of Proposed Rule Making copy either of these links and paste into your browser:

http://hraunfoss.fcc.gov/edocs_public/attachmatch/FCC-03-34A1.doc
http://hraunfoss.fcc.gov/edocs_public/attachmatch/FCC-03-34A1.pdf

Exhibit 2

Comparative Operating Ratios

Year	2002	2001	2000
Sales	1,233,466	1,089,269	1,108,687
Cost of Sales	722,395	591,104	610,708
Ratio	58.6%	54.3%	55.1%
Period Average	56.1%		
Net Expenses	298,183	283,505	299,335
Ratio	24.2%	26.0%	27.0%
Period Average	25.7%		
Income Before Taxes	67,706	75,948	72,370
Ratio	5.5%	7.0%	6.5%
Period Average	6.3%		
Discretionary Earnings	212,888	214,660	198,644
Ratio	17.3%	19.7%	17.9%
Period Average	18.2%		
Officer Compensation	120,000	120,000	100,000
Ratio	9.7%	11.0%	9.0%
Period Average	9.9%		

Exhibit 3

Ratios to Measure Safety and Liquidity
These ratios show the company to be financially strong and liquid.

Year	2002	2001	2000

Net Working Capital - Measures ability to meet short term obligations.

	2002	2001	2000
Current Assets	196,704	170,408	205,340
Current Liabilities	38,986	31,854	77,245
	157,718	138,554	128,095

Current Ratio - Measures ability to pay current liabilities as they mature. A ratio of 1:1 or greater equates to positive net working capital.

	2002	2001	2000
Current Assets	196,704	170,408	205,340
Current Liabilities	38,986	31,854	77,245
Ratio	5.05	5.35	2.66

Quick Ratio - Also known as the "Acid Test" ratio, it is a refinement of the Current Ratio and is a more conservative measure of liquidity. The ratio expresses the degree to which a company's current liabilities are covered by the most liquid current assets.

Cash, Accts & Notes	2002	2001	2000
Receivable	81,979	37,222	45,357
Total Current Liabilities	38,986	31,854	77,245
Ratio	2.10	1.17	0.59

Debt to Equity - Calculates balance between total equity and long term debt. The larger the percentage, the more the company is leveraged.

Long-term Debt000	2002	2001	2000
Stockholder's Equity	169,903	157,209	134,673
Ratio	0%	0%	0%

Debt Service Ratio - Indicator of a firm's ability to pay both interest and principal on its outstanding debt.

	2002	2001	2000
Adjusted EBIT	142,388	144,160	128,144
Interest & principal pmts	144,689	11,911	16,720
Ratio	9.7	12.1	7.7

Sales/Working Capital - Working capital is a measure of the margin of protection for current creditors. This ratio reflects the firm's ability to finance current operations.

	2002	2001	2000
Net Sales	1,233,466	1,089,269	1,108,687
Nct Working Capital	157,718	138,554	128,095
Ratio	7.8	7.9	8.7

Exhibit 4

Ratios Measuring Operating Efficiency

Collection Period - Calculates number of days' sales that are uncollected in average accounts receivables. Provides insight as to effectiveness in collecting customer debts.

Accounts Receivable	63,709	73,763	111,033
Daily sales	3, 379	2,984	3,037
days	18.9	24.7	36.6

# of Days Inventory - Amount of inventory maintained relative to company's sales.

Inventory	51,016	59,423	48,950
Daily cost of Goods	1,979	1,619	1,673
Days	25.8	36.7	29.3

Inventory Turns - Measures how quickly inventory turns.

Cost of Goods	389,212	539,914	794,211
Inventory	53,427	120,335	141,044
Times	7.3	4.5	5.6

Cost of Sales/Payables - This ratio measures the number of times trade payables turn over during the year.

Cost of Goods	389,212	539,914	794,211
Payables	25,597	13,395	43,288
Times	15.2	40.3	18.3

 # Days Payable - Same as above measured in days.

Payables	25,597	13,395	43,288
Daily Cost of Goods	1,066	1,479	2,176
Days	24	9	20

COMMENT

You probably have notice a consistency as well as differences between these two CBRs. The point to be made is that each company is unique representing a unique opportunity and therefore the CBRs will reflect the differences.

Important Points to Remember:

- Ratification of your opportunity by third parties adds credibility and value
- Obtaining lender pre-approval for acquisition funding is essential in obtaining maximum value
- Documentation of facts or opinions presented is crucial
- Keep your reader in mind as you write and present data

REMINDER

A blank piece of paper can be very intimidating and not everyone is comfortable writing. If writing is not your strong suit you should consider involving someone you trust to do the writing for you.

The next segment to be tackled is lender pre-approval. This should be a piece of cake as most all of the work required has already been completed ☺

What You Should Know

About financing the purchase of a small business

By: Edward McCormick, President
Alternative Funding Group

All SBA Programs are not the same. While the SBA eligibility criteria are the same across all lenders (size, type of business, number of employees etc.) the underlying credit criteria is left to the determination of each lender. For example, the following criteria may differ:

- Collateral - some require full collateralization of each dollar loaned while others are more concerned with cash flow. Some lenders require one to one collateral, while others require excess collateral i.e. $1.20 in collateral for each dollar loaned

- Years in Business - one lender requires a minimum of 2 years, while others require 3, 5 or more

- Direct Industry Experience - one lender requires some general management experience while others require a minimum of 2 or more years direct industry experience regardless of cash flow and collateral

- Rolling Stock (Vehicles) - some lenders like trucks and tractors while others will not touch them

- Single Purpose Real Estate - Some lenders will do restaurants, motels, gas stations etc. while others will not due to the limited market for single purpose real estate

- Business types - one lender likes bars and restaurants while others will not touch them

- Cash Flow - some lenders require certain multiples of cash flow over a two or more year period to qualify- i.e. If the debt payment is $1,000 per month, one lender will want net cash flow after new buyers salary of $1,200 while others require $1,500. This is referred to as 1.2x or 1.5x debt coverage.

- Some lenders will allow certain add backs to cash flow while others will not

- Lender may review personal credit of the borrower differently

- Some lenders will only do Franchised or Flagged Hotels, Gas Stations etc. while others will accept private Mom and Pop operations

- The list goes on and on and on

One might ask, "so what?" Well, if the SBA Officer at Bank of America turns down one business transaction is the deal dead as far as the SBA is concerned? It depends. For example, if the bank that declined the deal is a "Preferred Lender", then the SBA office did not see the deal and or reject it. This is because "Preferred Lenders" do not require the secondary underwriting approval of the SBA to approve or decline deals.

Preferred vs. Certified Lenders

If the lender were "Certified or a General" program lender then there is a possibility that the SBA office did see the loan and declined it. Taking the loan to another Certified or General Program Lender would be useless since they too have to send it to the SBA and we know that they have already declined it.

But, you could take the deal to a "Preferred Lender" and even if the SBA had viewed the deal through a Certified or General Lender, the Preferred Lender may still do the deal if they wish since as a Preferred Lender, it doesn't have to go through the local SBA for approval like the other two.

The SBA has a Standard Operating Procedure, which was revised as of October 1997 and still many banks and non-bank lenders have different interpretations of the requirements. Many "Certified and General' Lenders aren't even up to speed on the changes and as such may promise things that are subsequently denied when the local SBA office reviews the file. Typically, this is not the case with "Preferred" Lenders since to get this designation implies that the lender does a great deal of SBA volume and is current on these changes.

Some lenders specialize in "Low Doc" loans or loans requiring $150,000 or less in financing. Loans in excess of this amount are discouraged unless they could be underwritten using conventional policies plus they slap on an SBA Guarantee for additional insurance.

There are many lenders who only do SBA Lending. Typically, these are non-bank, national companies and most are "Preferred Lenders". Each of their policies differ however.

Let's consider a few deals

Most lenders will do *two tests* to determine loan approval and the size of the loan permitted. The first test is the "Asset Allocation Test". In this test, the lender looks at the hard assets versus goodwill that comprises the purchase price. If we have a business that has the following breakdown:

• Purchase Price		$275,000
• Inventory	$20,000	
• M&E	$73,000	
• Furniture	$15,000	
• Acct. Receivable	25,000	
• Sub total	$133,000	
• Goodwill	$142,000	
Total	$275,000	

Test 1

Under test one, we look at the hard assets and assume that if the cash flow is sufficient, the lender will advance up to 100% of hard asset value and 50% of Goodwill not to exceed 80% of the Purchase Price. Why? Because the SBA and Lenders usually look for a 20% down payment to provide some equity on the balance sheet of the new operation.

In the above case, 100% of the hard asset value is $133,000 plus 50% of the Goodwill, which is $71,000 for simplicity. Therefore, our potential loan under test one is $204,000. But wait; this loan is 84% of the purchase price and you'll remember I said that the maximum under this test is 80% of the price. Since 8o% of the purchase price or $275,000 is $220,000 our loan amount is okay for now.

Test 2

Test two determines if there is sufficient cash flow to cover a $240,000 loan. In recasting cash flow, let's assume, in 1997, we have positive earnings, depreciation, interest expense, officer salary and related payroll tax on the seller which totals $71,350. Let's assume in 2008, this same calculation results in $60,975.

The minimum historical cash flow coverage required by lenders is two years, so in this case we've looked at 2007 and '08 to determine our two years of cash flow. We always defer to the lower of the two years in order to assure ourselves that we get the two years of coverage. Exception: some lenders will average the cash flows for the two years if the business illustrates strong growth and the lower of the two years cash flow would not realistically give an appropriate picture of the businesses potential)

No lender is going to base a loan utilizing 100% of this cash flow. First of all, the new buyer will need a salary and by the way, every buyer may have significantly differing salary requirements due to their personal debt, number of family members, and lifestyle.

Salary Considerations

Let's assume a salary level for this buyer of $20,000. By subtracting this amount from our lowest cash flow year or $60,975 - $20,000 = $40,975. This is the dollar amount we will work with. But, we do not use the entire $40,975 because what if the new buyer has a small business downturn after purchasing the business or some other factor comes into play to negatively affect sales.

For this reason, lenders use a percentage of this number so as to provide a cash buffer in the event of problems. The most aggressive lenders use about 80% of this number or in this case $34,145 (we actually divide the number by 120% or 1.2) Therefore, our $25,812 represents a monthly amount of $2,151 ($25,812 /12).

We know the monthly payment allowed by the lender is $2,151 and we know that the SBA allows 10 years for business acquisitions and we know a reasonable interest rate is Prime (7.75%) plus 1.5% or 9.25%. With these variables, we can calculate a loan qualification amount of $222,241 or say $222,000. But wait, this amount is larger than Test One's amount of $204,000. We then defer to the lower of the two tests and the eligible loan amount is $204,000.

Now, if the SBA and lender require a minimum 20% down payment against the purchase price of $275,000 then the borrower must come in with $55,000 (plus closing costs). The purchase price of $275,000 less $55,000 from the buyer leaves $220,000 and our loan is $204,000. Where is the difference coming from? The answer is one of the following:

- The seller must finance a note for the difference
- The buyer must come up with more down
- A combination of the two
- A reduction in price
- Etc.

Let's look at this example in detail.
Example Business for Sale

Test 1 - Asset Allocation

$275,000 Selling Price

Assets:

M&E	73,000		
FF&E	15,000		
Inventory	20,000	Goodwill	42,000
Acct. Rec.	25.000	Non Compete	100.000
Hard Assets	133,000	Soft assets	142,000
	X 100%		X 50%
Loan Amount	**133,000**	**plus**	**71,000 =**

Maximum loan based upon assets $204,000

Test 2 - Cash Flow

	1 Year ago	Most recent year
Depreciation	9,000	8,000
Owner salary	28.000	22.000
Payroll tax - owner	3,150	2,475
Interest	3,200	2,500
Net cash benefit	71,350	60,975
Less new owner draw	20,000	20,000
Net cash for debt	**51,350**	**40,975**

(use lower number - Divide by 1.2)

Step 1

Calculate Cash $40,975 divided by 1.2 = $34,145 Eligible for

Available for debt service after cash buffer consideration

Debt Service Cash Available for Debt Service $34,145

Step 2

Calc. Monthly $34,145 divided by 12 months = $2,845 monthly payment

Payment

Step 3

Calc. Loan Amt. $2,845 Per month @ 9.25% for 10 years =

Maximum loan based upon Cash Flow = $220,000

Step 4

Determine Loan Amount   Use lower amount of Test 1 and Test 2
Probable Loan Amount $204,000

Step 5

Structure   Add loan amount and buyer down payment --
Transaction   Difference is seller financing, increased down payment or both

Heavy Assets - Poor Cash Flow

Sometimes a business, for whatever reason, has significant asset values but poor earnings. Let's say assets worth $300,000 versus a cash flow test indicating a borrowing capacity of $60,000. Can it be financed? Perhaps - If the business does not adequate cash flow, lenders treat the deal as it would a *"Start-Up"* business.

This means that we must meet the following Start Up criteria generally:

- What is the liquidated value of the assets

- What personal assets can be pledged in addition to the above to get us collateralized 100%

- Is the business trend upwards or declining - can a good case be made via a sound business plan that this business could probably repay a loan equal to 70% of the purchase price?

Note: In this, "projection based loan," the borrower must come in with 30% versus 20% in a cash flowing business, the business assets must be appraised, whereas in the cash flowing loan scenario, the lender accepts the agreed upon value between buyer and seller and personal assets will always come into play, if they exist.

Alert - The SBA may require outside assets to secure a cash flowing loan as well if the outside assets have 25% equity or more

Businesses with poor cash flow and few assets are good candidates for Seller Financing unless the borrowers have outside collateral and a plan to turn the business around.

Conclusion: The free pre-qualification offered by many lenders will provide you with vital information:

- Probable seller financing amount
- Whether the business can even be financed
- Provide a buyer profile including experience requirements, salary maximums and minimum down payment

CAUTION - Finally, the SBA and Conventional financing options in the marketplace are numerous and complicated. If you plan on handling the financing yourself, beware, this is a highly specializes business. Shopping loans around will leave a credit trail that other lenders will pick up on and this can sour a lender to the deal wondering why other lenders didn't do it.

How to Expedite a Financing Decision

Pre-qualification:

Contacting the lender early in the process is key. Lenders, we can do three important things to facilitate a smooth business transfer:

- First, check the buyer's personal credit worthiness and

- Second, assess the salary requirements of the buyer(s). Remember a salary requirement of $30,000 versus $80,000 can substantially affect cash flow available to service debt which affects debt level and seller financing.

- Third, we can assist with structuring the deal to fit the financing required. Our analysis, as discussed, will suggest additional down payment requirements and or seller financing needed to make the deal work as well as additional collateral that may be needed. Let's not tie up our time attempting a transaction or a sale structure that doesn't work

  Provide the lender with adequate information:

- Signed Offer to Purchase including terms and conditions of proposed seller financing

- Asset Addendum delineating specific asset values to be purchased versus Goodwill

- Three years of signed Tax returns from Seller

- Interim Financials on business within 45 days

- Recast cash flow to include supporting documentation for certain expense add-backs like two years of W-2s for non-essential employees, or non recurring expenses like unusual repairs or maintenance items etc.

- If real estate is involved, any previous appraisals, environmental reports, site plans, deed copy will help.

- If liquor license is involved, is there any local restrictions regarding the prohibition of assignment to lender

- Any special licensing information

- If the buyer does not have specific industry experience, does the contract call for seller training for some period of time?

- **Most Importantly**: Can the buyer renew the present lease for a term that mirrors the terms of the loan, typically 10 years, unless real estate is involved. (a 2 year lease with 4-2 year options, ~ any other combination is acceptable

- Any pictures or collateral brochures describing the business

- Any information that relates to competitive advantages, pricing, hours of operation, number of employees, proprietary products etc.

- Sales analysis for multi-product or multi-service companies help. i.e. Food versus beverage, Grocery versus Lottery, Room revenue versus food, etc.

Mr. McCormick is president of Alternative Funding Group of Framingham, MA and a licensed mortgage broker. He can be reached @ 800 249-2024 for private consultation.

Acquisition Lenders

There are scores of lenders who reportedly are active in the small business Acquisition Funding arena. We have chosen to list these companies as they have proven themselves to be pursuing this type business by their attendance at International Business Broker Association (IBBA) seminars and conventions.

Guidant Financial Group	www.guidantfinancial.com/
Business Loan Express	www.cienacapital.com/
Haskin Capital Group	www.haskincapital.com/v2/hask.php
Cedarcrest Capital	www.cedarcrestcapital.com/index.html
CIT Small Business Lending	www.cit.com/main/financial-solutions/corporate-finance/small-business-lending
Community South Bank	http://www.communitysouth.com/
First Heritage Capital	http://www.firstheritagecapital.com/
Popular Small Business Capital	http://www.popularsmallbiz.com/
Siegel Capital, LLC	http://www.siegelcapital.com
Siegel Financial Group	http://www.siegelfg.com
Stearns Bank	http://www.stearns-bank.com
UPS Capital	http://capital.ups.com/solutions/sbl_acquisitions.html
Wachovia Small Business Capital	http://www.wachovia.com/small_biz/page

Loan Proposal

Executive Summary

It is best to first complete all of the sections before you attempt to
create this summary.
The four subjects below should be addresed concisely and honestly
in no more than four (4) pages.

Description of Business

Describe this business/ How long established etc (Use Business
Profile sheet as a guide). Identify the opportunities and how your
Skills and background will enable you to capitalize upon the opportunity
the business represents.

Amount of Loan Requested

Explain why the funds are needed, how much and for how long.
Describe how the proceeds will be used.

How You Plan to Repay the Loan

When will payments be made? What do you want the payments to be? Will
there be balloon payments and what is the source of income to support repayment.

Collateral for the Loan

What will you pledge as security? What is the value of the collateral and how
value determined?

Business Profile

The Company

One or two paragraphs to describe The Company and its form

History

The companies beginnings -- how it got to where it is now -- date of incorporation.

The Industry

Industry outlook etc.

Market Served

Who are the customers, what is the outlook for their businesses etc.

Marketing Area

Outlook for the region served, demographics etc.

Customer Concentrations

What customer dependency exist if any?

Sales Segmentation

Revenues by product or business segment including target margin information

Operations

Hours and days of operation -- seasonality etc.

Staff

List by positions/functions. Include tenure, # hours worked/period, wage/salary, date of last raise? Will they stay or leave? -- identify family members.

Financial

Summary of key financial information

Facilities

Description of facility, lease etc.

Equipment

Suitability, age, FM Value age, condition......

The Opportunity

Highlight areas of opportunity. Areas where the aquirer can make a positive difference.

Management

Key People

Owner or manager

Name

Responsibility in company

Experience

Ownership

Title

Name

Responsibility in company

Experience

Ownership

Title

Name

Responsibility in company

Experience

Ownership

Title

Name

Responsibility in company

Experience

Ownership

Resume (One for Each partner/principal)

Name
Address
City, State Zip Code
Phone
Facsimile
Cell/Mobile

Personal

Education

Work experience

Experience relating to this business and industry

Personal references

Confidential Personal Financial Statement

Name
(Include spouse if married)
Address
City, State Zip Code
Facsimile, Email Web site
Telephone Cell/Mobile

Assets:

Cash (Bank/Money Funds)	$	-
Marketable Stocks/Bonds		0
Cash Value Life Insurance		0
Accounts/Notes Receivable		0
Real Estate- Residence		0
Real Estate Other		0
Other Assets		0
Total Assets	$	-

Liabilities:

Installment Debt	$	-
Real Estate Notes:		0
Residence		0
Other Real Estate		0
Other Debt		0
Total Liabilities	$	-

Net Worth	$	-

I/We understand that this Confidential Financial Statement is being submitted in order to obtain credit in conjuntion with the purchase of a business, I/We certify that the information provided above is complete and accurate to the best of my/our knowledge.

Signed

Date

Personal Draw
Calculation

	Monthly

Continuing income (pension, annuities etc.)
Spousal Income
Real Estate Rental Income
Other Income

Total Monthly Income	0
Total Annual Income	0

Expenses:
Mortgage Payment
(if home equity or refinance will be used to generate downpayment
please calculate based on new projected mortgage balance)
Rental Real Estate Mortgage Payment(s)
Rental Real Estate Expenses from Schedule E
Personal Residence Real Estate Taxes
Utilities
Telephone
Food & Clothing ($350 for 1st person in household and $150 per additional)
Personal Income Taxes last year (insert annual, it will compute monthly)   0
Auto Loans or Leases
Credit Cards (use 5% of Balance to determine monthly payment)
Medical Expenses
All Insurance (household, auto and medical)
Alimony
Child Support
Other   0
(automatically computes 10% of income)

Total Monthly Expenses	0
Total Annual Expenses	0
Owner draw required	0

Balance Sheet

Year	2003	2002	2001	2000	1999
Assets					
Current Assets					
Cash	12,500	10,451	15,447	13,554	12,541
Marketable Securities	0	0	0	0	0
Accounts Receivable	27,525	28,995	31,441	25,442	24,887
Inventories	35,784	36,888	35,773	39,881	42,554
Notes Receivable	10,000	0	0	0	0
Prepaid Expenses	2,578	3,155	2,750	2,954	2,799
Total Current Assets	**88,387**	**79,489**	**85,411**	**81,831**	**82,781**
Fixed Assets					
Leasehold Improvements	12,500	12,500	12,500	12,500	12,500
Equipment and Machinery	125,887	125,887	125,887	115,122	115,122
Vehicles	35,000	35,000	35,000	10,000	10,000
Office Equipment	15,899	15,899	14,500	14,500	12,000
Cash Value Officer Life Ins,	12,000	10,500	9,350	8,150	7,000
less Depreciation	(54,887)	(49,554)	(42,335)	(39,877)	(36,115)
Total Fixed Assets	**146,399**	**150,232**	**154,902**	**120,395**	**120,507**
Total Assets	**234,786**	**229,721**	**240,313**	**202,226**	**203,288**
Liabilities					
Current Liabilites					
Accounts Payable	14,552	15,423	16,622	13,578	15,221
Accrued Profit Sharing	-	-	-	-	
Accrued Taxes	5,887	6,521	9,128	7,229	6,554
Current Portion LT Debt	12,000	10,000	10,000	10,000	5,000
Line of Credit	10,000	5,000	6,500	8,500	9,500
Other	-	-	-	-	
Total Current Liabilities	**42,439**	**36,944**	**42,250**	**39,307**	**36,275**
Long term Liabilities					
Notes Payable - Bank	35,000	30,000	32,000	42,000	15,000
Notes payable - Other	-	-	-	-	-
Deferred Income Taxes	-	-	-	-	-
Capital Leases	-	-	-	-	-
Other	-	-	-	-	-
Total Long Term Liabilities	**35,000**	**30,000**	**32,000**	**42,000**	**15,000**
Total Liabilities	**77,439**	**66,944**	**74,250**	**81,307**	**51,275**
Owners Equity	**157,347**	**162,777**	**166,063**	**120,919**	**152,013**
Total Equity & Liabilities	**234,786**	**229,721**	**240,313**	**202,226**	**203,288**

Adjusted Balance Sheet

Assets	Book Value	FMV Transferable Assets	FMV Retained Assets
Current Assets			
Cash	12,500		12,500
Marketable Securities	-		-
Accounts Receivable	27,525		27,525
Inventories	35,784	35,784	
Notes Receivable	10,000		10,000
Prepaid Expenses	2,578		2,578
Total Current Assets	**88,387**		
Fixed Assets			
Leasehold Improvements	12,500	2,500	-
Equipment and Machinery	125,887	100,000	-
Vehicles	35,000	18,500	-
Office Equipment	15,899	7,500	-
Cash Value Officer Life Ins,	12,000		12,000
less Depreciation	(54,887)		
Total Fixed Assets	**146,399**		
Book Value Total Assets	**234,786**		
FMV of Transferable Assets		**164,284**	
FMV Value of Asssets Retained by Owner			**64,603**

Liabilities	Book Value	Transferable Liabilities	Retained Liabilities
Current Liabilites			
Accounts Payable	14,552		14,552
Accrued Profit Sharing	-		-
Accrued Taxes	5,887		5,887
Current Portion LT Debt	12,000		12,000
Line of Credit	10,000		10,000
Other	-		-
Total Current Liabilities	**42,439**		
Long term Liabilities			
Notes Payable - Bank	35,000		35,000
Notes payable - Other	-		-
Deferred Income Taxes	-		-
Capital Leases	-		-
Other	-		-
Total Long Term Liabilities	**35,000**		
Total Liabilities	**77,439**		
Owners Equity	**157,347**		
Value of Transferable Liabilities		-	
Value of Retained Liabilities			77,439
Residual Value			**(12,836)**

Beginning Balance Sheet

Assets	Book Value
Current Assets	
Cash	35,000
Accounts Receivable	
Inventories	35,784
Notes Receivable	
Prepaid Expenses	2,500
Total Current Assets	**73,284**
Fixed Assets	
Leasehold Improvements	2,500
Equipment and Machinery	100,000
Vehicles	18,500
Office Equipment	7,500
less Depreciation	
Total Fixed Assets	**128,500**
Other Assets	
Goodwill	75,000
Other	-
Total Other Assets	**75,000**
Book Value Total Assets	**276,784**

Liabilities	
Current Liabilites	**Book Value**
Accounts Payable	-
Accrued Profit Sharing	-
Accrued Taxes	-
Current Portion LT Debt	-
Line of Credit	-
Other	
Total Current Liabilities	**-**
Long term Liabilities	
Notes Payable - Bank	85,000
Notes payable - Former Owner	70,000
Deferred Income Taxes	
Capital Leases	
Other	20,000
Total Long Term Liabilities	**175,000**
Total Liabilities	**175,000**
Owner's Equity	**101,784**
Total Liabilities and Equity	**276,784**

Comparative Recast Income Statements

Year	2003	2002	2001	2000	1999
Revenue	535,112	547,087	544,593	616,750	578,966
Cost of Sales:					
Beginning Inventories	3,255	3,125	2,789	2,546	2,789
Purchases	172,114	176,251	159,267	135,308	124,889
Labor	170,255	165,784	229,599	275,855	258,998
less Ending Inventories	3,155	3,255	3,125	2,789	2,546
Cost of Sales Total	348,779	348,415	394,780	416,498	389,222
Gross Profit	186,333	198,672	149,813	200,252	189,744
Total Expenses	183,404	174,591	177,608	212,831	201,546
Income Before Taxes	**2,929**	**24,081**	**(27,795)**	**(12,579)**	**(11,802)**
Adjustments:					
Officer's salary	90,000	83,200	80,900	99,200	99,200
Depreciation	7,267	8,679	10,473	10,527	9,578
Interest	531	910	1,270	369	425
Personal auto	3,250	2,895	2,759	2,689	2,545
Personal Insurance	5,412	5,215	5,124	4,925	4,875
Total Adjustments	106,460	100,899	100,526	117,710	116,623
Net Expenses	76,944	73,692	77,082	95,121	84,923
Discretionary Earnings *	**109,389**	**124,980**	**72,731**	**105,131**	**104,821**
Adjusted EBIT **	55,889	71,480	19,231	51,631	51,321
EBITD ***	47,227	116,870	64,848	97,517	97,401
EBIT ****	39,960	54,691	875	33,490	34,323

---

*	Dollars available for new owner's compensation, acquisition debt service, actual depreciation reserves and return on invested capital.
**	Adjusted EBIT = Earnings Before Interest, Taxes plus Depreciation and Adjustments (less an Appropriate Owner/Manager salary)
***	Earnings Before Interest, Taxes and Depreciation
****	Earnings Before Interest and Taxes

Income Calculations

Year	Discretionary Earnings	Weight	Extension
2003	109,389	5	546,945
2002	124,980	4	499,920
2001	72,731	3	218,193
2000	105,131	2	210,262
1999	104,821	1	104,821
Totals	517,052	15	1,580,141

Most recent year   109,389

Straight Average   103,410

Weighted Average   105,343

Our estimate of earnings available for acquisition $ 105,000

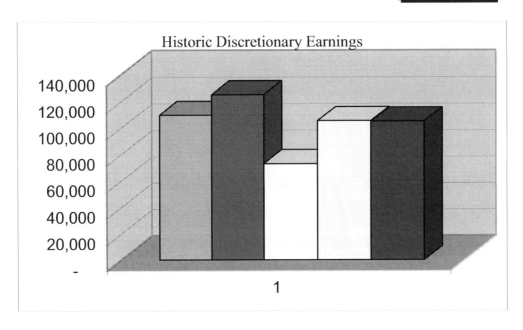

Historic Discretionary Earnings

Comparative Operating Ratio Review

Year	2003	2002	2001	2000	1999
Sales	535,112	547,087	544,593	616,750	578,966
Cost of Sales	348,779	348,415	394,780	416,498	389,222
Ratio	65.2%	63.7%	72.5%	67.5%	67.2%
Period Average	67.2%				
Cost of Goods	178,523	182,630	165,180	140,642	130,223
Ratio	33.4%	33.4%	30.3%	22.8%	22.5%
Period Average	28.2%				
Labor Cost	170,255	165,784	229,599	275,855	258,998
Ratio	31.8%	30.3%	42.2%	44.7%	44.7%
Period Average	39.0%				
Net Expenses	76,944	73,692	77,082	95,121	84,923
Ratio	14.4%	13.5%	14.2%	15.4%	14.7%
Period Average	14.4%				
Income Before Taxes	2,929	24,081	(27,795)	(12,579)	(11,802)
Ratio	0.5%	4.4%	-5.1%	-2.0%	-2.0%
Period Average	-0.9%				
Discretionary. Earnings	109,389	124,980	72,731	105,131	104,821
Ratio	20.4%	22.8%	13.4%	17.0%	18.1%
Period Average	18.3%				
EBIT	55,889	71,480	19,231	51,631	51,321
Ratio	10.4%	13.1%	3.5%	8.4%	8.9%
Period Average	8.8%				
Officer Compensation	90,000	83,200	80,900	99,200	99,200
Ratio	16.8%	15.2%	14.9%	16.1%	17.1%
Period Average	16.0%				

Comparative Ratio Analysis

Return on Equity Measures the return on the investments made by the owners

Net Income	2,929	24,081	(27,795)	(12,579)	(11,802)
Stockholder's Equity	157,347	162777	166063	120919	152013
Ratio	2%	15%	-17%	-10%	-8%

Return on Assets Measures the return on the gross investment of assets employed in the business.

Net Income	2,929	24,081	(27,795)	(12,579)	(11,802)
Total Assets	234,786	229,721	240,313	202,226	203,288
Ratio	1%	10%	-12%	-6%	-6%

Ratios to measure Safety and Liquidity

Net Working Capital Measures ability to meet short term obligations.

Current Assets	88,387	79,489	85,411	81,831	82,781
- Current Liabilities	(42,439)	(36,944)	(42,250)	(39,307)	(36,275)
	45,948	42,545	43,161	42,524	46,506

Current Ratio Measusres the ability to pay current liabilities as they mature. A ratio of 1:1 or greater equates to positive net working capital.

Current Assets	88,387	79,489	85,411	81,831	82,781
Current Liabilities	42,439	36,944	42,250	39,307	36,275
Ratio	2.1	2.2	2.0	2.1	2.3

Quick Ratio Also known as the "Acid Test" ratio, it is a refinement of the Current Ratio and is a more conservative measure of liquidity. The ratio expresses the degree to which a company's current liabilities arecovered by the most liquid current assets.

Cash, Accts & Notes Receivable	50,025	39,446	46,888	38,996	37,428
Total Current Liabilities	42,439	36,944	42,250	39,307	36,275
Ratio	1.2	1.1	1.1	1.0	1.0

Debt to Equity Calculates balance between total equity and long term debt. The larger the percentaage, the more the company is leveraged.

Long-term Debt	35,000	30,000	32,000	42,000	15,000
Stockholder's Equity	157,347	162,777	166,063	120,919	152,013
Ratio	22%	18%	19%	35%	10%

Debt Service Ratio Indicator of a firm's ability to pay both interest and principal on its outstanding debt.

Adjusted EBIT	55,889	71,480	19,231	51,631	51,321
Interest & principal paymts	12,531	10,910	11,270	10,369	5,425
Ratio	4.5	6.6	1.7	5.0	9.5

Sales/WorkingCapital Working capital is a measure of the margin of protection for current creditors. This ratio reflects the firm's ability to finance current operations

Projections

This exhibit estimates profitability at various revenue levels using historic Gross Profit data..

	Projected Current Yr.	Case 1	Case 2	Case 3	Case 4	Case 5
Target Revenues	600,000	625,000	650,000	675,000	700,000	725,000
Target % Cost of Sales *	67.2%	67.2%	67.2%	67.2%	67.2%	67.2%
Target $ Cost of Sales	403,406	420,214	437,023	453,832	470,640	487,449
Gross Profit	196,594	204,786	212,977	221,168	229,360	237,551
Target Net Expenses **	80,000	84,000	88,000	92,000	96,000	100,000
Target Manager's Salary	54,000	54,000	54,000	54,000	54,000	54,000
Adjusted EBIT	62,594	66,786	70,977	75,168	79,360	83,551
Discretionary Earnings	116,594	120,786	124,977	129,168	133,360	137,551
Target Ratios:						
Gross Profit	32.8%	32.8%	32.8%	32.8%	32.8%	32.8%
Net Expenses	13.3%	13.4%	13.5%	13.0%	13.1%	13.2%
Adjusted EBIT	10.4%	10.7%	10.9%	11.1%	11.3%	11.5%
Discretionary Earnings	19.4%	19.3%	19.2%	19.1%	19.1%	19.0%

* Period average ratio used in estimating expenses
** Estimated

Listing of Exhibits

Equipment List (signed by seller)

Signed Personal Tax Returns (3 years) with your Social Security #s showing

Company's Tax Return (3 to 5 years)

Corporate Articles of Incorporation and Corporate Resolution (to Sell)

Copy of Permits, Licenses and Environmental Surveys)

Signed copy of Sales Agreement indicating terms of sale

Pictures of Business

Company Literature and brochures

Copy of Premises Lease

Preparation for Due Diligence

If you want to sell your business quickly and quietly for the most money you must be ready to close a transaction before you start. You have invested a considerable amount of time up to this point in preparation for selling.

So far you have:

- Determined your Company's optimum value and probable terms of sale,
- Developed a profile of your ideal candidate,
- Conferred with your attorney and tax professional regarding the transaction,
- Written a Confidential Business Review and One Page Profile
- Identified Lenders willing to do a deal.

However, one crucial step is left to be completed. Leaving out this important step may cause all of your fine preparatory work to have been in vain.

Surprises and Time Kill Deals

Many a deal has been lost simply because buyers had to wait for requested information to become available or, were surprised when incomplete information allowed them to jump to wrong and alarming conclusions.

Compile a Due Diligence Book

The size and complexity of this book will obviously vary with the size and complexity of the business it represents. The data required for most businesses will fit nicely in a 2" loose leaf binder that can be obtained at any office supply store. Divide each heading with a tab for ease of reference and use. Headings and/or information to be included:

THE COMPANY

The CBR you created will do nicely and if a Corporation: List of shareholders, Number of shares owned by each, Number of shares outstanding

PERSONNEL AND POLICIES

List of employees with Job Description, Rate of Pay, Tenure, Stay/Leave?

Copy of employee's W-2, Employee benefits,

Incentive plans,

Pension plans,

Number of paid holidays,

Medical, life insurance, dental,

Copy of Operations Manual (if any),

List and summarize employment contracts,

Copy Union contract and expiration dates

INSURANCE

Copy of the Declaration page of all insurance policies

THE FACILITY

Copy of lease and all amendments/addendums or

Copy of Deed and plot plan if owned and part of the sale

ASSETS/EQUIPMENT

List of equipment including serial numbers (This will become part of the Bill of Sale)

List of tooling, dies, jigs, fixtures

Copy of vehicle registrations and titles

List patents, copyrights, trademark, and all new applications

SALES

Breakdown by product/service last 5 years

Percent of sales to top 5 customers

List top 20 customers and sales volume

FINANCIAL

Current interim financial statement

Financial statements past 5 years and/or Tax returns for past 5 years

Comparative Balance Sheet

Starting Balance Sheet

Comparative Ratio Analysis

Comparative Monthly Sales for past 5 years

ANALYSIS OF EARNINGS

Comparative Income and Earnings calculations

OUTSTANDING CONTRACTS

With suppliers, subcontractors, customers, unions, distributor/franchisors

COMPANY ADVISORS

Name, address, phone number of company's bank

Name, address, phone number of company's accountant

Name, address, phone number of company's attorney

Name and address of advertising agency

Name, address, phone number of other company advisors

Step Three - *FIRE*

To attract the most appropriate buyer:

- Write ad copy
- Identify best advertising medium(s)
- Field inquiries
  - Telephone
  - Internet
- Interview candidates
- Facilitate an offer

- Close the deal

Begin the Selling Process

You are finally ready to pull the trigger. You are fully prepared to begin selling your business. In preparation for arriving at this point you have:

- Ratified the timeliness of selling,
- Determined a fair price and suitable terms,
- Reviewed taxation consequences
- Identified the characteristics of your ideal buyer,
- Arranged for acquisition financing for your buyer, ,
- Prepared marketing materials that fully describe your opportunity,
- Compiled a complete Due Diligence package

Because you have created a Profile of your ideal buyer candidate you are better prepared to write appropriate ads and advertise and search in the right places.

Caution: Do not begin to sell your business before all of the above tasks have been completed. Doing so will drastically reduce your chances of success in selling your business

Attracting Your Buyer

Where to find and how to attract your buyer depends upon the type of buyer you are looking for. Buyers can be divided into essentially five groups:

- Individuals
- Employees/Family/Friends
- Investor Groups
- Synergistic Corporations
- Competitors (non-synergistic)

Individuals

A classified ad in your local newspaper might be the most effective way of finding a buyer for a small Main Street business. As the owner of a larger business however, you might find advertising in your region's edition of the Wall Street Journal more appropriate. The Wall Street Journal's national edition would be a good choice if your business can attract buyers from a national audience.

You can choose from scores of websites upon which to list your business for sale on the internet. Some websites specialize in larger businesses and others are geographically restricted, most charge a modest fee and a few are free. We have provided a list of the more popular websites for you at the end of this chapter.

Investor Groups

Few Individuals are able to afford a Company with earnings in the arena of $500,000. Additionally, many owners businesses of this size begin to realize that their business now needs leadership with the skills required to take the company to the next level. They realize their company has outgrown their abilities. This dynamic is not unlike the driver of a Camry comfortable driving at 70 miles per hour finding himself in a Porsche on the Autobahn doing 120 mph!

Scores of Investor Groups have been formed to address this dynamic. Some of these groups are industry specific and others have size and earnings criteria. Some will have what we refer to as "on the shelf CEOs." These are individuals who are exceedingly talented however, lack the capital required to buy a company worthy of their talents with their own financial resources. All of the companies listed below have a website where you will be able to obtain more information.

Alliance Holdings, Inc.
Allied Capital
Alpine Investors, LP
American Capital Strategies
American Industrial Partners
APAX Partners
Arbor Private Investment Company
Aureus Capital
Bayview Capital Partners, LP
Blue Point Capital Partners
Blue Sage Capital
Bolder Capital, LLC
Bradford Equities Fund, LLC
Branford Castle, Inc.
Brentwood Capital Advisors
Brookside Capital Partners
Calitus Mezzanine Partners
Calvert Street Capital
Cambridge Capital Partners
Capital For Business, Inc.
Capital South Partners
Carousel Capital
Castanea Partners
CHB Capital Partners
Cherington Capital
Christian Stanley, LLC
Chrys Capital
Churchill Capital
Clarion Capital Partners, LLC
Clearview Capital, LLC
CMS Companies
Context Advisors
Copeley Capital
Cornerstone Capital Holdings
Dubin Clark & Company
E&A Industries, Inc.
EBSCO Industries, Inc.
Eckford Group
Encore Consumer Capital
Entrepreneur Partners
Equitable Capital Management, LLC
Evolve Capital
FB Commercial Finance
FdG Associates
Ferro Management Group, Inc.
First Capital, LLC
Florida Capital Partners/FCP Investors, Inc.
Foreman Investment Capital, LLC
Friend Skoler & Co.
Gallagher Industries, LP
Gateshead Partners
Gen Cap America, Inc.
Generation Equity Investors
G.L. Ohrstrom & Co., Inc.
Goense Bounds & Partners

Graham Partners
Greenfield Commercial Credit
GUARDAIR CORP.
Hamilton Robinson, LLC
Hammond, Kennedy, Whitney & Co., Inc.
Hanover Partners, Inc.
Harbert Management
Harbour Group Industries, Inc.
Hastings Equity Partners, LLC
H.I.G. Capital
High Impact Structures, LLC
High Street Capital
Horizon Partners, Ltd.
ICV Capital Partners, LLC
Ironwood Capital
JMAC, Inc.
Jordan Industries, Inc.
JP Morgan Chase Bank
Key Principal Partners
Keystone Capital, LLC
KLH Capital, LP
KRG Capital Partners
LaSalle Capital Group, LP
Legg Mason Merchant Banking, Inc.
Lincolnshire Management, Inc.
Lineage Capital
Long Point Capital, Inc.
Lynwood Capital Partners
Mainsail Partners
MASCO Corporation
MCG Capital
MCM Capital Partners
Mercury Capital, Inc.
Merion Investment Partners, LP
Merit Capital Partners
Meriweather Capital Corporation
Merrill Lynch Financial Services, Inc.
Metapoint Partners
Mezzanine Management, LLC
MidCoast Financial
MIGG Capital, LLC
Milestone Partners
Montgomery, Shelton & Company
Moro Corporation
Nationwide Valuations
New England Capital Partners
Norwest Equity Partners
Onyx Capital International, Inc.
Oryx Capital Investments, Inc.
Pacific Partners
Palladium Equity Partners
Peachtree Equity Partners
Peninsula Capital Partners, LLC
Pfingsten Partners, LLC
Pinnacle Peak Capital Partners, LLC

PNC Bank
Polaris Venture Partners
Prairie Capital
Progress Equity Partners, Ltd.
Prometheus Partners
Prospect Partners, LLC
Prudential Capital Partners
RAF Industries
Ridgeview Capital
River Associates Investments, LLC
River Capital, Inc.
Riverside Partners, Inc.
Saunders, Karp & Megrue/SKM Growth Investors
SB Partners Capital Fund, LP
Seidler Equity Partners, LP
Silkroad Resources, LLC
Sowell & Co.
Sterling Investment Partners, LP
Stock Sale Compliance, LLC
Summer Street Capital Partners, LLC
Summit Partners
Sun Capital Partners, Inc.
Svoboda Collins, LLC
Swander Pace Capital
Swift River Investments
Synergy Investment Group, LLC
Technology Tree Group, Inc.
The Barish Fund
The Cambria Group
The Carlyle Group
The Columbia Group, LLC
The Compass Group
The Edgewater Funds
The Riverside Company
The Shansby Group
Thompson Street Capital Partners
Tonka Bay Equity Partners
Topspin Partners, LP
Transition Capital Partners, Ltd.
Triton Capital Partners
Trivest, Inc.
TSG Consumer Partners, LP
Unique Investment Corporation
Virginia Capital
Waveland Investments, LLC
Wells Fargo Mezzanine Capital
Westcap Partners Private Equity Fund
Westham Partners, LLC
Westview Capital Partners
WHI Capital Partners
Wingate Partners
Wynnchurch Capital, Ltd.
ZS Fund, LP

Synergistic Corporations

Attracting this type buyer demands a bit of research and imagination but is made easier through the Profiling exercise you completed earlier. What companies will have a need for your product or service? Who could benefit from access to the market you serve? Who has products or services that could be sold to your customers or could sell your product or service to their customers? It is often very surprising as to where this exercise takes you.

Find the names and addresses of target companies using directories such as the Thomas Register and Trade Associations lists. The internet is also a great assist in this regard.

Design a compelling letter to send along with the One Page Profile you created earlier to your targets. This is a blind mailing in that you do not identify yourself or your company at this time. You even might ask a friend or relative to mail them for you to prevent revealing your geographic location prematurely. We have done this for and with other intermediaries and brokers around the country from time to time when revealing a company's industry and regional location would jeopardize confidentiality.

Dear Ms Target BizOwner
Corporation A
123 A Street
Anytown, State 12345

                            Date

Dear Ms BizOwner:

Our research indicates that you are a leader in the field of MMMMMM and as such should be interested in considering the acquisition of our company. We believe you will recognize the benefits the addition of our service/product will provide Corporation A.

We have enclosed a brief summary our opportunity represents as well as a Confidentiality Agreement (CA). Please return the CA along with the appropriate contact person to whom we should send our Comprehensive Business Review.

Sincerely:

Name

Competitors

Usually this type buyer is to be avoided. However, sometimes this is the buyer of choice especially if the company's Asset value exceeds its Cash Flow or Goodwill value. Other reasons to choose this buyer might be to speed up the sale process. This is often the buyer of choice when moving on to life's next chapter by selling the business is more important than the extra dollars that might be obtain by attracting another type buyer.

You probably already know these people and could readily suggest getting together for lunch or a drink to explore the possibilities. Trade association lists will enable you to make contact with others outside your immediate geographic area and whom you may not know.

Employees/Family/Friends

It has been estimated that approximately five percent of business are sold to employees and fifteen percent to family members. Again the Profiling you completed will help you ratify that family member(s) or employee(s) posses the right combination of skills and talent required by the company.

Elimination of an employee from consideration because he/she lacks the required skill is really straight forward. If they lack what it takes then – well, that's it. With family members it is a completely different situation. Family is family and family dynamics can be complicated.

IDEA

What many founders have done to solve their succession issue is to bring in an outside person, one fitting the required profile, to be the new CEO and take the family business to the next level.

Advertising the Business for Sale

Your objective is to write a compelling ad and descriptive advertising copy without disclosing your identity. You never know who is reading the advertisement. Your ad could be discovered by: competitors, customers, staff, suppliers, lenders and others. Preserving confidentiality is usually extremely important in maintaining value.

The critical step to writing ads or copy to attract the best buy side candidates is to have a complete profile of the qualifications, interests, resources, and background your ideal buyer should posses. This knowledge and insight allows you to create copy in the "voice" of your buyer in such a way that they can recognize the opportunity your business represents. This is key to increasing your odds for success at the highest possible price and is why we have spent so much ink on the subject elsewhere in this guide.

Tips for Maintaining Confidentiality

Nothing good is achieve by allowing the fact your business is for sale to become general knowledge

To assist in maintain confidentiality you may wish to consider:

- ✓ Obtain a special email address from one of the free services provided by Google, Yahoo and others i.e.: mainebiz4sale@yahoo.com

- ✓ Use an email address instead of a telephone number in classified and other ads

- ✓ Do not use the business telephone number; instead consider obtaining a separate telephone line just for the purpose of receiving inquiries.

- ✓ Obtain a Post Office box in another town to use instead of the business or home address

- ✓ Avoid being too specific about your location. Providing several hints will allow prospects, as well as the just curious, to triangulate your position and identity

- o Use your county instead of your town for location

- o Say busy highway instead a specific road i.e. Route 66

- o Seaside community instead of Cape Ann

- ✓ Use a recorded message provided by the telephone company or message machine instead of your own voice in case the caller is a competitor, employee or anyone who might recognize your voice.

- ✓ For internet ads - write a concise headline that grabs attention and sets your headline apart from the scores of others in the list to increase click throughs to your complete ad.

- ✓ Highlight the opportunity your business represents in a few short sentences and sell the dream.

About Price

A business can be perceived as worth millions to one yet be considered worthless to another. As you have learned in prior sections, different buyers pay different prices and the first one to mention price generally looses. What to do?

- ✓ Avoid placing a price on the business. If necessary, provide information that the business is priced within a range or band of prices; $500K to $1 million.

- ✓ It is not the Price that matters it is the Terms or, not what you get but rather how you get it that counts.

- o *Example*: A price of $1 million under the terms of $1 a day for a million days would probably not be acceptable unless the payer could guarantee you would be around to collect the last dollar.

- ✓ Only the right buyer pays the right price therefore become as confident as possible that you have attracted a suitable buyer before going to far into the process.

Buyers won't pay any more than what they think the business is worth in any event. A buyer's perception of value depends entirely upon the scope of opportunity they perceive is available to them.

Buyers who do not recognize the full opportunity your business represents will not offer a full and fair price for it and thereby disqualify themselves from consideration. Good thing too for if they do not see the opportunity how will they take advantage of it? If they are buying the business because of the money it makes but do not understand how its run they will most likely run it into the ground.

Where to Place Ads

Several options are available and some are more effective than others depending upon the business and the type buyer you wish to attract. Newspaper classified ads are quite effective in attracting Lifestyle Buyers to "Main Street" businesses as potential buyers typically will be found within close proximity to the business making local papers a very appropriate medium. Main Street businesses can also use internet "Businesses for Sale" sites effectively.

Larger more complex businesses can attract buyers from a broader geographic territory making the internet and national or regional papers such as the Wall Street Journal especially appropriate mediums.

Businesses requiring special skills, degrees or licenses can be advertised discretely in trade or professional journals and magazines in addition to the internet.

Newspaper Classified Ads

Believe it or not the most effective ad is the least expensive yet one of the best ways to reach Financial or Lifestyle Buyers. No need for an expensive display ad because a well written three liner will do the job just as well. A three line ad allows your buyer to "discover" your offering whereas a large display ad connotes expensive and competition from other possible buyers.

What should be in the ad?

Remember that buyers generally do not know exactly what business they want to buy so no need to be too specific. Several key things to work into your ad if possible are:

- It's easy,
- Makes a lot of money,
- Reason for sale (preferably selling under duress), and
- Requires little cash down.
  The primary reason for the ad is to make the telephone ring, not to provide detail.

Sample classified ads

Coffee Shop in office bldg, easy 5 day wk, be home by 3, real $$$maker, low down, terms, baby due soon XXX YYY-ZZZZ

High End Retail, trained staff, revenues increasing, 25 yr owner will train and finance, Dr says sell biz4sale@gmail.com

Service Biz to Biz, 9 to 5 no weekends, 6 figure earnings, low down, easy terms, retiring seller will train XXX YYY-ZZZZ

Auto Repair 7 bays, run absentee, earn $100K+, low down, training, EZ financing poor health forces sale XXX YYY-ZZZZ

It is usually best to include your reason for selling in your ad to answer the first question everyone has: "If this is such a great business why are you selling it?" Reasons preferred by buyers are those that would appear to be forcing a sale i.e.
- Divorce,
- Death,
- Disease,
- Disability

Consider yourself fortunate if none of the above reasons fits your situation. Burned out and retirement works and also are reasons buyers like to hear. Other interests, recieved good job offer and the like do not fly with buyers.

Writing a compelling three line ad is not as easy as it might appear. To paraphrase Benjamin Franklin – *I apologize for writing such a lengthy letter but I had not the time to write a shorter one.*

Internet Ads

The internet allows the exchange of significantly more information than do newspaper classifieds and at a lower price. This can be both good and bad. Good in that you can provide more enticing ad copy and description. Bad potential buyers will think they fully understand your business from the ad copy and the numbers provided therein. The purpose of the ad is not to sell the business but rather entice possible buyers to contact you.

Change Your Ad Frequently

The average length of time required to sell a business is nine months according to an IBBA survey. So, if it takes a full time professional business broker/intermediary that long will it take you less? Probably not so be prepared to refresh your ad every so often because:

- Feedback and questions asked by responders point out need to either add or delete information

- Keep the ad fresh – Value is diminished when it becomes obvious you have been on the markct for any length of time

- Second chance to attract a buyer not enticed by your original advertisement

You want use different words to convey the same idea. For example, if you are selling a Sir Speedy Print Shop you could describe the type business as: Print Shop, Franchised Quick Print, Graphic Arts Franchise, Commercial Printer, Manufacturer, Biz to Biz Service Provider and so forth.

Some "biz for sale" websites will not allow you to change your ad so you may have to drop off those web sites and advertise again after a suitable period of time has passed. The objective is to keep your ad fresh. Again, value and interest diminish when it is obvious you have been on the market for awhile. The sample ad that follows contains the type of information that an internet ad should contain.

Type Business: **Computer, Sales and Service**

State/Region: Connecticut/Fairfield County

Annual Revenues: $900,000

Discretionary Earnings: $200,000

Price: Under $750,000 - Financing is in place with 20% down

Inventory: $200,000 + At cost included in the sale

Staff: Three F/Time Employees all are factory certified and trained - will stay

Established: 30 yrs

Summary Description: Manufacturer authorized sales and service provider. Warranty work referred by manufacturers. Several school contracts, extensive client list, 85% of annual revenues from repeat customers. Seller will provide training and transition assistance for suitable period

Location/Facility: Occupies 3,000 sq. ft. in a free standing building, ample parking on very busy Main Street in Fairfield county, low rent, room for expansion

The Opportunity: Expand into growing multimedia and home theatre sales, installation and service. Capitalize upon high visibility location to increase retail sales.

Reason for Sale: Thirty years is long enough and I've made my pile. It's time for young blood to take over and capitalize on what we have established.

Do not be tempted to provide so much information that a possible acquirer will believe a buy decision could be made upon information in the ad alone. The opportunity your business represents should be stressed over financial detail. Actually, financial statements are really a mystery novel even though there are some who believe they are operation manuals.

In actuality, financial statements and tax returns will remain mysterious until operations are fully understood so don't make the mistake so many make in flooding prospective buyers with reams of financial detail before they fully understand your operation.

Fielding a Telephone Response

Keep in mind that a buyer's main objective when responding to your ad is ***to eliminate it from consideration***. Can't you envision the Sunday paper's business opportunity page covered with circled ads? *The calls are being made to narrow the field. They are calling to eliminate your business, not to buy it.*

The first questions you probably will be asked is; Where is it and how much do you want for it?

Where is it? - Obviously you cannot answer this question and maintain confidentiality. You need to know something about them before you disclose your identity. Is this person a competitor? – Are they qualified to operate your business? You will need a bit more information before you can safely answer this question.

How much is it?! - The only valid reason to ask this question is to determine if they can afford the business. They certainly have absolutely no information upon which to base an opinion of whether the price is fair or not.

The person asking the questions is the one controlling the conversation and you want to be in control so you have to tactfully turn the table by asking a question of your own in response. *Example:*

Buyer: Can you tell me where the business is located?
You: Certainly, where do you live?

Buyer: In Fairlawn Park
You: Great! You are about 15 minutes away from my business

Buyer: How much are you asking for it?
You: We are asking a fair price and the financing is in place for a candidate qualified to operate this business. Tell me, what attracted you to this business?
Your objective is to obtain an initial feel as to the caller's background and experience and become comfortable enough to proceed to the next step.

Once satisfied you have a possible candidate you should suggest swapping information. Exchange email or snail mail addresses and explain that you are doing two jobs at the same time:

- Selling your business
- Interviewing for a suitable future company president.

The deliberate and controlled exchange of information begins. You will provide the inquirer with a One Page Business Profile describing your business. The One Page Profile contains enough information for a reasonable person to decide whether or not the business might fit their needs.

You request your candidate completed and returned the following before proceeding further.

- Signed Confidentiality Agreement,
- Personal Financial Statement
- Resume or summary of work experience

You are requesting this information in order to determine whether or not the candidate meets the qualifications of a new president for the business.

Alternative First Step would be to set up a face to face meeting preferably at a safe location such as a hotel, library, coffee shop etc. If you are satisfied with the candidate you then provide material listed above for completion and return before going to the next step which is to visit the business.

Fielding an Internet Response
Fielding an internet response may seem a lot less personal than either a face to face or telephonic meeting. You should keep this in mind and make email conversations as warm and personable as are your person to person communications.

Your objective is essentially the same as if fielding a telephone call. You want to obtain information from the applicant just as he/she wants information from you. The only difference may be that you are communicating by email instead of telephone.
You still must be in control of the process and dole out information only as is appropriate and not as may be demanded by an inquirer. You still do not know who you are dealing with so information exchange should be limited to the One Page Profile.

Draft a response that you can send to internet email inquiries. You still want as much information from your candidate as is possible before you schedule a meeting or send the Confidential Business Review.

Sample Response

Thank you for your interest in our business.

We have attached both a concise overview of the opportunity our business represents as well as a Non Disclosure or Confidentiality Agreement (CA). We ask that you review the Profile and, if our opportunity seems to be a match, please return a signed CA to the mailing address below along with your Personal Financial Statement and Resume or summary of your work experience.

We are not only selling our business but are actually interviewing the future president of our company. For your benefit, and ours, the new president should have the skills, background and experience with which to capitalize upon the opportunity our company represents. We hope you are this person.

CAUTION: Do not post your ad before you are completely ready. More often than not your best buyer will be your first responder. Best to be sure you are prepared before you begin. As with painting a house, you don't start by slapping on paint and then expect quality results.

Where to post your business for sale on line

Below is a compilation of websites where businesses can be listed for sale

Acquireo.com

Australian Business for Sale

BizBen - *California businesses for sale*

BizBuySell.com

Bizforsell.com

BizMLS.com

Bizquest

BSBX.com

BusiMarket.com

Business Nation

BusinessResaleNetwork

BusinessBroker.net

BusinessesForSale.com

BusinessMart.com

BuySellBiz.com – *Free listing*

Ebizsurf Australia

FranchiseGATOR.com

GlobalBX

Mergerplace.com

Sell-a-Biz.Com

USABizMart

These are the more popular sites on the web.. Most require a fee to list a business on their website. Some specialize in only larger businesses.

The Interview
Strategies for Success

As with most tasks in life, when approached with confidence and preparation, success is reasonably assured. Here are some suggestions to help you be prepared and to build your confidence in your ability to perform the task at hand.

Prior to the meeting certain basics must have been attended to.

Candidate has provided you:	You have provided candidate:
A signed Confidentiality Agreement	A concise overview of your business
Personal Financial Statement	(one page profile)

Prepare questions in advance
Create a list of questions before the candidate arrives. This upfront planning will keep the interview moving quickly and ensure you get the information you need. It will also help you avoid vaguely worded questions that may be difficult for candidates to answer.

Define your objectives before you start
The work you have done in the Profiling section of this work has taken care of this important element.

Listen more than you talk

When the interview begins, make candidate comfortable by asking a few general questions, and then let them do most of the talking. You should spend 80% of your time listening and 20% talking.

Preparation & Interviewing Tips
The Interview and Company tour should be a session of Give and Take, a sharing of foundational and background information. Ideally the session will be a "Know me, Like me, Trust me" session and not an inquisition on either parties part. Detailed financial and other sensitive information should not be revealed or discussed at this session.

Your job is to highlight the opportunity your business represents. The candidate's job is to provide you their qualifications and credential as the next president of your company.

Icebreakers: Start of with some Icebreaker questions. As their name implies, icebreakers are used to build rapport and set candidates at ease before beginning the interview. Examples:

- Did you have any trouble finding our place?
- Before we start, would you like a cup of coffee or glass of ice water?
- Was their much traffic?

General Questions: With these, you can gather general information about a candidate and their skills and experience. Examples:

- What do you find attractive about our industry?
- What in your background can be applied to this business?
- Do you have experience in this industry?
- What do you consider to be your greatest strengths and weaknesses?
- What qualifications do you have that make you think that you will be successful in business?
- What accomplishments have given you the most satisfaction? Why?
- How do you work under pressure?

Company Specific Questions: Questions you should consider asking to determine if your candidate is appropriate for your business.

- Why is my business attractive to you?
  Remember, you are interviewing for a potential new president and CEO of your business. Qualify means more than how much money they might have.

Situational Questions: Ask candidates what they would do in a specific situation relevant to the job at hand. These questions can help you understand a candidate's thought process. Examples:

- How do you deal with irate customers?
- How do you deal with stress on the job?

Behavior-Based Questions: This type question requires a candidate to share a specific example from their past experience. The candidate's answer should be a Situation, Action, and Result or SAR response. If a candidate skips any of these three elements, ask them to fill in the blanks. Examples:

- Crises usually require us to act quickly. Tell me how you resolve crises through your team members.
- In retrospect, how would you have handled a recent crisis differently, if you had been given more time to think before acting?

Other Thoughts

Attitude Trumps Skill - Among the qualities you'll want most is a fierce sense of optimism.

Results Over Potential - Never choose someone with good potential but questionable habits, thinking you can change him or her. As in choosing mates, what you see now is what you get forever.

Sense of Humor - A president who can't laugh easily, particularly at one's self, is going to be uninspiring and probably depressingly rigid.

Fill in the Blanks - Review carefully the aggregate strengths and skill gaps of your presidency, and go for the qualities and styles that are missing.

Listen - Ask quality questions and listen to the answers. Asking the right questions will go further in selling the opportunity your company represents than will any oratory, prospectus or brochure you might present. Listen for appropriate responses.

Investing quality time and effort in finding your ideal successor will pay off in two ways:

- Finding the ideal successor who will pay the best price plus be right for your company and
- Save you big bucks in fees and commissions paid to brokers..

What would it cost?

What would it cost to have someone do all of this for you? Here are some example costs of finding a candidate:

- Typical Executive Search - $34,844 *Source: SHRM/EMA*
- Business Broker/Intermediary – 8 to 12% of Company value

Never tell people how to do things.
Tell them what to do and they will surprise you with their ingenuity.

General George S. Patton

Close the Deal

All seems to be going quite well. You have attracted what appears to be a suitable buyer. Your candidate has all the qualifications needed to move your business forward and is very excited about the opportunity your business represents. You breathe a sigh of relief and think to yourself; that wasn't so difficult.

Remember back in the "Lay of the Land" section we pointed out that rookie business brokers and, **business owners selling on their own, had a success rate of only 2% selling a business!** Firsthand experience has taught us that one of the reasons for this poor performance is that too many thought the job was completed once an offer was received so they relaxed and waited for the attorneys or escrow to schedule a closing.

> ## *CAUTION*
> You are *only 10%* of the way to selling your business! This is not the time to relax; the real work lies ahead.

Do not be concerned however, because the work you have completed up to this point is about to pay off *Big Time!*

You have:

- Ratified the timeliness of selling and are ready to move on,
- Developed a Profile of your ideal candidate,
- Established a Fair price, workable terms and a prudent tax strategy,
- Completed a Due Diligence Book,
- Lined up Lenders ready to lend.

You are loaded for bear and prepared to complete a sale. All you need now is to be sure your buyer understands the unique environment and process involved in selling a Private company.

Your job now is to keep the deal on track with events occurring in the proper sequence:

- Meeting and facilities tour
- Offer to Purchase
- Investigation or Due Diligence
- Buyer Develops Business Plan - Secures Acquisition Funding
- Draw Closing Documents – Buyer Conducts Lien and Judgment Searches
- Closing
- After the sale support, training and compensation

Issues or problems are bound to arise as you move forward to a successful transfer and you should not be surprised when they occur. Your preparation and ability to keep things moving forward in the proper sequence will prevent many problems from arising at all.

Road Map to a Successful Transaction

Provide a "Road Map" and keep progress focused - You know buying a business is different than buying essentially anything else you can imagine. You have to make sure your candidate does also and that you both step off on the right foot and follow the same path. Therefore, we have developed a sort of procedural "Road Map" that you can share with your candidate and, hopefully start off on the same page and in step. A "Road Map" handout is provided for your use in the Exhibit section as well as at the end of this chapter..

IMPORTANT

When selling your business on your own you have to take on the job of **buyer education** that is usually performed by your broker. Successful brokers are talented educator first and finder last. We learned we had to provide our buyers with information they would need before they needed it. If we attempted to give buyers information when required they would ignore it and view our efforts as a typical salesman's ploy to gain a commission. Conversely, we were viewed as helpful professionals when information was provided before it was needed

Keep Focused on "A" Items

There must be an organized sequence of events to keep your deal on track and keep it from sliding into the weeds. It is human nature to avoid the big questions and focus instead upon the minuscule and unimportant; best to focus only upon the "A Items." "A Items" are the deal breaker issues. If your buyer can't get past one of them (earnings are too low) why would a small item such as the cost of trash removal be important?

You are helpful and professional if you provide information
before the information is needed.
Attempt to give the same information when it is needed and
you are viewed as a typical salesperson trying to make a sale

---

Keep your deal on track by focusing only upon the A Items. Certain sensitive A Items such as contact with customers, suppliers and employees, would be placed towards the end of the list and other events will not be addressed until price and terms are agreed upon. More critical issues, such as license transfers, are delayed until Due Diligence is completed, all contingencies removed and the deal is in Escrow with serious Earnest Money on Deposit.

A Items are simple, no-nonsense issues that must be addressed head on before moving forward. As one set of A Items is satisfied they are replaced by others, each being addressed in proper sequence. These are some examples of Buyer and Seller subjects of concern that must be satisfied early on and before too much time is wasted and sensitive information divulged.

Initial "A" Items:

- Can the business support the buyer's lifestyle?
- Can the Buyer afford the business?
- Can buyer see himself working at your business daily?
- Is the candidate qualified to move the business forward?
- Is there opportunity for growth/improvement?

Pre Facility Visit

Can the business support the candidate's lifestyle?

Your One Page Profile should have provided enough information for the candidate to make an accurate determination in this regard. The answer to the next question is one you must be satisfied with.

Can the Buyer afford the business?

You have requested a Personal Financial Statement from to obtain view of the candidate's financial strength and habits. Do they have the required capital to satisfy the down payment requirements of you and the acquisition lender you have lined up? Are they burdened with excessive credit card and other debt that would disqualify them from obtaining this financing?

No Problem – When candidates refuse to provide you with their Personal Financial Statement and respond instead "No problem." Both words are accurate and truthful i.e.:

- *No*, I don't have money and
- Money is a *Problem*.

CAUTION

Do not proceed without being satisfied with the candidate's financial abilities. The buying and selling of a business involves give and take by both parties. You provided a financial overview in your One Page Profile – They give you a Personal Financial statement.

Visit to the facility

Some questions can only be best satisfied by a tour of the business and/or a face to face meeting. A sale is often made when "the tires hit the curb."

Can buyer see himself working at your business daily?

Your One Page Profile presents your business as an attractive and profitable opportunity. However, will the candidate be comfortable actually working in your business? Some questions will be answered only by actually visiting the business. Is the neighborhood a bit too rough? Does your process give off an odor the candidate might find offensive? Will the candidate be at ease with your customers, employees? Is your facility old and worn or otherwise unattractive?

These and other questions are best resolved by a visit to the facility.

Is the candidate qualified to move the business forward?

You have requested your candidate provide you with a resume or work history. You have also developed a Profile of your target candidate. You confirm the candidate meets this Profile during a face to face visit preferably prior to touring the business if possible, otherwise during the tour of the business.

Is there opportunity for growth/improvement?

Does the candidate recognize the opportunity your business represents? Are all the right things wrong? If the opportunity does not excite your buyer, odds of completing a sale are close to nil.

IMPORTANT

> *A buyer needs a "White Heat Passion," fueled by the recognition of the opportunity your business represents, in order to overcome the many obstacle that will attempt to obstruct a successful purchase.*

Follow on "A" Items

The typical initial concerns as outlined above have been addressed and satisfied and are now replaced by a new batch. Usual follow on A Items include:

- Agree upon satisfactory price and terms
- Ratify perceived opportunity
- Review tax returns and other financial data to verify financial information
- Resolve possible environmental, OSHA, labor union, issues
- Confirm transferability of licenses, leases, distribution contracts, franchise agreements
- Confirm lack of concern re: Federal, state or local rules/regulation or other impending changes that might negatively affect the business
- Ratify business profile information re: customer concentrations, competition, breakdown of sales by product/service
- Ability to obtain financing

   As the process unfolds your candidate's suspicion and nervousness turns into enthusiasm and excitement, that is, as long as there are no unpleasant surprises. Your preparation should prevent unpleasant surprises from ever appearing.

Note – The Appendix and CD-Rom include blank Conditional Offer to Purchase and Letter of Intents that you could give your candidate in order to demystify and facilitate the process of making the offer on their own. The last thing you need to happen is to have your deal "go legal" prematurely.

Road Map

Step 1 – **Owner and Candidate Meet, Tour Facility** - After meeting and touring the facility the candidate can answer these A Item questions: Does the business feel right? Are you comfortable with the owner? Do you recognize an opportunity? If yes proceed – If seller is satisfied with candidate's qualifications a Comprehensive Business Review containing enough information upon which one can make an offer is provided.

Step 2 **-** **Make a *Non Binding* Offer** – Offer will not be binding upon either the buyer or the seller until each is satisfied;

- Buyer's satisfaction with Seller's business and the financial condition of same
- Seller's satisfaction with Buyer's credit worthiness, character and ability to operate the business successfully

Both Buyer and Seller will make the offer binding only after each is satisfied (as outlined above) during "Due Diligence" as evidenced by their signing an "Authorization to Close."

The Letter of Intent (LOI) or Offer to Purchase

The buyer outlines the terms and price they are prepared to pay in a written, nonbinding document, and promises confidentiality so that you'll allow further investigation of your company. It is usual to have a bit of back and forth using Counter Offers or Addendums to the LOI before a final understanding is reached.

Non-Binding – The LOI or Offer to Purchase is not intended to be a binding contract at this time.

- **Seller** - You certainly want to affirm the candidate's credit worthiness, qualifications to operate your business etc before you are bound by a contract to sell
- **Buyer** – Does not want to be forced to purchase if the business does not meet their needs or expectations

Exception - One part of the letter of intent is binding on the buyer wherein promises are made to keep confidential the fact that negotiations are proceeding, and not to disclose any information learned during due diligence or negotiations.

Conditional Purchase and

Sale of Assets Agreement

Date _____ / _____ / _____

1. The Purchaser agrees to buy business assets from the Seller, including all furniture, equipment, trade fixtures, inventory, goodwill, trademarks, trade names and other intangible assets of the business known as: _____

_____

_____

Located at _____

2. The purchase price of $_____ shall be paid as follows:

    a. Deposited with Seller on the date of this Agreement. $ _____

    b. Additional deposit with Seller in certified funds upon or before acceptance by Seller. $ _____

    c. Balance of down payment due at the closing in certified funds. $ _____

Total Down Payment. $

_____

    d. Assumption of existing obligation

$ _____

    (Payable at $ _____ per month (including _____ % interest).

    e. Balance to be paid to Seller pursuant to a secured Promissory Note

$ _____

    payable $ _____ (or more per month, without penalty), including _____% interest, secured by assets being purchased.

f. Additional terms:_____

$ _____

$ Total Purchase Price

$ _____

3. The full purchase price shall include inventory of $_____ at Seller's cost. If the actual amount is more or less, up to a maximum amount of $_____, the purchase price and down payment or note to Seller shall be adjusted at the closing accordingly.

4. The closing shall take place on or before _____ 2 _____ at _____ AM   PM at the offices of _____.Closing costs shall be shared equally by Purchaser and Seller.

NOTE - A Conditional Purchase and Sale of Assets Agreement you can give to your candidate is included on the Business Selling System CD-ROM and the Appendix

Counter Offers – Generally involve price and/or terms. If you wish to have a higher down payment or purchase price the Counter Offer is the format to be employed.

Counter Offer

Sample Company
123 Main Street
Your Town, State, Zip Code

Between: Appropriate Name as Seller(s)

and: Buyer's Name as Purchaser(s)

I/We accept all of the terms and conditions of the Letter of Intent dated _____except as follows:

Down Payment to be $150,000

Purchase Price to be $500,000

2007 Ford F250 excluded from sale

Should the Purchaser, fail to accept this counter offer on or before 6 o'clock PM, on Date, this counter offer may be terminated.

Receipt of a copy of this Counter Offer is hereby acknowledged.

Purchaser: _____

Date: _____

Will Seller
President

Month, day, Year

Notice – All terms and conditions remain unchanged except for those that are detailed in the counter offer. This allows for forward movement while avoiding the need to redraft the entire document. Simple is good, complex is bad.

The secret to managing is to keep the guys who hate you away from the guys who are undecided.

Casey Stengel

130

Addendum or Amendments to the LOI are typically used for clarification or procedural issues. For example, use an Addendum if the LOI lacks language regarding:

- Confidentiality
- Non-binding nature of the agreement
- Time limit on length of time for Due Diligence

Amendment/Addendum

To a certain Letter of Intent dated Month/Day/Year identified below between:

Earnest Byers - Buyer

on that business known as: Sample Company
and located at: 123 Main Street, Your Town, State Zip Code

This Amendment /Addendum shall constitute an integral part of that Agreement, and all its terms and conditions not otherwise modified below are hereby confirmed and accepted.

This Agreement shall be construed as non binding upon either party, excluding the Confidentiality Agreement executed earlier, until said parties sign the Authorization to Close

Interview of Suppliers, Employees and Customers will occur only after Buyer receives written permission from Seller to do so.

This offer may by withdrawn after 6:00 p.m. on <u>Date</u> if not previously accepted below, and Buyer's deposit shall be promptly and fully refunded. Receipt of a copy of this Amendment/Addendum is hereby acknowledged.

_____	_____
Purchaser	Date

Will Seller
President
Sample Company

<u>Dated</u>

Notice – The Addendum/Amendment also specifies that "all terms and conditions not otherwise modified are confirmed and accepted."

If you don't do it excellently, don't do it at all. Because if it's not excellent, it won't be profitable or fun, and if you're not in business for fun or profit, what the hell are you doing there?

Robert Townsend

Earnest Money Deposits - The protocol regarding Earnest Money varies with the size of your company and the format your buyer uses when presenting his offer.

- **Letters of Intent** (LOI) - Typically used by Sophisticated or Corporate Buyers, are not always accompanied by an Earnest Money Deposit however, we would counter that a deposit would be required at the end of the Due Diligence period in order to 'take the business off the market"
- **Offers to Purchase** - Preferred by Financial or Lifestyle buyers are typically accompanied by an Earnest Money deposit

Use an Addendum/Amendment to assure significant Earnest Money is on deposit before you begin drawing final closing documents, notifying creditors, landlords and others of the impending sale.

> **Sample language** to assure commitment on the Buyer's side
>
> An additional deposit of $X0,000, bringing the total deposit to 10% of the Purchase Price, will be place on deposit concurrent with executing the Authorization to Close.

Items you may wish to have included in the letter of intent by using either the Addendum/Amendment or Counter Offer format.

- ➢ A specified period of time in which to conduct their due diligence investigation, seven days for small businesses and up to thirty days for larger businesses

- ➢ Additional deposit upon completion of Due Diligence and signing the Authorization to Close – 10% of Purchase Price is usual

- ➢ Add Confidentiality language

- ➢ Location where and when closing will be held

- ➢ The full purchase price shall include inventory of $_____ at Seller's cost. If the actual amount is more or less, up to a maximum amount of $_____, the purchase price and down payment or note to Seller shall be adjusted at the closing accordingly.

- ➢ Inventory to be taken by Professional Inventory Company – cost to be shared by Buyer and Seller equally

- ➢ Assumption of existing obligation payable at $ _____ per month (including ـــــ % interest)

- ➢ The following adjustments and pro rations shall be made at closing: rent security deposit, rent, utilities, _____

> ➤ This offer shall not be binding upon either Purchaser or Seller until both have executed the "Authorization to Close," signifying the Seller's satisfaction with Purchaser's credit worthiness, character and abilities and the Purchaser's satisfaction with Seller's business and the financial condition of same.

Multiple Offers

It sometimes happens and brings to mind the time four associates each took an offer on the same business, all with identical terms, on the same day. What was our client to do? We made Counter Offers to all four allowing them to proceed with their Due Diligence (it was a simple operation) and the first to remove all contingencies and place the total purchase price Down Payment and proof of financing into escrow would be the buyer.

It turned out that the last buyer to make an offer was the one who prevailed. The others either could not obtain the needed financing or were frightened of during due diligence.

Note: There are several "Bump Clauses" covering numerous "what if" scenarios in the Special Wording section on your *Business Selling System's* CD-ROM.

Step 3 - **Investigation** or **Due Diligence** – Buyer conducts an operational and financial review of the company and its records. Seller conducts a credit and background check on buyer.

Upon completion of their independent reviews:

- Seller either accepts the Buyer and signs the Authorization to Close or not
- Buyer has three options from which to choose:
  1. Return all materials provided by seller and walk away from the deal – Earnest Money Deposit is returned
  2. Express satisfaction with the proposed transaction and execute the Authorization to Close and deposit additional deposits, if required, into escrow
  3. Counter Offer – After investigation buyer may wish to modify price and or terms i.e.:
     - A - Lower Purchase Price and/or Down Payment
     - B - Increase Purchase Price and lower Down Payment
     - C - Change terms of Note(s)
     - D - Postpone purchase of certain assets thereby reducing initial price

Upon final agreement, execute the Authorization to Close and deposit any additional deposits into escrow

---

The problem is not that there are problems. The problem is expecting otherwise and thinking that having problems is a problem.

Theodore Rubin

Due Diligence

During this period the parties have a limited time period in which to investigate each other thoroughly, to see whether they will proceed with the deal.

Seller

Conduct your own due diligence. If you are providing some or the entire purchase price financing one of your primary concerns will be the buyer's credit record. Obtain authorization to check the credit history of all parties to the contract.

AUTHORIZATION TO
OBTAIN CREDIT INFORMATION

For the purpose of obtaining credit, the following statement is made intending that it be relied on as being correct.

PERSONAL INFORMATION

LAST NAME:_____   **SPOUSE'S INFORMATION**

FIRST NAME: _____   _____

MID. INITIAL:._____   _____

SOCIAL SEC. # _____   # _____

CURRENT ADDRESS

STREET_____   _____

CITY _____   _____

STATE/ZIP _____   _____

PREV. ADDRESS   (if current address less than 2 years)

STREET_____   _____

CITY _____   _____

STATE/ZIP _____   _____

(Your Firm) may verify the information above, check my credit history and secure follow up credit reports on me. Note: I understand that my credit report will be obtained through (Credit Bureau's name and address) and it will be this report that will be used to evaluate my credit history.

AUTHORIZATION signed by: _____

SPOUSE _____

DATE: _____

Of equal concern are your candidate's business experience, education, skills talents and the resources he/she will bring to your business. Essentially you will want to verify that you have attracted the right person(s) or company – verify that they fit the profile of your ideal buyer.

Buyer

This is where your earlier preparation really pays off. Much to the pleasant surprise of your buyer and their team of advisors, you are able to immediately provide them:

A complete Due Diligence book containing all the essential information a buyer and advisors can be predicted to request i.e.:

- Copies of all leases, contracts, and loan agreements in addition to copious financial records and statements.

- Management reports you use, such as sales reports, inventory records, detailed lists of assets, facility maintenance records, aged receivables and payables reports, employee organization charts, payroll and benefits records, customer records, and marketing materials.

- Pending litigation, tax audits, or insurance disputes. Depending on the nature of your business, you might also consider getting an environmental audit and an insurance checkup.

- Financial analysis of your company; including your key financial ratios

Name(s) and contact information of lender(s) willing to provide Acquisition Funding

A comprehensive outline of the information and data the lender(s) require, all of which, except the buyer's personal and financial information, you have included in the Due Diligence book

---

Note: Sample documents and loan proposal are
found in the Appendix section and
on the ***Business Selling System*** CR-ROM

The measure of success is not whether you have a tough problem to deal with, but whether it's the same problem you had last year.

John Foster Dulles

Authorization to Close

Both buyer and business owner have some checking to do before the LOI is converted into a binding contract. Once each side has satisfactorily completed their Due Diligence review they will sign off on their satisfaction with;

- **Seller**: Buyer's credit history, creditworthiness, references, and police records etc.
- **Buyer**: Financial and operational suitability of the business to his/her needs.

Once this document has been executed final documents can be drawn final steps of the transfer can begin.

Authorization to Close

Re: Letter of Intent Dated: _____

BusinessName: _____

Purchasers Authorization – "My independent investigation and analysis of the subject Business and the Information provided by the Seller having been favorably concluded, and all contingencies and conditions of the sales contract having been resolved to my satisfaction, I hereby re-affirm said contract and all of my obligations there-under. I expressly waive any and all rights that I may have to rescind said agreement and agree to hold myself ready, willing and able to close this sale as soon as the appropriate documents have been prepared."

_____

Purchaser

Date _____

_____

Sellers Authorization - "I hereby re-affirm the above referenced Agreement and hold myself ready, willing and able to close this sale as soon as appropriate documents have been prepared" (after check buyer's credit history, creditworthiness, references, and police records etc.).

_____

Seller

Date _____

The fewer data needed, the better the information. And an overload of information, that is, anything much beyond what is truly needed, leads to information blackout. It does not enrich, but impoverishes.

Peter F. Drucker

Step 4 – **Develop Business Plan - Secure Acquisition Funding** – At this point in the process your candidate is now very familiar with your business and is fully aware of the markets you serve, its customer base and most importantly – the opportunity the business represents. Your candidate will be able to answer any questions posed by a lender with full knowledge and confidence.

Note - We have included an SBA loan package outline you can provide your candidate. Also, much of the financial and profile information found in the Due Diligence Book you provided your candidate can be used to complete the SBA Loan Proposal.

Step 5 - **Draw Closing Documents – Conduct Lien and Judgment Searches**

In the western states this stage is called "Opening of Escrow." Most eastern states do not use escrow agents and buyers and sellers employ lawyers instead. This is unfortunate as most attorneys are unfamiliar with the business transfer process. Accordingly, transfers take longer to complete, costs are unnecessarily high and the quality of work is lower.

> ## *SUGGESTION*
>
> Contact your regional Business Broker Association, or the International Business Broker Association (IBBA) www.ibba.org for names and contact information of Attorneys, Accountants and Lenders who are proficient and experienced with small business transfers.

Earnest money deposit from Buyer is placed in a third party escrow account or a special bank account established by the Seller for this purpose only.

Many items can be collected, signed and completed before the business transfer is completed. Purchase and sale agreement, licenses, franchises, leases, transferable contracts and notes etc. can be placed in Escrow pending actual closing

Some items might be executed only *after* or at the *same time* all conditions and terms have been met and the deal is done. Liquor license transfers, for example, should not be completed until everything else is done. Otherwise you run the risk of transferring the license to the buyer and then having negotiations breakdown with the license in the buyer's name.

> ## *CAUTION* – Some leases and licenses should be transferred only after everything else has been settled and signed with all monies on deposit in escrow. Otherwise your license or lease may end up in the buyer's name should negotiations breakdown.

What is Escrow?

Escrow is the process whereby buyers and sellers deposit documents and money with a third party (Escrow Agent) with instructions for distribution when certain conditions and terms are met.

In California and other Escrow jurisdictions the Escrow Officer will:

- Receive, deposit, and distribute funds for both parties,
- Prepare closing documents
- Perform a lien and judgment search on Sellers business.
- Publishes and files Notice to Creditors and other applicable documents
- Requests releases/clearances from State Agencies evidencing taxes are up to date
- Conducts State and County Lien Searches
- Clearances and/or Claims are received and acknowledged
- Escrow cannot close until liquor licenses are transferred by Liquor Boards.
- Any liens or judgments that arise must be satisfied before closing.

Closing costs are split between Buyer and Seller. Typical cost of a $500,000 business transfer would approximate $1,000.

The Bulk Sale Escrow Process

The Bulk Sale Code contained in the Uniform Commercial Code of California and a few other states governs the escrow process for businesses. The Code requires the publication of a Notice to Creditors for a mandatory minimum publication period. The close of escrow must take place **on or after** the date specified on the Notice.

The Notice to Creditors, and all necessary documents, are all prepared at the beginning of the escrow. These documents are signed by all parties and put into escrow along with buyer's deposit, funds for payment of up front expenses for publication and filing fees, etc. before the Notice to Creditors is recorded or published. It is usual, and in fact the Uniform Commercial Code of California requires, that no funds are released to the seller prior to the close of escrow.

Step 6 – **Closing** – In non Escrow states a "Closing" typically occurs when the parties meet with their respective lawyers to sign all the documents in each other's presence. In Escrow states where an escrow agent is used each party signs the necessary documents as they become available, and forwards them to the escrow agent over a period of days or weeks. When the agent has everything from both parties, he or she will release the funds to the seller and the deal is "closed." Whether an escrow agent or a closing ceremony is used really depends on the custom in your geographic locality, and the preference of your lawyer.

Documentation to be reviewed and signed at closing generally include:

- **Purchase and Sale Agreement** – Purchase price and terms of sale are outlined as well as Representations, Warranties, Covenants and Agreements by Seller and Buyer are the primary items covered by this contract.
- **Bill of Sale** - This document conveys all rights, title and interest of the specific assets listed (equipment, fixtures, vehicles and furniture) to the Buyer as agreed in the Purchase and Sale Agreement
- **Promissory Note** - This document is an agreement whereby the Buyer (Debtor) agrees to make payments under specific terms and conditions over a predetermined time period.
- **Security Agreement** - A Security Agreement grants the Seller (Secured Party) a Lien or Security Interest in the assets of the business, until such time as the loan is paid in full. A Security Agreement can be compared to "mortgage" or "deed of trust" on a home.
- **UCC-1 Financing Statement** - This document is filed with the Secretary of State on behalf of the Secured Party to record their security interest on the business assets until the Promissory Note is paid in full.

Note - Blank closing documents can be found in the Document Pack of your *Business Selling System* **CD-ROM.**

Step 7 – **After the sale support, training and compensation** - The required training/support period and after sale compensation changes as the complexity and size of the business increases.

Buyers of smaller businesses will typically receive two weeks of onsite training and transition support at no additional cost as this is built into the purchase price.

- Acquirers of larger companies often request longer periods and transition periods of one year are not uncommon. Compensation for this transition assistance is usually in addition to the purchase price.

- Owners are often asked to remain for a period of years by Public companies acquiring smaller Private businesses. Many agreements contain provisions for the seller to share in increased profits.

- Other acquirers, usually Private Equity Groups (PEGs), who plan to "flip" the company after they add their "magic", will offer a sort of joint venture arrangement where the seller participates in the increased value upon re-sale of the company.

Road Map

Step 1 – **Owner and Candidate Meet, Tour Facility** - After meeting and touring the facility the candidate can answer these questions: Does the business feel right? Are you comfortable with the owner? Do you recognize an opportunity? If yes proceed

If Seller is satisfied with a candidate's qualifications a Comprehensive Business Review containing enough information upon which one can make an offer is provided.

Step 2 - **Make a *Non Binding* Offer** – Offer will not be binding upon either the buyer or the seller until each is satisfied;

- Buyer's satisfaction with Seller's business and the financial condition of same
- Seller's satisfaction with Buyer's credit worthiness, character and ability to operate the business successfully

Both Buyer and Seller will make the offer binding only after each is satisfied (as outlined above) during "Due Diligence" as evidenced by their signing an "Authorization to Close."

Step 3 - **Investigation or Due Diligence** – Buyer conducts an operational and financial review of the company and its records. Seller conducts a credit and background check on buyer.

Upon completion of their independent reviews:

- Seller either accepts the Buyer and signs the Authorization to Close or not
- Buyer has three options from which to choose:
    1. Return all materials provided by seller and walk away from the deal – Earnest Money Deposit is returned
    2. Express satisfaction with the proposed transaction and execute the Authorization to Close and deposit additional deposits, if required, into escrow
    3. Counter Offer – After investigation buyer may wish to modify price and or terms i.e.:
        - A - Lower Down Payment and/or Purchase Price
        - B - Lower Down Payment and Increase Purchase Price
        - C - Change terms of Note(s)
        - D - Postpone purchase of certain assets thereby reducing initial price

Upon final agreement, execute the Authorization to Close and deposit any additional deposits into escrow

Step 4 – **Develop Business Plan - Secure Acquisition Funding** – At this point in the process your candidate is now very familiar with the business and is fully aware of the markets served, the customer base and most importantly – the opportunity the business represents. The candidate will be able to answer any questions posed by a lender with full knowledge and confidence.

Step 5 - **Draw Closing Documents – Conduct Lien and Judgment Searches**

In the west this stage is called "Opening of Escrow." Most eastern states do not use escrow agents and buyers and sellers employ lawyers instead.

Earnest money deposit from Buyer is placed in a third party escrow account or a special bank account established by the Seller for this purpose only. Most items must be collected, signed and completed before a business transfer can be completed. Purchase and sale agreement, licenses, franchises, leases, transferable contracts and notes etc. can be placed in Escrow pending actual closing

Some items might be executed only *after* or at the *same time* all conditions and terms have been met and the deal is done. Liquor license transfers, for example, should not be completed until everything else is done.

Step 6 – **Closing** – In non – Escrow states a "Closing" typically occurs when the parties meet with their respective lawyers to sign all the documents in each other's presence. In Escrow states where an escrow agent is used each party signs the necessary documents as they become available, and forwards them to the escrow agent over a period of days or weeks. When the agent has everything from both parties, he or she will release the funds to the seller and the deal is "closed." Whether an escrow agent or a closing ceremony is used really depends on the custom in your geographic locality.

Documentation to be reviewed and signed at closing generally includes:

- **Purchase and Sale Agreement** – Purchase price and terms of sale are outlined as well as Representations, Warranties, Covenants and Agreements by Seller and Buyer are the primary items covered by this contract.
- **Bill of Sale** - This individual document conveys all rights, title and interest of the specific assets listed (equipment, fixtures, vehicles and furniture) to the Buyer as agreed in the Purchase and Sale Agreement
- **Promissory Note** - This document is an agreement whereby the Buyer (Debtor) agrees to make payments under specific terms and conditions over a predetermined time period.
- **Security Agreement** - A Security Agreement grants the Seller (Secured Party) a Lien or Security Interest in the assets of the business, until such time as the loan is paid in full. A Security Agreement can be compared to "mortgage" or "deed of trust" on a home.

- **UCC-1 Financing Statement** - This document is filed with the Secretary of State on behalf of the Secured Party to record their security interest on the business assets until the Promissory Note is paid in full.

Step 7 – **After the sale support and training** Business buyers of smaller businesses will typically receive two weeks of on site training and transition support as part of the selling price. The required training/support period increases as the complexity and size of the business increases. One year is not uncommon in the case of the larger companies. Owners are often asked to remain for a period of years by Public companies acquiring smaller Private businesses.

Appendix

Section Three – Closing the deal

Additional clauses

Agreement to pay accounts payable

Assumption Agreement

Bill of Sale

Bulk Sale Addendum to the Offer to Purchase

Bulk Sale Agreement

Bulk Sale Notification

Bulk Sale Release

Bulk Sale Waiver

Closing Worksheet

Covenant Not to Compete

Escrow Agreement

Guaranty

Inventory Completion Agreement

List of Creditors for Bulk Transfer

Mutual Release

Note - Balloon

Note – Convertible

Note - Demand

Promissory Note – secured by real estate

Note - Unsecured

Promissory Note

Pledge Agreement

Power of Attorney

Purchase and Sale Agreement - Short

Purchase and Sale Agreement – Stock

Purchase and Sale Agreement – Long

Security Agreement

Training Agreement

Section Four – Leases and lease assignment paperwork

Short Lease

Medium Lease

Long Lease

Assignment of Lease as Collateral Security

Assignment of Lease

Authorization to Sublease

Get Ready to Sell Documents

Skills and Knowledge desired of the New President

Listed below are specific areas where you can rate levels of skill and comfort on a scale of 1 – 10 with 10 being the highest. Use this matrix first to measure your levels and then, do it again with the new president in mind.

	Low				Medium				High	
Accounting	1	2	3	4	5	6	7	8	9	10
Finance	1	2	3	4	5	6	7	8	9	10
Artistic	1	2	3	4	5	6	7	8	9	10
Taxes	1	2	3	4	5	6	7	8	9	10
Selling	1	2	3	4	5	6	7	8	9	10
Marketing	1	2	3	4	5	6	7	8	9	10
Sales Mgmt	1	2	3	4	5	6	7	8	9	10
Managerial	1	2	3	4	5	6	7	8	9	10
Motivational	1	2	3	4	5	6	7	8	9	10
Analytical	1	2	3	4	5	6	7	8	9	10
Verbal	1	2	3	4	5	6	7	8	9	10
Writing	1	2	3	4	5	6	7	8	9	10
Mechanical	1	2	3	4	5	6	7	8	9	10
Design	1	2	3	4	5	6	7	8	9	10
Computer	1	2	3	4	5	6	7	8	9	10
Programming	1	2	3	4	5	6	7	8	9	10
Systems	1	2	3	4	5	6	7	8	9	10
Controls	1	2	3	4	5	6	7	8	9	10
Concepts	1	2	3	4	5	6	7	8	9	10
Manual	1	2	3	4	5	6	7	8	9	10
Athletic	1	2	3	4	5	6	7	8	9	10
Task Oriented	1	2	3	4	5	6	7	8	9	10

Social	1	2	3	4	5	6	7	8	9	10
Investigative	1	2	3	4	5	6	7	8	9	10
Enterprising	1	2	3	4	5	6	7	8	9	10
Other:										
	1	2	3	4	5	6	7	8	9	10
	1	2	3	4	5	6	7	8	9	10
	1	2	3	4	5	6	7	8	9	10
	1	2	3	4	5	6	7	8	9	10
	1	2	3	4	5	6	7	8	9	10

Business Experience/Education

Required	Helpful

Skills

Hard Skills	Soft Skills

Work Style

Personality Traits

Acquirer Profile (Confidential)

This questionnaire is for use by one or more individuals. A separate questionnaire for public and private companies and established private investment groups is available upon request.

Contact Information

Name:

Home Address: City: State: Zip:

Business Phone: Home Phone: Fax:

Background Information

Education:

College(s)   Degree(s)

Business experience: (Circle as Appropriate)

Sales   Manufacturing   Accounting   Retail   Engineering   Finance
Service   Marketing   Distribution Operations   Other

Industries: Position(s):

Present Employer: Position: Salary:

Address: City: State: Zip:

Business Ownership

Do you own any businesses presently?: ___ Yes   ___ No

If yes, what type(s) of business(es)?

Approximate total annual revenues(s): $

If no, is this your first acquisition for your own portfolio?   ___ Yes   ___   No

Are you interested in acquiring less than 100% ownership? __ Yes __ No

Will you be an: __ Active Manager __ Passive Investor

How long have you been seeking an acquisition?

How soon is acquisition desired?

Purpose for acquiring:

Are you the sole buyer/investor? __ Yes __ No

If no, how many others? ___

Please provide information and resumes for all investors.

Name: Name:

Address: Address:

City: State: Zip: City: State: Zip:

Phone: Phone:

Financial Information

Combined Net Worth of all investors: $

Amount of investment equity available:

List and describe all cash sources: (current as of: /   /   )

ASSETS	LIABILITIES
Cash	Notes Payable
Securities	Accounts Payable
Treasury Notes	Mortgages
Real Estate	Other Loans
Receivables	Other Liabilities
Other	
Total Liabilities	Total Assets
Net Worth	

Bank Line of Credit Available:

Financial References

Financial Institution:

Address:

City: State: Zip:

Contact Person: Title: Phone:

Other:

I certify that the above information is complete and accurate as of the date of this document and I authorize you to verify such information through reference and credit checks.

Signature: _____

Name: (Print) _____

Date: _____

Authorization To
Obtain Credit Information

For the purpose of obtaining credit, the following statement is made intending that it be relied on as being correct.

PERSONAL INFORMATION

LAST NAME:_____   **SPOUSE'S INFORMATION**

FIRST NAME: _____   _____

MID. INITIAL:._____   _____

SOCIAL SEC. # _____   # _____

CURRENT ADDRESS

STREET_____   _____

CITY _____   _____

STATE/ZIP _____   _____

PREV. ADDRESS   (if current address less than 2 years)

STREET_____   _____

CITY _____   _____

STATE/ZIP _____   _____

(Your Firm) may verify the information above, check my credit history and secure follow up credit reports on me. Note: I understand that my credit report will be obtained through (Credit Bureau's name and address) and it will be this report that will be used to evaluate my credit history.

AUTHORIZATION signed by:

_____

SPOUSE

_____

DATE: _____

Business Profile

Business Name:_____

(Use separate sheets for additional information as may be necessary.)

The Business:

Form of Ownership: Individual _____ Partnership _____ # Partners _____

S Corp. _____ or C Corp._____ Business established in _____ Present Owner acquired in _____ If acquired amount paid $ _____ Down Payment $ _____

Describe this Business:

_____

_____

_____

_____

_____

Square footage Business occupies: _____ Number of Seats: _____

Special licenses required, vending contracts, franchise or license contracts: _____

_____

_____

_____

Lease:

Presently Tenant at Will? Yes _____ No _____

Current lease has ____months remaining at $_____ per month with option to renew for an additional period of_____years.

Current Lease expires on ___/___/___ Option to renew expires on ___/___/___

Rent under option to be $_____/ Month

Does lease contain option to buy Real Estate? _____

Landlord's Name _____

Telephone # _____

Address_____

Is Lease assignable? _____ New Lease available? _____

What is the rent per square foot next door? _____, across the street? _____

Owner's estimate of Values, (Orderly Liquidation Value (OLV))

	$ Value	Average Age
Furnishings, Fixtures and Equipment (FFE)	_____	_____
Leasehold Improvements	_____	_____
Inventory	_____	_____
Vehicle(s) to be included in sale	_____	_____
Patents, Franchises, Licenses etc. (explain in notes)	_____	_____
Accounts Receivable	_____	_____
Other	_____	_____
Total OLV $	$_____	_____

Staff:

Number of family members active in Business _____. List below:

Name	Job Description	Pay Rate	Hrs/Wk	Stay/Leave
_____	_____	_____	_____	_____
_____	_____	_____	_____	_____
_____	_____	_____	_____	_____
_____	_____	_____	_____	_____
_____	_____	_____	_____	_____
_____	_____	_____	_____	_____

Number of non-family employees: Full-time_____ Part-time_____

Name	Job Description	Pay Rate	Hrs/Wk	# yrs
_____	_____	_____	_____	_____
_____	_____	_____	_____	_____
_____	_____	_____	_____	_____
_____	_____	_____	_____	_____
_____	_____	_____	_____	_____

Operations

Hours Open: _____ # days open _____

How much would you have to pay a manager in order to run this Business "absentee"?
$_____

What percentage of supplies or inventory would be considered as dead or obsolete?

What percent of your FFE should be replaced yearly to maintain a good image and productivity?
_____

As a new Owner, how long would it take to be functional in this Business? _____

From start up, how long to reach current level of profitability(months) _____

How accurately can you predict Revenues (explain) _____
_____
_____
_____

How much training is required to perform and understand this company's
operations_____
_____
_____

What is your Liability exposure level_____

How important is the Owner to the Revenues of this Business? _____
_____

Over last three years, how have Gross Sales been trending? _____

_____

New business is obtained by: (Owners influence, walk in, direct mail, etc.) _____

_____

What special license, degree or skills would a new owner need? _____

_____

_____

How do you price your product or service? _____

_____

_____

_____

Present marketing strategy?_____

_____

_____

_____

_____

Most businesses can be segmented and profit margins identified by segments. Identify below.

Major Categories or Segments	Target Gross Profit	% of Volume

_____

_____

_____

Customers:

How many Customers does the Business serve?_____

What number of Customers account for 25% of Volume? _____

Industry:

Considering social status, visual appeal, profits, etc. how desirable is this Business or Industry?

Have liability insurance rates gone up? _____ How much? _____

What is the trend for this Industry?_____

What is the status of local labor pool for this Business? _____

Does your industry have a "Trade Association?" _____ Are you a member? _____ Association (s)
:_____

_____

_____

Overview:

What are the businesses strong points?_____
_____
_____
_____
_____

What are the opportunities? _____
_____
_____
_____
_____

How could the Business be improved? _____

_____
_____
_____
_____

Competition:

How many Competitors in marketing area?_____ How many have failed in last two years ?
_____ How many are new (within last two years)? _____

Impending Changes:

Traffic flow, government regulations, zoning and competition etc.? _____ If yes, how would the
Business be affected positively and/or negatively?_____

_____
_____
_____
_____

Banking:

Have lenders loaned on the assets of the Business alone? _____

Which Bank(s) does the Business use and what is the relationship?

Bank	Service Utilized	Loan	Officer	Phone

Outstanding Notes:

Assumable? Indicate with an X if No

Lender	Security	% Interest	Term	Current Payoff?

Business Profile

Business Name _____

Address _____

City _____ State _____ Zip Code _____

Business Phone _____ Facsimile _____

Cell Phone _____ Email _____

Home Address _____

City/Town _____ State _____ Zip Code _____

Home Phone _____

Form of Ownership:

Individual _____ Partnership _____ #Partners _____ S Corp. _____ or C Corp._____

Partners/Shareholders Names   % ownership or #Shares

_____

_____

_____

_____

_____

_____

Location:

Is there a Lease? Yes _____ No _____

Current lease has _____months remaining at $_____ per month with option to renew for

an additional period of _____ years. Current Lease expires on ___ /___ /___

Option to renew expires on ___ /___ /___ # Options _____

Rent under: Option 1 $_____ / Month Option 2 $_____ / Month Option 3 $_____ / Month

Does lease contain option to buy Real Estate? Yes _____ No _____

If owned and to be included in sale need copies of: Deed ____ Tax bill _____ and Plot plan _____

Landlord's Name _____

Address_____

Telephone # _____ Is Lease assignable? _____ New Lease available? _____

What is the rent per square foot next door? _____ Across the street? _____

Parking: # cars _____ In lot _____ On street _____

History

Date founded _____ and/or date acquired _____

If acquired, the price paid was $ _____

Total down payment was _____ Note was _____

Security for note was _____

162

Give a brief overview of the company from its founding to the present. Note major changes and stages in its evolution to its present structure. Use additional sheet if required.

The Business:

Describe this business:

Hours/Days Open:

Square footage business occupies:

Number of seats (if applicable):   Number of shifts:

Special licenses required?   Vending contracts?

Assets

Owner's estimate of Values, Orderly Liquidation Value (OLV) and Average Age of:

	Orderly Liquidation	Replacement Value	Age/Condition
Furnishings, Fixtures and Equipment (FFE)			
Leasehold			
Improvements			
Inventory (at time of sale)			
Vehicle(s)			
Patents, Franchises, Licenses etc.			
Accounts Receivable			
Other			
Totals			

Provide a list of all assets to be transferred. Include serial numbers where available.

Staff

Family

Number of family members active in Business: Full-time_____ Part-time_____ List below:

Name	Job Description	PT FT	Pay Rate	Hours/Wk	Stay or Leave

Non Family

Number of non-family employees: Full-time___ Part-time _____

Name	Job Description	PT FT	Pay Rate	Hours/Wk	Stay or Leave

Benefits provided and cost per employee

Employee employment contracts? If yes provide a copy of same:

Copy of W-2s and 1099s for latest tax year:

What is the status of the labor pool for the company?

Is the company unionized?   If not, is unionization likely in the future?

How much of your industry is unionized?

Operations

How much would you have to pay a general manager in order to run this business "absentee"?

Salary	_____
Payroll taxes	_____
Insurance	_____
Automobile	_____
Bonuses	_____
Other	_____
Total	$_____

What percentage of supplies or inventory would be considered dead or obsolete? _____%

As a new owner, how long would it take to be functional in this business? _____

From start up, how long to reach current level of profitability? (months) _____

How accurately can you predict revenues? (explain seasonal variations etc.)

How much training is required to perform and understand this company's operations?

How important is the owner to the revenues of this business?

Explain how new business is obtained: (Owners influence, walk in, direct mail, etc.)

What special license, degree or skills would a new owner need?

Does the business have room for expansion?

Owner's Background:

Owner's background prior to founding or acquisition:

Education

Special skills or interests

Prior positions held

Owner's duties and hours devoted to each per week

Personnel Management		Customer service	
Administration		Sales/Marketing	
Production		Financial Mgmt	
Other			

Sales Segmentation

How do you price your product/service?

Details of sales and target gross profit by segment:

Segment	Volume/Revenue	Target Gross Profit

Have there been recent price changes?

Customer Base

List the top10 customers by volume for the past three years:

Year		Year		Year	
Customer	Volume	Customer	Volume	Customer	Volume

Describe your typical customer.

What other industries, businesses or customers could you serve?

Have you lost any significant customers/accounts in the past two years? If so why?

Do you expect to loose any significant customers/accounts in the future? If so why?

Competitors

Name	Major Strength/Weakness	Distance

How many competitors have gone out of business in the last three years and why?

Does your industry have a trade association(s)? Include name(s) and contact information.

What is the outlook for your industry?

Government Regulations

Are there anticipated or actual changes in government regulations that will impact your business?

Environmental

Are there environmental risks or hazardous materials used in or by this business? If so provide details.

Do you produce anything that is considered hazardous? If so provide details.

Liability

How common are lawsuits within your industry?

What do the lawsuits generally entail?

Do you have product/professional liability insurance?   How have the premiums been trending?

Do you have any pending litigation?

Sales and Marketing

What efforts do you expend to grow the business?

What do you need to grow the business further?

Equipment

Staff

Financial

Other

Liens/Debts/Encumbrances

Lender	Amount	Collateral

Miscellaneous

Copies of pension/profit sharing plans

Declaration pages of all insurance policies

Copies of independent party reports:

Copies of OSHA reviews and reports

Copies of environmental audits or reports

Copies of sales, state, and federal tax reviews, audits or reports

Advisors

Name	Address	Telephone and Facsimile	Email
Attorney			
Accountant			
Insurance Agent			
Other			

FIXTURES, FURNITURE

& EQUIPMENT LIST

Company:

Quantity	Item	Serial/Model Number

Buyer Release

Business Name:

Conditional Offer to Purchase Dated:

Between

Buyer:

and

Seller:

I, the undersigned potential Buyer, in the above referenced Conditional Offer to Purchase, acknowledge receipt of the sum of $_____, return in full of my earnest money deposit in the above transaction and hereby release and discharge the Seller, its principals, agents or employees, from any and all liabilities, contractual or otherwise, in connection with this transaction.

_____

Buyer

_____

Date

Confidential
Financial Statement

Name (First, Middle, Last) (include spouse if married)

Address

City   State   Zip   Tel No.

Facsimile   Email   Web site

Assets
Cash (Banks/Money Funds) $ _____
Marketable Stocks/Bonds   _____

Cash Value Life   _____

Insurance   _____

Accounts/Notes Receivable   _____

Real Estate-Residence   _____

Real Estate-Other   _____

Other Assets   _____

Total Assets $ _____

Liabilities
Installment Debts   _____
Real Estate Notes -   Residence   _____

Other   _____

Other Debts   _____

Total Liabilities $ _____

Net Worth $ _____

I/We understand that this Confidential Financial Statement is being submitted in order to obtain credit in conjunction with the purchase of a business. I/We certify that the information provided above is complete and accurate to the best of my/our knowledge.

The reverse side of this page may be used for additional details

Signed _____ Date _____

Due Diligence Check List

THE COMPANY
A comprehensive overview of the company, the CBR you created will do nicely and if a Corporation: List of shareholders, Number of shares owned by each, Number of shares outstanding

PERSONNEL AND POLICIES
List of employees with Job Description, Rate of Pay, Tenure, Stay/Leave?
Copy of employee's W-2, Employee benefits,
Incentive plans,
Pension plans,
Number of paid holidays,
Medical, life insurance, dental,
Copy of Operations Manual (if any),
List and summarize employment contracts,
Copy Union contract and expiration dates

INSURANCE
Copy of the Declaration page of all insurance policies

THE FACILITY
Copy of lease and all amendments/addendums or
Copy of Deed and plot plan if owned and part of the sale

ASSETS/EQUIPMENT
List of equipment including serial numbers (This will become part of the Bill of Sale)
List of tooling, dies, jigs, fixtures
Copy of vehicle registrations and titles
List patents, copyrights, trademark, and all new applications

SALES
Breakdown by product/service last 5 years
Percent of sales to top 5 customers
List top 20 customers and sales volume

FINANCIAL

Current interim financial statement

Financial statements past 5 years and/or Tax returns for past 5 years

Comparative Balance Sheet

Starting Balance Sheet

Comparative Ratio Analysis

Comparative Monthly Sales for past 5 years

Comparative Income and Earnings calculations

OUTSTANDING CONTRACTS

With suppliers, subcontractors, customers, unions, distributor/franchisors

COMPANY ADVISORS

Name, address, phone number of company's bank(s), accountant, attorney, advertising agency and other company advisors

Mutual Non-Disclosure and Confidentiality Agreement

This Agreement is between _____ (BUYER) and

_____ (SELLER) regarding the exchange of confidential business and personal information. Both BUYER and SELLER understand and agree:

- That information to be exchanged by SELLER and BUYER is sensitive and confidential and that its disclosure to others would be damaging to the businesses and to the individuals involved.
- That SELLER and BUYER will not disclose any Information provided to any other person who has not also signed and dated this agreement, except to secure their advice and counsel, in which case their consent to maintain such confidentiality will be obtained.
- "Information" shall include the fact that the business is for sale plus other data. The term Information does not include any information, which is, or becomes, generally available to the public.
- All Information provided to review the business will be returned to SELLER without retaining copies, summaries, analyses or extracts thereof in the event the review is terminated.
- That no contact of employees, suppliers or customers and the like will be made without the express written consent of the parties.

If the foregoing is acceptable to you please indicate your agreement by your signature below.

Agreed to and accepted:

FOR   :   FOR

----------------------------------   ----------------------------------

Name, Title   Name, Title

Date   Date

Non-Disclosure and
Confidentiality Agreement

Business Acquisition protocol requires that we obtain a non-disclosure and confidentiality agreement and evidence of financial ability before disclosing the name and location of this business. This information will be kept confidential. In compliance with the above, please read and complete the following Non-Disclosure and Confidentiality Agreement.

AGREEMENT

I, the undersigned potential investor, in consideration your providing me with information on the business you have offered for sale, understand and agree: That information provided on this businesses is sensitive and confidential and that its disclosure to others would be damaging to the businesses.

That I will not disclose any Information regarding these businesses to any other person who has not also signed and dated this agreement, except to secure their advice and counsel, in which case I agree to obtain their consent to maintain such confidentiality. "Information" shall include the fact that the business is for sale plus other data. The term Information does not include any information which is, or becomes, generally available to the public or is already in your possession.

All Information provided to review the business will be returned without retaining copies, summaries, analyses or extracts thereof in the event the review is terminated.

That I will not contact the Company's employees, suppliers or customers except with written permission.

That, prior to finalizing an agreement to purchase a business, it is my responsibility to make an independent verification of all Information.

That, should I enter into an agreement to purchase this business, I grant to the Seller the right to obtain, through standard reporting agencies, financial and credit information concerning myself or the companies or other parties I represent and understand that this information will be held confidential by Seller and will only be used for the purpose of Seller extending credit to me.

Agreed to and accepted:

Name (Signature)   Date

Name (Please Print) _____   Telephone _____

Address_____

City _____ State _____ Zip _____

Section Two

Get the Deal on the Road or

Offer Documentation

Conditional Purchase and
Sale of Assets Agreement

Date _____ /_____ /_____

1. The Purchaser agrees to buy business assets from the Seller, including all furniture, equipment, trade fixtures, inventory, goodwill, trademarks, trade names and other intangible assets of the business known as:

_____

Located at

_____

2. The purchase price of $_____ shall be paid as follows:

a. Deposited with Seller on the date of this Agreement. $ _____

b. Additional deposit with Seller in certified funds upon

        or before acceptance by Seller. $ _____

c. Balance of down payment due at the closing in certified funds. $ _____

Total Down Payment. $ _____

d. Assumption of existing obligation $ _____

(payable at $ _____ per month (including _____ % interest).

e. Balance to be paid to Seller pursuant to a secured Promissory Note $ _____

payable $ _____ (or more per month, without penalty), including ____% interest, secured by assets being purchased.

f. Additional terms:_____ $ _____

$ Total Purchase Price $ _____

3. The full purchase price shall include inventory of $_____ at Seller's cost. If the actual amount is more or less, up to a maximum amount of $_____, the purchase price and down payment or note to Seller shall be adjusted at the closing accordingly.

4. The closing shall take place on or before _____ 2 _____at_____ AM   PM at the offices of _____ Closing costs shall be shared equally by Purchaser and Seller.

5. This offer shall not be binding upon either Purchaser or Seller until both have executed the "Authorization to Close," signifying the Seller's satisfaction with Purchaser's credit worthiness, character and abilities and the Purchaser's satisfaction with Seller's business and the financial condition of same.

Conditional Purchase and
Sale of Assets Agreement (Cont.)

6. Purchaser's offer is further contingent upon obtaining a valid lease or assignment of lease at Seller's business location for a period of _____ years, including option years, at a base rent not to exceed $_____ /month.

7. Additional Purchaser contingencies are contained in attached addenda. ___ yes ___ no.

8. Seller will train Purchaser at no cost for ___ consecutive weeks after closing.

9. Seller will not compete with Purchaser within _____ miles for _____ years after closing.

10. Seller warrants that at the time physical possession is delivered to Purchaser all equipment will be in working order and that the business will meet all licensing requirements necessary to conduct the business as presently run.

11. Seller warrants that it has clear and marketable title to the business assets being sold, except as otherwise disclosed in writing. Seller will pay all business debts at closing or shall make other arrangements with creditors satisfactory to Purchaser. Seller shall hold Purchaser harmless from any undisclosed, pre-closing business obligations.

12. All deposits shall be held until closing in separate Trustee Account. At Seller's option Purchaser's initial deposit check may be held in an un-cashed form until this Agreement and any Addenda have been signed by both Purchaser and Seller.

13. The following adjustments and pro rations shall be made at closing: rent security deposit, rent, utilities, _____

14. Purchaser agrees that if he/she should fail in good faith to complete this transaction after timely acceptance by Seller, and after Purchaser's written satisfaction of the business and its financial condition, as evidenced by the Authorization to Close, then any funds on deposit with Broker shall be forfeited as liquidated damages. If Purchaser's review of the business and its financial condition or if Seller's review of the Buyer's credit worthiness, character and ability cannot be satisfied in writing then Seller agrees that Purchaser's deposit shall be promptly refunded in full..

15. This agreement, including any addenda, contains the entire understanding of the parties and there are no oral agreements, understandings or representations relied upon by the parties. Any modifications must be in writing and signed by all parties.

16. If the Seller fails to accept this offer by 6:00 o'clock P on _____ 2 ____, then the Purchaser may revoke Purchaser's offer and the deposit refunded in full.

17. The foregoing constitutes the entire Agreement.

_____   _____

(Purchaser)   Date

_____

Witness

_____   _____

(Seller)   Date

_____

Witness

Counter Offer

Business Name:_____

Address: _____

City: _____ State,_____Zip_____

Between:

_____asSeller(s)

and:_____as Purchaser(s)

I/We accept all of the terms and conditions of the Conditional Offer For Purchase and Sale of Assets Agreement dated _____except as follows:

_____
_____
_____
_____
_____
_____
_____
_____
_____
_____
_____
_____
_____
_____
_____
_____
_____

Should the Purchaser, Seller, fail to accept this counter offer on or before ____ o'clock __ AM __ PM, on _____, 2____, this counter offer may be revoked and deposit returned to Purchaser.

Receipt of a copy of this Counter Offer is hereby acknowledged.

Purchaser: _____

Date:_____ At: _____ __ AM __ PM

Seller:_____

Date:_____At:_____ __ AM __ PM

Clauses and Contingencies

Assets

F.F. & E. to be Valued at Later Date

Purchaser and Seller shall advise escrow holder at a later date of the valuation of the furniture, fixtures and equipment as listed on the Bill of Sale.

Accounts Receivable Included In Purchase Price

The accounts receivable of the business herein are included for the consideration of (*). The Seller agrees to furnish up to date accounting, in escrow of all of the accounts receivables (Note to Broker: This will be before date of possession.) of the business up to and including _____, 2XXX . Seller agrees to furnish additional like information up to and including the date of closing. The Purchaser reserves the right to audit the accounts and verify the existence thereof and to approve same. If purchaser does not disapprove the accounts in writing within 15 days of mutual acceptance it shall be deemed as purchaser's approval.

Conditions of Assets

All assets of SELLER's business being transferred to PURCHASER shall be in good working order at the closing. SELLER shall be responsible for repairing any items found defective prior to the closing.

Purchaser Purchasing Closed Business

The Purchaser herein is purchasing the equipment only of a closed business, and is purchasing said equipment with all faults.

All implied warranties, including the implied warranties of merchantability and fitness for a particular purpose are hereby disclaimed. Seller makes no express warranty of any kind in connection with such furniture, fixtures, equipment and assets. Purchaser acknowledges that he/she has had ample opportunity to inspect all such items and that he/she has done so to his/her satisfaction.

Purchaser Purchasing Equipment only "AS IS "

Purchaser is purchasing the subject business including its furniture, fixtures, equipment and miscellaneous assets located in subject premises "AS IS" and with all faults. All implied warranties, including the implied warranties of merchantability and fitness for a paticular purpose, are hereby disclaimed. Seller makes no express warranty of any kind in connection with such furniture, fixtures, equipment and assets. Purchaser acknowledges that he/she has had ample opportunity to inspect all such items and that he/she has done so to his/her satisfaction.

Approval and Possession

Subject to Approval of Third Party

This Agreement is contingent upon written approval from (^) within (*) days from execution of this agreement by (buyer) and (seller). In the event (^) does not notify buyer and seller in writing of his/her approval of this agreement within said (*) day period, it shall be deemed that purchaser has not approved this agreement and this agreement shall no longer continue in its full force and effect.

Seller Agrees to Grant Early Possession - To be used rarely and with only with Broker's approval. *Suggest this clause not be used under most circumstances.*

Seller will grant possession of subject business prior to close of escrow if all funds required including estimated costs, are on deposit. Purchaser herein agrees to be personally and financially responsible for any indebtedness incurred by him while in operation of the business from date of possession and the Seller shall be relieved of any liability in connection therewith. Both Purchaser and Seller agree to hold harmless (Name of VR Office Corporate Inc.) and escrow holder from any and all liabilities arising from possession prior to the close of escrow.

Trial Period before Closing - *Suggest this clause not be used under most circumstances*

Seller represents that he has been grossing (*) per month, and that during a trial period of (*) working days he will prove a gross volume of (*) with a lesser variance of % allowable. If the above trial period figures prove to be true, then Purchaser waives further proof of income. If the business should be closed any day or days during the trial period due for any reason then a like day or days of the preceding or succeeding week which has been observed by Purchaser will be substituted for purpose of the trial period of computation. During the trial period, Seller or his agent will remain with Purchaser to acquaint Purchaser in the manner in which Seller has conducted the business.

Closing Adjustments

Adjustment Clause - Used with two-part note and Security

The parties agree that the total payment due under this Agreement shall be adjusted on the date of closing to equal the total of: (a) the then unpaid balance on seller's underlying Note, a copy of which is attached hereto; and (b) the difference between the adjusted total of payments due under the attached schedule in the approximate sum of (*) and the sum of (*)

Only One Spouse at Closing (Note to Broker - All sellers and buyers not signing final documents must sign Purchase and Sale Agreement)

Escrow holder is authorized and instructed to accept any one of the signatures of the Sellers, if more than one, and any on one of the signatures of the purchasers, if more than one, for the purpose of consummating the transaction contemplated by this escrow in strict accordance with its terms with the exception of all documents drawn in connection with these instructions, without liability on the part of the escrow holder for so doing.

Prorations, Deposits, Utilities and Adjustments

Utilities - SELLER and PURCHASER shall arrange to notify all utility companies to take final readings as of the day of closing, and PURCHASER shall have the obligation to advise such utilities to provide services in PURCHASER's name.

Deposits and Prepayments - SELLER shall be entitled to be reimbursed for all deposits and prepayments which are held by depositees for the benefit of PURCHASER.

Pro-ratable Items - All pro-ratable items shall be prorated at the closing.

Inventory-Adjustment to Purchase Price - The purchase price provided for herein includes current and saleable inventory to be transferred to the PURCHASER at the closing at SELLER's wholesale cost of_____DOLLARS ($_____). In the event the amount of inventory transferred to PURCHASER is more than or less than such figure, the purchase price shall be increased or decreased, as the case may be.

Closing Conditions

On or prior to the closing, SELLER shall obtain any necessary consents from third parties required for the transfer of the assets to PURCHASER, including, but not limited to, consent from the landlord, if applicable, and consent from any holders of mortgages against the assets of the business being assumed by PURCHASER.

Witholding Tax Affidavit

I (Seller) owner of that business known as (Business Name) and located at (Business Address) do depose and swear that I have not and do not sell any products, food or drink nor have any employees and therefore do not qualify for Meals, Sales or Witholding Tax collection or payment.

Seller to Keep Business Open until Escrow

The Seller agrees to keep the business in operation during the regular business hours until time of closing.

Handle Employee benefits outside of Escrow

Escrow holder is not to be concerned with the transfer of vacation pay, pension funds, or any other fringe benefits accrued as of the date of possession. These employee benefits are to be handled outside of escrow by the Purchaser and Seller.

Escape Clauses

Escape "Bump" Clause

It is understood and agreed that in the event Seller receives a bonafide, non-contingent offer on the assets of the subject business during the term of this agreement, seller agrees to give written notice of such an offer to purchaser and or agent herein, and purchaser shall have (*) days from receipt of such notice to remove all purchaser's contingencies contained herein. In the event purchaser is unable to remove all said contingencies within (*) day period, this agreement shall be rendered null and void and Earnest Money Deposit shall be returned to purchaser.

Bump Clause

A primary offer exists. This a secondary offer. The seller reserves the right to accept, reject or counter this offer. Should this offer become a contract it shall be valid only upon forfeiture or nullification of the primary offer.

Multiple Offer - Bump Clause

The Seller has received multiple offers and is now presenting counter offers to all prospective buyers. In the event more than one Buyer accepts the counter offer, then the Buyer(s) have three (3) working days to remove all contingencies.

In the event more than one Buyer removes the contingencies within the above time period, then the Seller will make his/her decision, based upon subjective factors as to who shall proceed so as to satisfy the conditions of sale i.e. landlord approval.

Buyer's Bump Clause

It is understood that the Buyer has made a Contingent Offer for the purchase of another business. In the event that the parties thereto reach an agreement this Agreement shall be rendered null ana void and Earnest Money Deposit returned to Purchaser. It is also understood and agreed that inspection of Company books, records, leases and other Due Diligence' data by the Buyer shall not occur until the Contingent Offer referenced above has been rendered null and void and this Agreement shall become effective immediately upon communication to the Seller of such fact.

Back up Clause - Only one backup offer

It is understood that seller has accepted a contingent offer from a third party for the purchase of subject business. In the event that seller or third party negotiate the removal of the contingencies contained in said offer within the time periods allowed, this Agreement shall be rendered null and void and Earnest Money Deposit returned to purchaser. However, in the event that said contingencies are not removed within the time periods allowed, this agreement shall become effective immediately. For all purposes herein, the date of mutual acceptance shall be the date on which this Agreement becomes effective as provided in this paragraph.

(Note: Acceptance must be communicated to buyer - no deal until then.)

Back up Clause - More than One Offer

It is understood that seller has accepted offer(s) from (*) different third parties for the purchase of the subject business. In the event that seller and one of the third parties negotiate for the removal of the contingencies contained in one of said offers within the time periods allowed, this Agreement shall be rendered null and void and Earnest Money Deposit returned to purchaser. However, in the event that such contingencies are not removed within the time periods allowed, this Agreement shall become effective immediately. For all purposes herein, the date of mutual acceptance shall be the date on which this Agreement becomes effective as provided in this paragraph.

(Note: Acceptance must be communicated to buyer - no deal until then.)

One Counter offer

It is understood that seller has executed a counter offer to a third party for the sale of subject business. In the event that said counter offer is accepted and seller and said third party negotiate the removal of the contingencies contained in said counter offer within the time periods allowed, this Agreement shall be rendered null and void and Earnest Money deposit returned to purchaser. However, in the event that said counter offer is not accepted nor the contingencies removed within the time periods allowed therein, this Agreement shall become time periods allowed therein, This Agreement shall become effective immediately upon communication to buyer of such fact. For all purposes herein, the date of mutual acceptance shall be the date on which this Agreement becomes effective and was so communicated as provided in this paragraph.

More than one Counter offer

It is understood that seller has executed (*) counter offers to third parties for the sale of subject business. In the event that Seller and one of the third parties negotiate for the removal of the contingencies allowed, this Agreement shall be rendered null and void and Earnest Money deposit returned to Purchaser.

However, in the event that such contingencies are not allowed therein, this agreement shall become effective immediately upon communication to buyer of such fact. For all purposes herein, the date of mutual acceptance shall be the date on which this Agreement becomes effective and was so communicated as provided in this paragraph.

Lease

No Lease - Purchaser to negotiate

Purchaser is aware that there is no lease and has made his own arrangements outside of escrow. Escrow holders are not to be concerned with lease or rental arrangements.

Cross Default Clause

Purchaser and Seller agree that any default by Purchaser under the terms of Real Property lease which Purchaser is to assume herein shall constitute a default under the Note and security agreement which Purchaser is to execute in favor of Seller in accordance with this agreement.

Lease Assignment

SELLER presently possesses a lease for the premises of the business being sold to PURCHASER. Such lease is a valid lease, is current and in good standing, and SELLER has the right, subject to any consent required to be obtained by the lessor under the terms of the lease, to assign the lease to PURCHASER. Such lease shall be assigned to PURCHASER at the closing. The present term of the lease extends until_____ 19__. The current monthly rent payable under the terms of the lease

Purchaser to Negotiate New Lease

The parties hereto agree that a new lease for a period of (*) years at a monthly rental rate of (*) has been (or will be) negotiated outside of escrow, between the Lessor and the Purchasers herein, and escrow is not to be liable or concerned with same.

Financial

Inspection Clause - Financial Records; (Purchaser to write disapproval or offer becomes binding)

This agreement is contingent upon purchaser's final inspection of subject's financial records pertaining to the operation thereof within (*) days from mutual acceptance of this agreement, and in the event the purchaser does not notify in writing his disapproval of subject financial records within (*) days of mutual acceptance, it shall be deemed that purchaser has approved said records and this agreement shall continue in its full force and effect unless Seller has not made the records available so as to give Purchaser a reasonable opportunity to inspect within such time period. Seller agrees to make subject records available to purchaser for his inspection during said (*) day period.

Seller Warranty Financial Records - Stock Sale

The Seller warrants that the books and accounts of the Corporation are a true representation of the financial condition of the Corporation. The Purchaser acknowledges that he has made his own independent investigation of the business. The Purchaser understands that upon the transfer of the Corporate securities for the consideration and terms stated herein, he is accepting the assets and the liabilities of the said Corporation on the basis of the Sellers warranty. Purchaser agrees to hold harmless (Corporate Name of VR Office) and escrow holder for any conditions not specifically stated herein.

Purchaser's Offer not Contingent on Financial Records

Purchaser acknowledges that he has made his own independent investigation of subject business and has satisfied himself that he can properly operate same. No representations have been made by the Seller or the Broker other than specifically set forth herein.

Seller's Approval of Purchaser's Financial Statement

This offer is contingent upon seller's approval of purchaser's financial statement and failure of purchaser to deliver his financial statement to the seller and/or seller's agent herein within (*) days from mutual acceptance of this offer shall render this agreement null and void and Earnest Money deposit shall be returned to purchaser. If seller does not notify in writing his disapproval of subject financial statement within (*) days of mutual acceptance, it shall be deemed that seller has approved said statement and this agreement shall continue in its full force and effect

Inspection Clause - Financial Records; (Purchaser to Remove Contingency)

This Agreement is contingent upon purchaser's final inspection of subject's financial records pertaining to the operation thereof within (*) days from mutual acceptance of this agreement, and failure of the purchaser to remove this contingency in writing within said (*) day period shall render this agreement null and void and earnest money deposit shall be returned to purchaser. Seller covenants to make said financial records available to purchaser for his inspection during said (*) day period.

Inspection of Property, Books and Records.

For a period of ten (XX) calendar days following the execution of this Agreement by both parties, PURCHASER shall have the right at mutually agreeable times to inspect the assets and records of SELLER. If PURCHASER is not satisfied with such review, PURCHASER shall have the right to cancel this Agreement for any reason and receive a return of the deposits paid if written notice of PURCHASER'S objection is received by SELLER and <Your Firm> within ten (XX) calendar days of the date of this Agreement. Upon any such cancellation, all deposits paid shall be returned to PURCHASER and each of the parties shall have no further obligation to each other.

Subject to Financing

This offer is contingent upon the purchaser being able to obtain financing satisfactory to him within (*) days from mutual acceptance of this offer, and failure of the purchaser to obtain a commitment in writing for such financing within said (*) day period and remove this contingency in writing, shall render this agreement null and void and the Earnest Money Deposit shall be retuned to purchaser.

Default

In the event SELLER refuses or is unable to consummate the sale of the assets provided for herein, the earnest money deposit received by the <YOUR FIRM> shall be returned to PURCHASER upon demand..

In the event PURCHASER fails to complete the purchase after all terms and conditions have been met by SELLER, fifty percent (50%) of the deposits paid by PURCHASER shall be retained by <YOUR FIRM> as liquidated damages, and the remaining fifty percent (50%) shall be paid to SELLER as liquidated damages.

Waiver Bulk Transfer

Purchaser and seller acknowledge having been informed by Broker of the requirement of notification of creditors in accordance with the Bulk Transfer Provision of the (state) Uniform Commercial Code. Seller agrees to hold harmless and indemnify purchaser of any and all claims or liabilities of seller under this provision. Purchaser agrees to waive such requirement of notification of creditors. Purchaser and seller mutually agree to jointly and severally hold harmless and indemnify Broker of any and all liabilities either may suffer as a result of said waiver.

(Note: Use only after buyer(s) and seller(s) have had an opportunity to discuss this with counsel.)

Lease

No Lease - Purchaser to negotiate

Purchaser is aware that there is no lease and has made his own arrangements outside of escrow. Escrow holders are not to be concerned with lease or rental arrangements.

Cross Default Clause

Purchaser and Seller agree that any default by Purchaser under the terms of Real Property lease which Purchaser is to assume herein shall constitute a default under the Note and security agreement which Purchaser is to execute in favor of Seller in accordance with this agreement.

Lease Assignment

SELLER presently possesses a lease for the premises of the business being sold to PURCHASER. Such lease is a valid lease, is current and in good standing, and SELLER has the right, subject to any consent required to be obtained by the lessor under the terms of the lease, to assign the lease to PURCHASER. Such lease shall be assigned to PURCHASER at the closing. The present term of the lease extends until_____ 19__. The current monthly rent payable under the terms of the lease

Purchaser to Negotiate New Lease

The parties hereto agree that a new lease for a period of (*) years at a monthly rental rate of (*) has been (or will be) negotiated outside of escrow, between the Lessor and the Purchasers herein, and escrow is not to be liable or concerned with same.

Liabilities

Seller to Assign Existing Encumbrances

Seller agrees effectively to transfer and assign to the Purchaser the existing encumbrances as stated herein.

Purchaser not to Assume Encumbrances - Seller to remain responsible

If for any reason the Purchasers are not approved by the beneficiaries of the encumbrances herein, Seller agrees to remain responsible f6rs aid encumbrance as guarantor for the Purchasers. If for any reason the beneficiary's statements are not received by the close of escrow, the escrow agent is hereby instructed by the Purchaser and Seller to accept the balance given by the Seller as the amount owing. The Seller warrants that the given balances will be correct.

Purchaser to Acknowledge Existing Contract - Purchaser to assume
(Use when there is existing contracts on equipment, etc.)

The Purchaser acknowledges the existence of the attached contract on (*) and agrees to assume same.

Seller to Promise no Other Lease Obligations

Seller does covenant to the Purchaser that there are no continuing contracts or lease, financing or service agreements which the Purchaser shall be obligated to assume except as follows

Assumptions of Liabilities

PURCHASER shall not be obligated and will not assume or become liable for any obligations or liabilities of SELLER. At the closing, all of SELLER's accounts payable, liens, liabilities of any type and other encumbrances of SELLER affecting the business being transferred which are existing on or arise prior to the closing shall be paid from the proceeds of the sale contemplated herein. The parties intend PURCHASER shall acquire ownership of the assets being purchased free and clear of all claims, liens and other encumbrances, except as set forth herein.

License and Permit Transfer

Purchase Subject to License or Permit Transfer - both parties agree to steps to accomplish transfer. In the event this Agreement is subject to the transfer or acquisition of any license, permit, interim appointment, bond or any document requiring the approval of a third party or governmental agency, Purchaser and Seller agree that all necessary steps to expedite such transfers or acquisitions of such documents will be take by Purchaser and Seller as required.

Subject to Transfer Liquor License

This Agreement is subject to the Purchaser obtaining a (Name of State) State Liquor license to operate the subject business. Buyer shall apply invariably for such permit and pay all expenses relative thereto. Should the Purchaser intercede to cancel the application for said license, or, if license is denied because of any willful act or omission of the Purchaser, then all monies deposited herein shall be forfeited in accordance with this Agreement.

Liquor License to be Transferred Outside of Escrow

This escrow is not subject to the Purchaser obtaining a (State Name) State Liquor license, however, Purchaser is aware that he must obtain said license in order to operate that portion of the business.

Closing Date Liquor License

It is mutually understood and agreed by and between the parties hereto that the actual close of this escrow shall be three days after written approval of license transfer to Purchaser by the Liquor Control Board but in no event later than _____ In the event such license is not transferred by such date, then this Agreement shall be of no force and effect and the Purchaser's deposit shall be returned to the Purchaser unless the failure to transfer was caused by the Purchaser's negligent, wrongful or intentional misconduct.

Purchase Conditions

Purchaser to Purchase as Corporation - To furnish Corporate Resolution

Purchaser shall furnish escrow holder with Corporate Resolution, authorizing the purchase of the assets of business by a corporation to be formed by the buyer under the terms and conditions specified herein, and shall designate (*) as authorized signatory to execute all documents as called for herein to consummate the purchase and sale of the business.

Purchaser to Take Title in Name of Corporation

Purchaser reserves the right to take title in the name of his/her corporation providing the Purchaser agrees to remain personally responsible for all conditions of this agreement including signing the promissory note referenced herein

Amendment

This Agreement may be amended at any time in writing executed by SELLER and PURCHASER; however, no such amendment shall affect the <YOUR FIRM> unless <YOUR FIRM> joins in the execution of any such amendment.

Agreement Rewritten

This Earnest Money Agreement supercedes any conditions set forth in that certain Earnest Money Agreement dated (*) by and between the parties herein.

Contract Review

From the date of execution of this contract, Buyer and Seller shall have five (5) Business days to have this contract, which includes any addenda or amendments to it, reviewed by their respective attorneys to verify that the forms and Language only used herein adequately protects their respective clients and to have the necessary changes made within such time, so long as the substance of and material terms in this contract shall remain unchanged.

Seller to Continue to Operate Business - with no changes

Seller agrees to conduct business as he is presently conducting same until the earlier of _____, 200_ or until the Purchaser agrees to take possession of same.

Seller to Provide list of Suppliers

Seller agrees to hand Purchaser a list of purveyors (suppliers) of the business, and to instruct the Purchaser as to the manner of ordering supplies and dealing with said purveyors (suppliers).

Consent to Sell Clause - Where consent to sell is required

Purchaser acknowledges that there are "consent to sell" clauses or other terms or conditions encumbering Seller's ability to transfer and convey the subject business which may affect seller's ability to do so without penalty and/or acceleration. This offer is subject to seller being able to negotiate terms satisfactory to him with the holder of any such encumbrance for the sale described herein within (*) days from mutual acceptance hereof, and failure of seller acknowledge in writing to purchaser and/or the agent herein that he has negotiated such terms within said (*) day period shall render this Agreement null and void and Earnest Money Deposit returned to Purchaser.

Consent to Sell Clause - Acknowledge that there may be consent to sell

In the event that there are any "consent to sell" clauses or other terms or conditions encumbering Seller's ability to transfer and convey the subject business or otherwise affecting seller's right to convey subject business without acceleration and/or penalty, seller agrees to give written notice of the same to the purchaser and/or the agent herein within 7 days from mutual acceptance of this offer. In the event that seller gives such notice within said 7 day period, and not otherwise, this offer shall be subject to seller being able to negotiate terms satisfactory to him with the holder of any such encumbrance for the sale described herein within (*) days any from mutual acceptance hereof, and failure of seller to acknowledge in writing to the purchaser and/or agent herein that he has negotiated such terms within said (*) day period shall render this Agreement null and void and Earnest Money Deposit returned to Purchaser, unless Purchaser elects to assume those terms and conditions with the holder of such encumbrance and subject to acceptance by such holder.

Non-Disclosure

Non-Disclosure Clause

Buyer shall not disclose to any unauthorized person any information pertaining to the purchased business including information concerning customers, business methods and other   and any other information represented as confidential by the Purchaser or Seller, without the Seller's specific written consent

Non-Compete

Non-Compete Clause

As part of the consideration herein paid, the Seller (or the Seller's principals if the Seller is a non-individual) does covenant to the Purchaser that he will not engage, either directly or indirectly, in this type of business within a radius of (*) miles from subject premises for a term of (*) years from date of Purchaser's possession.

Agreement Not To Compete

SELLER and all stockholders and/or partners of SELLER shall agree at the closing in writing not to compete with the business being sold to PURCHASER hereunder for a period of_____ (__) months following the closing date within <Distance or Area>.

Non-Compete - (use when Seller is a corporation)

The Seller agrees that neither it nor any officer, shareholder, or their respective affiliates shall compete, directly or indirectly, in the same or a similar business within (*) miles radius of the business sold for a period of (*) years from the close of escrow. Seller recognizes that his agreement not to compete is a material inducement to the Purchaser concerning the purchase of this business.

Seller and its officers, shareholders, partners, principals and employees shall not be involved directly or indirectly, as employee, consultant, owner, representative or in any other capacity, in any business or business activity which is engaged wholly or partially in the business of _____ or any business substantially competitive with the business purchased or sold, for a period of one or two year(s) after the date hereof, within a radius of _____ miles of the location of the business, unless and only to the extent modified under applicable law.

Notes

Payment Schedule for Step Payments

($ Amount) approximately, payable at the rate of (Amount) per month, or more at purchasers option, for the 1st through the (Number) month, inclusive, including interest at the rate of (percent*) per annum; thence payable at the rate of (Amount) per month, inclusive, including interest rate of (Percent) per annum thereafter, payable at the rate of (Amount) per month, or more at Purchaser's option, including interest at the rate of (Interest rate) per annum, interest computed on the diminishing principal balance, first payment due 30 days after date of closing, and which payment schedule purchaser agrees to pay in full on or before (Number) years after date of closing.

Chattel Mortgage

All notes assumed or executed by PURCHASER for the benefit of SELLER shall be secured by security agreement and chattel mortgage on all of the assets of the business being transferred to PURCHASER.

Purchaser is a Corporation

In the event PURCHASER is a corporation, all promissory notes executed/assumed by the PURCHASER shall be personally guaranteed by all stockholders of PURCHASER.

Grace Period

All promissory notes executed by PURCHASER to SELLER shall provide for a grace period of ten (10) days and shall allow for pre-payment without penalty

Security

Notes

All notes assumed or executed by PURCHASER for the benefit of SELLER shall be secured by security agreement and chattel mortgage on all of the assets of the business being transferred to PURCHASER.

In the event PURCHASER is a corporation, all promissory notes executed/assumed by the PURCHASER shall be personally guaranteed by all stockholders of PURCHASER.

All promissory notes executed by PURCHASER to SELLER shall provide for a grace period of ten (10) days and shall allow for pre-payment without penalty

Additional Security

Purchaser further agrees, as additional security for the performance of said Note, to execute and deliver to seller a Note and Mortgage or Deed of Trust on Purchaser's principal residence or other formal security agreement and note acceptable to Seller. (Insert legal description)

Training

Training Period

Seller is to remain with Purchaser, without compensation, a sufficient length of time to enable the Purchaser to become acquainted with the business, but in no case shall the Seller remain with Purchaser for more than (*)   Seller's duties during this period will be as follows:

Contingency Removal

Date _____ / _____ / _____

We, the undersigned Purchasers of that certain business known as _____

_____

and located at:

Address:

City:

State: Zip:

do hereby remove the contingencies from that certain Conditional Purchase and Sale of

Assets Agreement dated_____

_____

Purchaser

Date _____

Authorization to Close

Re: Letter of Intent Dated: _____

Business Name: _____

Purchasers Authorization – "My independent investigation and analysis of the subject Business and the Information provided by the Seller having been favorably concluded, and all contingencies and conditions of the sales contract having been resolved to my satisfaction, I hereby re-affirm said contract and all of my obligations there-under. I expressly waive any and all rights that I may have to rescind said agreement and agree to hold myself ready, willing and able to close this sale as soon as the appropriate documents have been prepared."

_____

Purchaser

Date _____

_____

Sellers Authorization - "I hereby re-affirm the above referenced Agreement and hold myself ready, willing and able to close this sale as soon as appropriate documents have been prepared".

_____

Seller

Date _____

Corporate Resolution
Of Authority

I, hereby certify that I am the duly elected and qualified Clerk/Secretary of
_____, a lawful corporation in the JURISDICTION, and
have custody of the official records of said corporation and that the following is a true copy
of the resolution adopted by the Board of Directors thereof at a meeting of the board duly
called and held on _____, at which a quorum was present, and hat such
resolution is now in full force and effect.

RESOLVED: That the _____
and_____ are/is hereby authorized to sign any and all lawful
documents necessary to list, transfer and/or sell the real estate, fixtures, goodwill,
trademarks, tradename, leasehold rights, equipment and inventory. I further certify that
the foregoing resolution conforms to all applicable provisions of the by-laws of said
corporation relative to such a transaction, and the party/parties named herein are
empowered to act for this corporation as provided herein. In witness thereof I have
hereunto set my signature and affixed the corporate seal this _____ day of _____
20____.

_____

Clerk/Secretary

I _____, a director of said corporation hereby confirm the
correctness of the contents of the foregoing certificate

_____

Director

Letter of Intent

<Date>

<Business Owner>, <Title>

<Business Name>

<Address>

<City/Town>, <State> <Zip Code>

Dear <Salutation:>

This Letter of Intent, when countersigned by <Business Owner> (the "Owner"), d/b/a <Business Name>, (the "Company") will confirm our recent discussions with regard to the intent of <Purchaser's Name> M. Miller (the "Purchaser"), or his nominee, to acquire substantially all of the assets, properties and business of the Owner. If the terms set forth herein are acceptable to the Owner, this Letter of Intent will serve as a basis for the continuation of our due diligence review and the preparation of a definitive written asset purchase agreement in form and substance satisfactory to Purchaser and the Owner and in accordance with the terms and provisions hereof (the "Purchase Agreement").

This Letter of Intent is intended as an expression of certain basic understandings of the parties and, except for the provisions of Section III herein, shall not be considered a binding commitment or obligation of the parties. Other than as set forth in Section III herein, it is agreed that no legally binding obligation shall arise between the parties until the Purchase Agreement covering all aspects of the proposed transaction shall have been executed by the parties.

I.   SUMMARY OF PURCHASE TERMS

1.   Purchase of Assets.

The Purchaser will purchase from the Owner, and the Owner will sell to the Purchaser, substantially all of the assets, properties and business of the Owner (the "Assets"). The Assets shall include, but not be limited to, any and all machinery, equipment, and other tangible assets (the "Tangible Assets") and customer lists, trade names, business phone numbers, licenses, and other intangible assets (the "Intangible Assets") of the Owner.

2.   Purchase Price and Payment.

The purchase price (the "Purchase Price") for the Assets shall be the aggregate sum of <Spell out amount> ($XXXXXX) Dollars and shall be allocated <Spell out> percent (XX%) to the Tangible Assets. <Spell out amount> ($XXXXXX) Dollars of the Purchase Price shall be paid by the Purchaser to the Owner on the Closing Date (as hereinafter defined) in cash or certified funds, and the balance shall be paid pursuant to a subordinate promissory note (the "Promissory Note") to be delivered on said Closing Date from the Purchaser to the Owner. The Promissory Note shall be in the principle amount of <Spell out amount> ($XXXXXX) Dollars, shall have a payment term of <Number> (X) years and shall bear interest at a rate of <Number> percent (X%). The amount paid by the Purchaser on the Closing Date will be conditional upon the Purchaser successfully obtaining senior debt financing for a minimum of <Spell out amount> ($XXXXXX) Dollars.

3.   Closing Date

The closing of the transactions contemplated hereby (the "Closing") will be as soon as possible, but in no event shall such date (the "Closing Date") be later than six (6) weeks from the date that this Letter of Intent shall have been executed by all of the undersigned parties.

4.   Purchase Agreement

Counsel for the Purchaser will prepare and submit to the Owner an initial draft of an asset purchase agreement and related agreements embodying the transactions contemplated hereby. The parties and their respective counsel will then proceed to finalize and execute in good faith a definitive asset purchase agreement as soon as possible, which agreement will include such representations, warranties, agreements, indemnification and offset provisions and conditions as are customarily contained in an agreement for the acquisition of assets of a business and which are consistent with the terms and intent of this letter.

II.   OTHER AGREEMENTS AND COVENANTS

5.   Consulting Agreement

As a condition precedent to Purchaser's obligation to close, the Owner shall enter into an agreement with the Purchaser (the "Consulting Agreement") based upon the terms and conditions set forth in subparagraphs (a) and (b) below.

(a)   The term (the "Term") of the Consulting Agreement shall be for a total of <Number> (X) weeks. The Term shall consist of <Number> (X) consecutive weeks commencing on the Closing Date.

(c)   During the Term, the Owner shall be available and (i) report to and work with the Purchaser so as to maintain and transition existing customer relationships of the Company, expand the customer base and profitability associated with the sold business of the Company, render technical assistance and perform such other related duties as said Purchaser requests; (ii) maintain a work schedule that is agreeable to both parties; (iii) be reimbursed only for normal and customary expenses incurred while traveling at the request of the Purchaser during the Term.

6.   Non-competition Agreement.

The Purchase Agreement shall contain non-competition provisions which shall prohibit the Owner directly or indirectly from (a) soliciting clients or customers of the Purchaser, or associated with the sold business of the Owner, except on behalf of the Purchaser, or otherwise competing with the businesses of the Purchaser in the states of <State's) and (1)) interfering or attempting to interfere with any employees, representatives or agents of the Purchaser or inducing or attempting to induce any of them to leave such employ, until <Number> (X) years after the Closing Date.

7.   Conditions Precedent to the Owner's Obligations.

The obligation of the Owner to consummate the transactions set forth herein will be subject to the following conditions precedent and to such other conditions upon which the Purchaser and the Owner may agree:

(a)   the Purchaser will have represented and warranted in the Purchase Agreement (i) the Purchaser's due organization and good standing, (ii) the Purchaser's due authority to enter into the Purchase Agreement, and the due execution ,delivery and binding effect of the Purchase Agreement, subject to customary exceptions for bankruptcy and the like, (iii) the absence of proceeding seeking to affect the Purchase Agreement, and (iv) such other matters as may be agreed to by the Purchaser, Owner and the Company;

(b)   the Purchaser will have executed and delivered to the Owner the Consulting Agreement; and

(c)   the Purchaser will have executed and delivered to the Owner the Promissory Note.

8.   Conditions Precedent to the Purchaser's Obligations.

In addition to the other conditions set forth herein, the obligation of the Purchaser to consummate the transactions set forth herein will be subject to the following conditions precedent and to such other conditions upon which the Purchaser and the Owner may agree:

(a)   the Purchaser will have conducted such investigation of the properties, business, operations, stock records and affairs of the Owner as it deems appropriate, and will have approved the results of such investigation in its sole and absolute discretion;

b)   the Owner will have represented and warranted in the Purchase Agreement (i) the accuracy of all financial statements and other information furnished by the Owner to the Purchaser, (ii) the Owner's due authority to enter into the Purchase Agreement, and the due execution, delivery and binding effect of the Purchase Agreement, subject to customary exceptions for bankruptcy and the like, (ii) the Owner's title to all of its properties included in the Asset addendum to the Purchase Agreement, (iv) the absence of proceedings seeking to affect the Purchase Agreement, (v) the absence of contracts, unpaid taxes or other obligations other than those, if any, already disclosed to the Purchaser and which would not adversely affect any of the rights or interests of the Purchaser as contemplated under the Purchase Agreement, (vi) the absence of default by the Owner under any material contract, and of notice from any governmental agency of any violation of any statute, regulation or ordinance, other than those, if any, already disclosed to the Purchaser and which would not adversely affect any of the rights or interests of the Purchaser as contemplated under the Purchase Agreement, (vii) the absence of any material adverse change in the financial condition or business of the Owner since <Date>, (viii) pending or threatened litigation , (ix) a list of all customers (and the contact names therein) that have made payments to the Owner within the last five (5) years and (x) such other matters as may be agreed to by the Purchaser and the Owner;

(c)   the Owner will furnish to the Purchaser an opinion of its counsel as to matters customary in transactions of this nature satisfactory to the Purchaser; and

(d)   the Purchaser shall be satisfied that all agreements and covenants contemplated under Paragraphs 5 through 7 of Article II hereof, and Paragraphs 9 through 12 of Article III hereof, shall have been executed and performed by or on the Closing Date including, but not limited to, the completion by Purchaser of all due diligence hereunder, the results of which are satisfactory to Purchaser in its sole and absolute discretion.

III.   MISCELLANEOUS

9.   Conduct of Business.

From and after the date hereof and until the Closing, the Owner shall not, without prior written consent of the Purchaser, (i) dispose of or make changes in its assets or incur liabilities, other than in the ordinary course of business, (ii) make any material changes in its methods of operation, or (iii) enter into any employment contracts. The Owner agrees that, from and after the execution of this Letter of Intent until the termination hereof in accordance with Paragraph 17 below or the completion of the transactions contemplated hereby, the Owner's business will be operated in such a manner so as not to adversely affect any of the rights or interests of the Purchaser as contemplated hereunder or under the Purchase Agreement. For purposes of this Letter of Intent, contract negotiations that are being conducted by the Owner as of the date hereof with existing or potential customers shall be considered to be within the Owner's "normal course of business."

10. Confidentiality.

In connection with the parties' efforts to bring the transactions contemplated hereby to a successful completion, the Owner may, at his option, furnish the Purchaser with certain information concerning the Owner's business affairs, operational and marketing plans and financial affairs, prospects, appraisals, market surveys, customers, suppliers, employees, business operations and the contents of contracts, books and other records, all of which materials and/or information (the "Information") the parties hereto acknowledge is of a confidential and secret character and of immeasurable value to the Owner.

The Purchaser hereby agrees that all Information which it obtains will be kept confidential, will not be utilized except in connection with the joint efforts of the parties hereto to complete the transactions contemplated hereby, and will not be disclosed to any person in such connection or otherwise other than those directors, officers, employees, attorneys, accountants and representatives of the Purchaser who require such material for the purpose of evaluating the transactions contemplated hereby. This confidentiality shall be so maintained notwithstanding the failure of the parties to compete the transactions contemplated hereby.

If the transactions contemplated hereby are not completed, then, upon the Owner's request, the Purchaser will, except as otherwise required by law, destroy or return to the Owner any document or other materials furnished

by the Owner, or its agents without retaining any copy thereof and will destroy any notes, analyses or other materials prepared by the Purchaser which contain any Information.

The Purchaser acknowledges and agrees that in the event of any breach of the provisions of this Paragraph 10, the Owner will be irreparably and immediately harmed and could not be made whole by monetary damages. It is accordingly agreed that in the event of any breach hereof, the Owner shall have, in addition to any other rights under law or equity, rights to injunctive relief and to payment by Purchaser of all costs incurred by the Owner in enforcement of the provisions of this Paragraph 10.

11. Due Diligence.

After the execution of this Letter of Intent by all of the undersigned and until the Closing Date, the Owner will give the Purchaser and its representatives full access during ordinary business hours to the premises and personnel of the Owner and to all accounting, financial and other records applicable to the Owner and shall furnish all information with respect to the business and affairs of the Owner as the Purchaser may request. Purchaser shall have the opportunity, up to the date of the Closing, to conduct such other examinations, inspections and diligence as Purchaser deems necessary or advisable with respect to the assets, liabilities, business and affairs of the Owner. In the event the transactions contemplated hereby are not consummated, the Purchaser and its representatives shall return all documents, contracts and papers received from the Owner or any of its representatives and any copies thereof and shall not disclose to any third person other than its professional advisors or to the public any of such information.

12. No Shopping.

The Owner understands that the Purchaser will expend considerable efforts in the preparation of definitive agreements and conducting its due diligence and, therefore, the Owner hereby agrees not to sell, or solicit potential purchasers of, or negotiate to sell, the business or any material portion of its assets from the date of this Letter of Intent until termination of the Letter of Intent pursuant to the provisions of Paragraph 17 herein.

13. Indemnification.

(a)   the Owner shall indemnify the Purchaser from and against (i) any liability for sales or income tax liabilities of the Owner for periods ending on or prior to the Closing Date; (ii) any obligation with respect to any pending or threatened claim or litigation, or any claim or litigation hereafter arising with respect to periods prior to the Closing Date which is not specifically disclosed to Purchaser prior to the Closing Date; (iii) any liabilities and costs relating to the treatment, handling, storage, use, transportation or disposal on or prior to the Closing Date of any hazardous or toxic substance or pollutant and the assessment, containment or removal of same; (iv) any liability with respect to any warranty for services performed on or prior to the Closing Date and (v) any liability, claim, damages, costs or other loss with respect to any misrepresentation, or the proving false or breach of any representation or warranty or covenant or non-fulfillment of any agreement on the part of the Owner under the terms of this Letter of Intent, the Purchase Agreement or in any closing document executed by any party other than the Purchaser pursuant to or in connection with the Purchase Agreement.

b)   Any claim for indemnification hereunder may be satisfied by off-set against the balance of the Purchase Price due the Owner and/or by any other right or remedy available to Purchaser at law or in equity, at Purchaser's option.

14.   Legal Fees and Other Expenses.

The Owner and Purchaser shall each bear their own legal fees and expenses incurred in connection with the execution of the Purchase Agreement and the closing of the transactions set forth herein. The Purchaser will not be responsible for any broker's, finder's or other such fee incurred by the Owner in connection with this transaction, and the Owner will indemnify the Purchaser for all amounts expended in investigating, defending against or satisfying any such claim.

15.   Public Announcements.

The Owner and the Purchaser each agree not to disclose to any person or entity or to make any public statement of this proposed transaction or of the Letter of Intent without the prior written consent of all parties hereto, except any disclosure required by law prior to Closing. In addition and in the event that the transactions contemplated hereby are not consummated, the parties hereto agree not to disclose to any person or entity or to make any public statement of this proposed transaction or Letter of Intent without the prior written consent of all parties hereto.

16.   Notices.

All demands, notices and communications hereunder and under the Purchase Agreement shall be in writing and shall be given by hand-delivery, United States mail (certified, return receipt requested), overnight courier service or other means, in each case with all postage or delivery charges prepaid, to the party entitled thereto at such party's address set forth below:

If to the Purchaser: <Purchaser>

          <Address>

          <City>, <State> <Zip>

          <Telephone>

          <Facsimile>

With a Copy to: <Purchaser's Counsel>.

          <Address>

<City>, <State> <Zip>

<Telephone>

<Facsimile>

If to the Owner: <Owner>

<Address>

<City>, <State> <Zip>

<Telephone>

<Facsimile>

With a Copy to: <Owner's Counsel>

<Address>

<City>, <State> <Zip>

<Telephone>

or at such other address as such party may hereafter furnish to the other party by notice conforming to the requirements of this Paragraph 16. Any demand, notice or communication hereunder shall be deemed to have been given upon delivery to the appropriate address if delivered other than by mail and, if delivered by mail, upon depositing the same in the United States mail as above stated (as evidenced by the date noted on the return receipt).

17.   Termination.

Except with respect to Paragraphs 10, 13, and 15 (the obligations under which Paragraphs shall survive termination of the Letter of Intent for any reason), the obligations of the parties under the paragraphs of this Letter of Intent will terminate on the earlier of (i) six (6) weeks from date that this Letter of Intent shall have been executed by all of the undersigned parties, or (ii) the date on which all of the parties hereto shall have agreed in writing not to pursue further the transactions contemplated hereby; provided, however, that such termination shall not relieve the parties of liability for the breach of any obligation occurring prior to such termination.

18.   Successors and Assigns; Assignment.

The Purchase Agreement and the Promissory Note shall be binding on the successors and assigns of the parties thereto.

Please indicate your agreement to the above summary of discussions set forth in Paragraphs 1 through 18 by signing and returning a copy of this letter to the undersigned.

Very truly yours,

By:

<Purchaser's Name>

Accepted on this _____ day of <Month>, <Year>:

By:

<Owner's Name> <Title>

<Company>

Section Three

Closing the Deal

AGREEMENT TO PAY ACCOUNTS PAYABLE

The Undersigned _____ Bulk Sale Creditor of that

business known as_____

acknowledge the total indebtedness due as of _____to be $ _____.

I understand that _____, owner

of that business known as _____

and located at _____ is

transferring ownership of said business. I hereby agree, to

accept _____ (owner's) note (no interest) in

the above amount payable in _____days/month from the date of transfer

and release the buyer of said business from payment and any obligation for this debt thus
waiving my rights under the Bulk Sale provision of the Uniform Commercial Code.

Company/Individual   _____

Authorized Signature _____

Date   _____

I hereby acknowledge receipt of above referenced Promissory Note

Company/Individual   _____

Authorized Signature _____

Date   _____

Assumption Agreement

For value received (and in consideration of the written consent and acknowledgement of the Secured Party, if any) having acquired title to the assets of that certain business known as (Business name), located at (Business Address) subject to a security interest created by a Security Agreement securing a note dated (Date) in the original face amount of $ (Amount) payable in installments of $ _____ or more, including interest at (_%), on which the unpaid balance is $ _____ with interest paid to date, do/es hereby assume, warrant and agree to pay when due all payments as prescribed in said notes, to indemnify and hold the make, and any prior successor of maker of said note of and from any default under the said note and security agreement, commencing with that payment due (Date).

If this assumption agreement is signed by more than one party, the liabilities of the undersigned shall be joint and several and in the language above set forth, the singular shall include the plural where the context so requires.

_____

Print Name

_____   Date

Signature

Secured Party's Agreement

For value received the undersigned Secured Party under the aforesaid Note and Security Agreement does hereby consent to the foregoing Agreement to assume liability for the payment of said Note upon transfer of said business, but does not thereby waive any rights under said Note or Security Agreement, nor shall this consent be construed as a release of the maker or any prior successors, nor as consent to subsequent assumptions.

_____   Date

Secured Party

Bill of Sale

FOR VALUE RECEIVED, the undersigned_____

of_____ hereby sells and transfers

unto_____of_____(Buyer), and its successors and
assigns forever, the following described goods and chattels:

_____

_____

Seller warrants and represents that he/she has good title to said property, full authority
to sell and transfer same and that said goods and chattels are being sold free and clear of
all liens, encumbrances, liabilities and adverse claims, of every nature and description.

Seller further warrants that it shall sully defend, protect, indemnify and save
harmless the Buyer and its lawful successors and assigns from any and all adverse claim,
that may be made by any party against said goods.

It is provided, however, that Seller disclaims any implied warranty of condition,
merchantability or fitness for a particular purpose. Said goods being in their present
condition "as is" and "where is."

Signed this_____ day of_____, 20__.

In the presence of:_____

_____

_____

_____ _____
Witness Seller

Bulk Sale Addendum to the

Offer to Purchase

(Waiver of bulk sale compliance)

The undersigned Purchaser(s) and Seller(s), of that business known as (Business Name) (Business Address) are aware that pursuant to Section 6-104 of the Uniform Commercial Code, commonly known as the Bulk Transfer, provision of the Bulk Sales Law, the Seller(s) shall provide upon demand a list of creditors with business addresses to each and the amount of the indebtedness due or owing by said Seller(s) to each, and also listing all other persons known to be asserting claims (even though disputed) with their address and amounts asserted all duly certified by the Seller(s) under oath as provided in said statue.

Both parties are aware that said "Bulk Sales Law" may apply too this transaction and both parties desire to waive compliance with the provisions of said Act.

For and in consideration of the Purchaser's agreement to waive compliance with the "Bulk Sales Act" the Seller(s) will provide an affidavit as to the creditors and the amount now owed and direct the escrow holder to reserve $_____ and to pay all creditors out of the funds held, with the remainder to the seller, and will hold the Purchaser(s) harmless from any creditor should any funds be due such creditors by the Seller, and grants the Purchaser(s) the right of set off against any unpaid balance then due the Seller under purchase price note in the original amount of $_____.

Buyer agrees to indemnify and hold harmless Seller for any loss they or any of them may suffer by reason of their acquiescence in said waivers.

_____   _____

(Purchaser)   Date

_____   _____

(Seller)   Date

Bulk Sale Agreement

The Undersigned _____ Bulk Sale

Creditor of that business known as

_____

acknowledge the total indebtedness due as of __ / __ / __ to be $ _____

I understand that _____, owner

of that business known as _____

and located at _____ is

transferring his ownership of said business. I hereby agree, to

accept _____ (owner's) note

(no interest) in the above amount payable in ____days/month from the date of transfer and release the buyer of said business from payment and any obligation for this debt thus waiving my rights under the Bulk Sale provision of the Uniform Commercial Code.

Company/Individual _____

Authorized Signature _____

Date   _____

I hereby acknowledge receipt of above referenced Promissory Note

Company/Individual _____

Authorized Signature _____

Date   _____

Bulk Sale Notification

Dear Credit Manager,

Please be advised of the intended BULK TRANSFER of the assets of the business known as:

The Transferor is:

Date of transfer: on or before

All other business names and addresses used by the transferor in the past three years, so far as the transferee knows, are as above.

The Transferee is:

It is the intention of the parties that all debts of the transferor be PAID IN FULL as they fall due as a result of this transaction. Please provide invoice or letter stating amount currently owed along with one copy of this notice to:

NAME OF ESCROW SERVICE

ADDRESS, CITY, STATE, ZIP

This notice complies with the bulk transfer provisions of the Uniform Commercial Code-Section 6-107. Your reply within 10 days of this notice is required to protect your rights under the above mentioned code.

Very truly yours,

for: NAME OF ESCROW SERVICE

Recieved by_____

for   _____

Company Name

Date   _____

CERTIFIED MAIL #<enter cert. #>

Agreement

(Bulk Sale Release)

The Undersigned _____ Bulk Sale Creditor of that

business known as_____

acknowledge the total indebtedness due as of _____to be $ _____.

I understand that _____, owner

of that business known as _____

and located at _____ is

transferring ownership of said business. I hereby agree, to

accept _____ (owner's) note (no interest) in

the above amount payable in _____days/month from the date of transfer

and release the buyer of said business from payment and any obligation for this debt thus
waiving my rights under the Bulk Sale provision of the Uniform Commercial Code.

Company/Individual   _____

Authorized Signature _____

Date   _____

I hereby acknowledge receipt of above referenced Promissory Note

Company/Individual   _____

Authorized Signature _____

Date   _____

Addendum To The Offer To Purchase

(Bulk Sale Waiver)

The undersigned Purchaser(s) and Seller(s), of that business known as (Business Name) (Business Address) are aware that pursuant to Section 6-104 of the Uniform Commercial Code, commonly known as the Bulk Transfer, provision of the Bulk Sales Law, the Seller(s) shall provide upon demand a list of creditors with business addresses to each and the amount of the indebtedness due or owing by said Seller(s) to each, and also listing all other persons known to be asserting claims (even though disputed) with their address and amounts asserted all duly certified by the Seller(s) under oath as provided in said statue.

Both parties are aware that said "Bulk Sales Law" may apply too this transaction and both parties desire to waive compliance with the provisions of said Act.

For and in consideration of the Purchaser's agreement to waive compliance with the "Bulk Sales Act" the Seller(s) will provide an affidavit as to the creditors and the amount now owed and direct the escrow holder to reserve $_____ and to pay all creditors out of the funds held, with the remainder to the seller, and will hold the Purchaser(s) harmless from any creditor should any funds be due such creditors by the Seller, and grants the Purchaser(s) the right of set off against any unpaid balance then due the Seller under purchase price note in the original amount of $_____.

Buyer agrees to indemnify and hold harmless Seller, (Your Firm, for any loss they or any of them may suffer by reason of their acquiescence in said waivers.

_____   _____

Purchaser   Seller

_____   _____

Witness to All   Date

Closing Worksheet

ADJUSTMENTS AND

PRORATIONS	TOTAL AMT	BUYER	SELLER
Rent	_____	_____	_____
Security Deposits	_____	_____	_____
Electric Deposits	_____	_____	_____
Natural Gas/Fuel Oil Deposits	_____	_____	_____
Telephone Deposits	_____	_____	_____
Water Deposits	_____	_____	_____
Leased Equipment Deposits	_____	_____	_____
Business Property Taxes	_____	_____	_____
Real Estate Taxes	_____	_____	_____
Insurance	_____	_____	_____
Estimated Inventory Adj.	_____	_____	_____
Employee Wages	_____	_____	_____
Miscellaneous	_____	_____	_____
TOTALS	_____	_____	_____

BUYER - TOTAL ANTICIPATED CASH NEEDED AT CLOSING

Total above adjustments and prorations   _____

Escrow attorney's fees   _____

Total Down Payment on Business   _____

Sub-Total   _____

    Less funds on deposit in Escrow   _____

Total Anticipated Cash Needed $ _____

SELLER - TOTAL ANTICIPATED CASH NEEDED AT CLOSING

Total above adjustments and prorations   _____

Escrow attorney fees   _____

Franchise Transfer fee   _____

Broker's Commission   _____

Sub-Total   _____

      Less Down Payment on Bus. in Contract   _____

Total Anticipated Cash Needed (Provided) $ _____

Covenant Not to Compete

FOR GOOD CONSIDERATION, the Undersigned jointly and severally covenant and agree not to compete with the business of (Company) and its lawful successors and assigns.

The term "not compete" as used herein shall mean that the Undersigned shall not directly or indirectly engage in a business or other activity described as: not with standing whether said participation be as an owner, officer, director, employee, agent, consultant, partner or stockholder (excepting as a passive investment in a publicly owned company).

This covenant shall extend only for a radius of ___ miles from the present location of the Company at___ and shall remain in full force and effect for ___ years from date hereof. In the event of any breach the Company shall be entitled to full injunctive relief without need to post bond, which rights shall be cumulative with and not necessarily successive or exclusive of any other legal rights.

 This agreement shall be binding upon and inure to the benefit of the parties, their successors, assigns and personal representatives.

Signed under seal this __ day of ____ , 2___ .

Escrow Agreement

This agreement is between _____ (Seller) and _____ (Buyer) regarding the purchase of _____ (Company) of Town/City, State and Your Firm (Escrow Agent).

1.   The Buyer and Seller have signed a Letter of Intent, providing that the Business shall be transferred to the Buyer upon satisfaction of certain contingencies and conditions.

The Buyer and Seller have requested Escrow Agent to hold Buyers deposit in Escrow, pending transfer of the Business.

The Buyer and Seller agree that the Escrow Agent shall hold Buyers deposit (Escrow Funds) in the amount of TEN THOUSAND DOLLARS ($10,000).

Upon written notice mutually given by Buyer and Seller, the Escrow Agent shall disperse the Escrow Funds pursuant to such notice.

C.   The Escrow Agent shall not hold Escrow Funds after the passage of Two (2) months after receipt (Escrow Deadline), unless:

        1)   The Buyer and Seller enter into a Purchase and Sale Agreement setting forth disposition of the Escrow Funds, which will supersede this Agreement, or

        2)   The Buyer and Seller provide mutual written notice to the Escrow Agent that they request an extension to the Escrow Deadline to a specified date (the Extended Deadline), or

        3)   Buyer and Seller advises Escrow Agent that there is a dispute regarding disbursement of the Escrow Funds.

D.   If Buyer and Seller have not entered into a Purchase and Sale Agreement setting forth disposition of the Escrow Funds, and the Escrow Agent has received no notice regarding disbursement of the Escrow Funds by the Extended Deadline, the Escrow Agent shall return Escrow Funds to the Buyer.

E.   1)   If, prior to the Escrow Deadline, the Escrow Agent receives notice pursuant to paragraph C (2) above, the Escrow Agent shall hold the Escrow Funds up to but no later than the Extended Escrow Deadline.

        2)   If prior to the Escrow Deadline, the Escrow Agent receives notice pursuant to C. (3) above, the Escrow Agent shall hold the Escrow Funds until he receives notice mutually given by Buyer and Seller or notice of resolution of any dispute between Buyer and Seller by a court of competent jurisdiction.

F.   Interest on the Escrow Funds shall be credited to Buyer - Social Security #

_____

G.   All notices required to be given to the Escrow Agent shall be by Certified Mail, Return Receipt Requested.

Executed by:

(Name) _____   Date _____

Buyer

(Name) _____   Date _____

Seller

(Name) _____   Date _____

Escrow Agent

Guaranty

FOR GOOD CONSIDERATON, and as an inducement for_____ (Creditor), from time to time extend credit to _____ (Customer), it is hereby agreed that the undersigned does hereby guaranty to Creditor the prompt, punctual and full payment of all monies now or hereinafter due Creditor from Customer.

Until termination, this guaranty is unlimited as to amount or duration and shall remain in full force and effect notwithstanding any extension, compromise, adjustment, forbearance, waiver, release or discharge of any party obligor or guarantor, or release in whole or in part of any security granted for said indebtedness or compromise or adjustment thereto, and the undersigned waives all notices thereto.

The obligations of the undersigned shall be at the election of Creditor be primary and not necessarily secondary and Creditor shall not be required to exhaust its remedies as against Customer prior to enforcing its rights under this guaranty against the undersigned.

The guaranty hereunder shall be unconditional and absolute and the undersigned waive all rights of subrogation and set-off until all sums under this guaranty are fully paid. The undersigned further waives all suretyship defenses or defenses in the nature thereof, generally.

In the event payments due under this guaranty are not punctually paid upon demand, then the undersigned shall pay all reasonable costs and attorney's fees necessary for collection, and enforcement of this guaranty. If there are two or more guarantors to this guaranty, the obligations shall be joint and several and binding upon and inure to the benefit of the parties, their successors, assigns and personal representatives.

The guaranty may be terminated by any guarantor upon fifteen (15) days written notice of termination, mailed certified mail, return receipt requested to the Creditor. Such termination shall extend only to credit extended beyond said fifteen (15) day period and not to prior extended credit, or goods in transit received by Customer beyond said date, or for special orders placed prior to said date notwithstanding date of delivery. Termination of this guaranty by any guarantor shall not impair the continuing guaranty of any remaining guarantors of said termination.

Each of the undersigned warrants and represents it has full authority to enter into this guaranty. This guaranty shall be binding upon and inure to the benefit of the parties, their successors, assigns and personal representatives. This guaranty shall be construed and enforced under the laws of the state of _____.

Signed this____ day of _____, 20__.

In the presence of:

_____ _____
Witness   Guarantor

Inventory

Completion Agreement

Business

Address

City

State   Zip

The undersigned Buyer(s) and Seller(s) of the above referenced Business, having together on this date completed a physical inventory of the Business Inventory, agree upon an Inventory value of $ _____, (at cost). We hereby affirm that we agree upon the calculations and methods utilized in completing said inventory.

Buyer_____

Seller_____

_____

Witness to All   Date

List of Creditors

For Bulk Transfer

I _____ do on oath depose and say that the following is a complete and accurate list of creditors to the best of my knowledge, information and belief for the business I operate known as _____. I further understand these creditors will be notified of the transfer of the above mentioned business prior to the transfer date.

CREDITORS NAME	BUSINESS ADDRESS	AMOUNT
_____		
_____		
_____		
_____		
_____		
_____		
_____		
_____		
_____		
_____		
_____		
_____		
_____		

Signed: _____   Date_____

Title: _____

Mutual Release

Business Name:

Conditional Offer to Purchase Dated:

Between:

Seller -

and

Buyer -

I, the undersigned potential Seller, in the above referenced Conditional Offer to Purchase, hereby acknowledge the return of the Buyer's earnest money deposit in the above transaction and hereby release and discharge the Buyer, its principals, agents or employees, from any and all liabilities, contractual or otherwise, in connection with this transaction.

I, the undersigned potential Buyer, in the above referenced Conditional Offer to Purchase, acknowledge receipt of the sum of $_____, return in full of my earnest money deposit in the above transaction and hereby release and discharge the Seller, its principals, agents or employees, from any and all liabilities, contractual or otherwise, in connection with this transaction.

_____   _____

Seller   Date

_____   _____

Buyer   Date

Balloon Note

FOR VALUE RECEIVED, the undersigned promise to pay to the order of
_____ the sum of _____ Dollars ($), with annual
interest of _____% on any unpaid balance.

This note shall be paid in _____consecutive and equal installments of $_____ each with a
first payment one ____ from the date hereof, and the same amount on the same day of
each_____ thereafter, provided the entire principal balance and any accrued but uupaid
interest shall be fully paid on or before _____, 20__.

This note may be prepaid without penalty.

All payments shall be first applied to interest and the balance to principal.

This note shall be due and payalbe upon demand of any holder hereof should the
undersigned default in any payment beyond ____ days of its due date.

All parties to this note waive presentment, demand and protest, and all notices thereto.

In the event of default, the undersigned agree to pay all costs of collection and reasonable
attorney's fees. The undersigned shall be jointly and severally liable under this note.

Signed this ____ day of _____, 20__.

Signed in the presence of: _____

_____ Witness Maker _____

Convertible Note

_____ (the "COMPANY") for value received hereby promises to pay to _____ (the "HOLDER") and its registered assignees, the sum of

_____ Dollars ($_____.00), ("principal") plus _____ percent (____%) interest ("interest").

1. Payment Terms: Principal plus interest accrued is payable, in one lump sum, _____ (__) Months from the date of signature on this Series A Convertible Note.

2. Right to Convert: The HOLDER of this Note shall have the option to convert any portion thereof of the unpaid principal of this Note into shares or interests pledged to this Note. Shares made available for

conversion are _____ _____, common stock.

3. Conversion Price: The principal amount of the Note, if converted, shall be converted to such number of shares equal to _____ percent (___%) of the principal & accrued interest amount of the Note, at either the market price of the shares on the day of conversion or _____ dollars ($____.00) per share, whichever is less.

4. Conversion Date: This Note is convertible _____ (____) days from the date of signature on this Note upon written request by Holder.

5. Manner of Exercise of Conversion Rights: In order to exercise the conversion rights of this Note, the HOLDER must give written notice to the COMPANY no later than thirty (30) days after the Conversion Date of its intention to exercise its conversion rights. HOLDER'S conversion rights shall be automatically exercised if COMPANY defaults on the terms of this Note.

6. Prepayment: The COMPANY may prepay principal plus the accrued interest portion of this Note upon providing the HOLDER thirty (30) days notice to effect conversion. After notice is provided, COMPANY may prepay principal plus accrued interest without penalty.

7. Default: In the event the COMPANY fails to pay the Note when due, the Note shall automatically convert as set forth above in Paragraph 3.

8. COMPANY to Reserve Collateral: The COMPANY shall deposit into the Attorney Trust Account of_____, Atty., sufficient shares of _____ stock to effect

conversion of this Note, prior to the conversion date.

9. Notices: All notices given pursuant to this Note must be in writing and may be given by (1) personal delivery, or (2) registered or certified mail, return receipt requested, at the respective addresses of the parties set forth below. Any party hereto may by notice so given change its address for any future notices:

10. Arbitration: The parties hereby submit all controversies, claims and matters of difference arising out of this Note to arbitration in XXXX County, State, according to the rules and practices of the

American Arbitration Association from time to time in force. This submission and agreement to arbitrate shall be specifically enforceable. The Note shall further be governed by the laws of the State of XXXXXX.

11. Attorney Fees: If any legal action or any arbitration or other proceeding is brought for the enforcement of this Note, or because of an alleged dispute, breach, default or misrepresentation in

connection with any of the provisions of the Note, Attorneys Fees shall be reimbursed to Holder, if HOLDER prevails. HOLDER shall be entitled to recover reasonable attorney fees and other costs incurred in that action or proceeding, in addition to any other relief to which it may be entitled.

IN WITNESS WHEREOF, the COMPANY has caused this Note to be executed by any one member of the Board of Directors of _____.

Signature: _____

Dated: _____

By: _____

Title: _____

NOTE HOLDER INFORMATION:

NAME (PLEASE PRINT): _____

ADDRESS: _____

CITY, STATE & ZIP: _____

PHONE: _____

Demand Note

$_____

Date:_____

On demand, the undersigned, for value received, jointly and severally promises to pay to the order of _____ the sum of _____ dollars ($) together with interest thereon from the date hereof until paid at the rate of _____% per annum.

In the event this note is not paid when due, the undersigned shall pay all attorney's fees and reasonable costs of collection.

_____

Promissor:

Promissory Note

$XXX,XXX.XX

City, State

Date

FOR VALUE RECEIVED, the undersigned (the Borrowers) promise to pay to the order of <Name> of <Full Address>, (the Lender) the sum of <Spell out Amount Borrowed> and No/100 ($Expressed in Numerals) Dollars, together with interest in arrears at Eight (8%) percent per annum.

Payment of this Note shall be as follows: Sixty (60) consecutive monthly payments of <Monthly Payment>, commencing on <Date>.

Provided that the Borrowers are not then in default, the Borrowers may prepay all of any part of this Note without penalty.

In the event of a default under the terms hereof, which default is not cured within thirty (30) days after written notice of such default to the Borrower, the Lender may, without further notice, declare the entire principal balance of this Note together with all interest accrued thereon, to be immediately due and payable. Failure to exercise this option shall not constitute a waiver of the right to exercise the same at any other time.

Every maker, endorser and guarantor of this Note hereby waives presentment, demand, notice and protest and consents to any and all extensions or other indulgences and no discharge or release of any other party primarily or secondarily liable on, or of any collateral securing, this Note shall affect the liability of such maker, endorser or guarantor. If this Note is signed by more than one person, all references to the undersigned shall apply to each of them and their liabilities hereunder shall be joint and several.

This Note shall be construed in accordance with the laws of the <Your jurisdiction> and shall take effect as a sealed instrument.

This Note is secured by Mortgage of even date herewith on the premises owned by <Name of Owner(s)> located at <Location of Property>, as more particularly described in said Mortgage. Notwithstanding such security, however, in the event of a default under the term hereof, the Lender shall not seek satisfaction hereof from such mortgaged premises until Lender has sought satisfaction hereof from the liquidation of the business assets which were the consideration hereof, which assets are more particularly described in said Exhibit A (Equipment List).

      This Note is subject to a right of setoff contained in an agreement of even date herewith a copy of which is attached hereto and marked Exhibit B and made a part hereof.

_____

Borrower

                                     _____

                                     Borrower

_____

Witness

Note

(Unsecured)

$_____   _____ , 20__

     FOR VALUE RECEIVED, the undersigned promise(s) to pay to
_____ the principal sum of
_____ DOLLARS ($_____)
and interest from _____ on the balance of principal remaining from time to
time unpaid at the rate of _____ per cent per annum, such principal sum and
interest to be payable in installments as follows:_____

_____DOLLARS ($ _____) on the   __ day of _____, 2___,
and _____ DOLLARS ($_____)
on the _____ day of each and every month thereafter until this Note is fully paid, except that
the
final payment of principal and interest, if not sooner paid, shall be due on the _____ day of
_____, 2_____, All such payments on account of the indebtedness evidenced by this
Note shall be applied first to accrued and unpaid interest on the unpaid principal balance and the
remainder to principal.

    Payments are to be made at _____

_____, or at such other place as the legal holder of this Note may from time
to time in writing appoint.

    And to secure the payment of said amount, the undersigned hereby authorizes, irrevocably,
_____ any attorney of any Court of Record to
appear for the undersigned in such Court, in term time or of collection, including reasonable
attorneys fees and to waive and release all errors which may intervene in any such proceedings,
and consent to immediate execution upon such judgment, hereby ratifying and confirming all that
said attorney may do by virtue hereof.

    At the option of the legal holder hereof and without notice, the principal sum remaining
unpaid hereon, together with accrued interest thereon, shall become at once due and payable at
the place of payment aforesaid in case default shall occur in the payment, when due, of any
installment of principal or interest in accordance with the terms hereof.

    All parties hereto severally waive presentment for payment, notice of dishonor, protest and
notice of protest.

Promissory Note

Principal amount $_____

Date:_____

FOR VALUE RECEIVED, the undersigned hereby jointly and severally promise to pay to the order of _____ the sum of _____ Dollars ($), together with interest thereon at the rate of _____% per annum on the unpaid balance.

Said sum shall be paid in the following manner: All payments shall be first applied to interest and the balance to principal. This note may be prepaid, at any time, in whole or in part, without penalty. This note shall be at the option of any holder thereof be immediately due and payable upon the occurrence of any of the following: 1) Failure to make any payment due hereunder within days of its due date. 2) Breach of any condition of any security interest, mortgage, loan agreement, pledge agreement or guarantee granted as collateral security for this note. 3) Breach of any condition of any loan agreement, security agreement or mortgage, if any, having a priority over any loan agreement, security agreement or mortgage on collateral granted, in whole or in part, as collateral security for this note. 4) Upon the death, incapacity, dissolution or liquidation of any of the undersigned, or any endorser, guarantor to surety hereto. 5) Upon the filing by any of the undersigned of an assignment for the benefit of creditors, bankruptcy or other form of insolvency, or by suffering an involuntary petition in bankruptcy or receivership not vacated within thirty (30) days. In the event this note shall not be in default and placed for collection, then the undersigned agree to pay all reasonable attorney fees and costs of collection.

Payments not made within five (5) days of due date shall be subject to a late charge of _____% of said payment.

All payments hereunder shall be made to such address as may from time to time be designated by any holder.

The undersigned and all other parties to this note, whether as endorsers, guarantors or sureties, agree to remain fully bound until this note shall be fully paid and waive demand, presentment and protest and all notices hereto and further agree to remain bound notwithstanding any extension, modification, waiver, or other indulgence or discharge or release of any obligor hereunder or exchange, substitution, or release of any collateral granted as security for this note.

No modification or indulgence by any holder hereof shall be binding unless in writing; and any indulgence on any one occasion shall not be an indulgence for any other or future occasion. Any modification or change in terms, hereunder granted by any holder hereof, shall be valid and binding upon each of the undersigned, notwithstanding the acknowledgement of any of the undersigned, and each of the undersigned does hereby irrevocably grant to each of the others a power of attorney to enter into any such modification on their behalf.

The rights of any holder hereof shall be cumulative and not necessarily successive.

This note shall take effect as a sealed instrument and shall be construed, governed and enforced in accordance with the laws of the State of _____.

_____ Borrower _____ Borrower

Pledge Agreement

This agreement is made between _____ (Secured Party)
and _____ (Debtor); and
_____ of _____ (Escrow Agent" or Trustee);
in consideration of the following consideration and the mutual covenants and agreements made as
follows.

1. Debt. Debtor is indebted to the Secured Party in accordance with the

terms of a promissory note dated ___ / ___, 2____ in the amount of _____
payable in _____ (__) years.

2. Description of Collateral. Simultaneously with the execution of that note and this Pledge Agreement,
the Debtor causes to be delivered _____ _____shares of _____ (symbol) as
collateral to Escrow Agent pursuant to the Terms of this Agreement.

3. Appointment of Escrow Agent. The Debtor and the Secured Party do hereby accept possession of
that pledged property (Held in Trust or in Escrow) and to hold it for the purposes and under the
conditions set forth herein.

4. Acceptance by Escrow Agent. The Escrow Agent hereby acknowledges receipt of the pledged
property, which shall be held, kept and preserved by it in its possession until the payment in full of the
promissory note; or until the Debtor defaults in the payment of the note or in any of the Debtors

Under takings there under.

5. Return of property on performance. When the note is paid in full according to its terms, the Escrow
Agent shall return the collateral to it'sowner, upon written demand of the Debtor and the Secured
Party and receipt of the owner.

6. Return of property on nonperformance. If the Debtor defaults in the payment of the note or in any
of the Debtor's undertakings thereunder, the Escrow Agent shall, upon written demand by Secured
Party, sell the pledged property in an amount sufficient to pay the note and shall transfer proceeds
sufficient to pay the note from any such sale to the Secured Party.

7. This Agreement shall be governed by the laws of the State of _____ and the parties agree that
the Courts of _____ shall have exclusive jurisdiction over this agreement.

8. In the event that any dispute arises under this agreement, the at fault party shall be liable for all
attorney's fees and costs of the other parties.

9. In the event that any clause or portion of this Agreement shall be found to be invalid, the Agreement
shall continue in force without such clause as if the clause had never existed. If such clause is later
made valid either by function of law or by a court, that clause shall be reinstated and fully enforceable
as of the date of its becoming valid.

Dated this _____ day of _____, 20XX

Secured Party Debtor

By: _____   By: _____

By: _____   By: _____

Power of Attorney

TO ALL PERSONS, be it known that, ("Principal"), of Address: hereby appoints of: ("Advisor") to act in and perform in said fiduciary capacity consistent with my best interests; as he is his best discretion deems advisable, and I affirm and ratify all acts so undertaken. THIS IS A DURABLE POWER OF ATTORNEY AND THE RIGHTS HEREIN SHALL CONTINUE DESPITE THE INCAPACITY OR DISABILITY OF THE PRINCIPAL:

SPECIAL DURABLE PROVISIONS:

The undersigned constitutes and appoints the Advisor with full power and authority to act for and on behalf of the Account(s), established, or to be established, in the behalf of the Principal through:

The Advisor shall have full power to arrange and execute transactions as directed in

This power of attorney shall be in effect for a period of one year and shall automatically renew each year, on January 1st of the year, unless superseded or otherwise canceled in writing, by the Principal.

_____ Date _____

Attorney-In-Fact and Advisor.

_____ Date _____

Principal and Grantor.

Notary Public

STATE OF _____. COUNTY OF _____

On_____ before me _____,Notary, the Principal and Grantor, personally appeared_____ personally known to me (or proved to me on the basis of satisfactory evidence) to be person(s) whose name is/are subscribed to the within instrument and acknowledged to me that he/she/they executed the same in his/her/their authorized capacity(ies), and that by his/her/their signature(s) on the instrument the person(s) or the entity upon behalf of which the person(s) acted, executed this instrument. Witness my hand and official seal:

Signature _____ Date _____

Purchase and Sale Agreement

THIS AGREEMENT is made and entered into by:

    A. SELLER's Name, Address: ("SELLER"); and

    B. PURCHASER's Name, Address: ("PURCHASER").

PURCHASE AND SALE OF ASSETS. SELLER agrees to sell to PURCHASER, and PURCHASER agrees it will purchase from SELLER all of SELLER's assets and properties pertaining to the business known as "Company Name", located at Address, City, State . The assets to be conveyed to PURCHASER by SELLER at the closing include all inventory, customer records, materials, supplies, equipment, machinery, leasehold improvements, furniture, furnishings, fixtures, transferable licenses, business name, telephone numbers, leasehold interest, goodwill, and other assets used in the business.

This sale does not include the SELLER'S, accounts receivable, cash on hand and _____.

PURCHASE PRICE

$ _____The total purchase price for the assets to be transferred by SELLER to PURCHASER

PAYMENT OF PURCHASE PRICE

$ _____ Deposit paid by PURCHASER to the escrow account of <Your Firm> to be included in down   payment.

$_____ Represents the balance of the down payment (subject to prorations and adjustments), payable by cash or certified check at the closing.

$_____ TOTAL DOWN PAYMENT

$_____ of the purchase price shall be paid by PURCHASER'S assumption of an existing obligation in such amount to payable DOLLARS ($_____) per month at an interest rate of percent (%) per annum.

$_____ shall be paid by PURCHASER'S execution of a promissory note to SELLER, bearing interest at _ percent (%) per annum, amortized in equal installments of principal and interest of DOLLARS ($) over ( ) months.

$_____

TOTAL PURCHASE PRICE is _____DOLLARS ($_____).

LIABILITIES PURCHASER shall assume:

WARRANTIES AND REPRESENTATIONS OF SELLER

SELLER warrants and represents that at the closing, all sales taxes, interest and penalties which may be owing to the <YOUR STATE> Department of Revenue will have been paid and satisfied in full. Following the closing, SELLER agrees to indemnify the PURCHASER and hold the PURCHASER harmless from any and all sales taxes, interest and penalties that may be asserted against the PURCHASER as a result of the activities of SELLER prior to the closing.

SELLER also represents to PURCHASER that:

SELLER is the owner of and has good and marketable title to all of the assets, free and clear of any liens, encumbrances or claims whatsoever, except as set forth in Section 6 above with respect to the existing obligations (if any) to be assumed by PURCHASER.

SELLER possesses all licenses necessary to operate the business being transferred to PURCHASER.

There are no judgments, liens, actions or proceedings pending or threatened by or against SELLER.

The business of SELLER will be conducted up to the date of closing in accordance with all laws, rules and regulations, and SELLER will operate and maintain the business in regular course and not violate the terms of any contracts with third parties.

TRAINING PERIOD

SELLER agrees to provide assistance to PURCHASER to transfer management and operation of the business during normal business hours at the location of the business for a period of_____ (__) days following the closing, all without additional consideration payable by PURCHASER to SELLER.

FURTHER COOPERATION

Each of the parties agrees to take whatever actions as may be necessary to carry out the terms of this Agreement following the closing.

SURVIVAL OF REPRESENTATIONS

All representations, warranties and agreements of the parties contained in this Agreement shall survive the closing.

ATTORNEYS' FEES

In the event any party shall be forced to retain the services of legal counsel to enforce the terms of this Agreement whether suit be brought or not, the prevailing party shall be entitled to be reimbursed for all attorneys' fees and court costs incurred.

PURCHASER:

_____

Date:_____ Time:_____

SELLER:

_____

Date:_____ Time:_____

Witness to all:

_____

This Agreement is made on <Date>, between <Shareholder(s)>, hereinafter referred to collectively as "Sellers", and <Acquirers>, hereinafter referred to collectively as "Buyers".

Sellers agree to sell to Buyers, and Buyers agree to purchase from Sellers, (Number of shares) shares of capital stock of <The Corporation, Inc.>, a <Your State> <The Corporation, Inc.> hereinafter referred to as "Company", at the price and on the terms and conditions herein set forth.

Sec. 1. Purchase Price

(a) The purchase price to be paid by Buyers to Sellers for said XXX shares of capital stock shall be determined on the closing date according to the following calculation:

$X,XXX,XXX	Agreed gross value of Company
- XXXXXX	minus current portion of Long Term Debt on the closing date
- XXXXX	minus notes to officers
- XXXXX	minus Long Term Debt on the closing date
- XXX	price per share to be paid for said XXX shares

(b) For informational purposes, the calculation of the price per share as of <Balance Sheet Date>, according to the information provided by Company to the Buyers, would be as follows:

$XXXXXX	Agreed gross value of Company
- XXXXX	current portion of Long Term Debt as of <Balance Sheet Date>
- XXXXX	Notes to officers
- XXXXX	Long Term Debt
XXXXXX	gross value minus debt
- XXX	
XXXXX	price per share for said XXX shares

(c) As of <Balance Sheet Date>, the working capital (Current Assets Minus Current

Liabilities) of Company was $, which included $XX,XXX in cash and $ non-cash working capital. On the closing date, cash working capital must be $XXXXXX. If non-cash working capital is greater than $ (non-cash working capital as of <Balance Sheet Date>) then the excess shall be divided by (Number of shares) and added to the price per share calculated pursuant to Sec. 1 (a). If the non-cash working capital is less than $ (non-cash working capital as of <Balance Sheet Date>) the deficiency will be divided (Number of shares) and deducted from the price per share calculated pursuant to Sec. 1 (a). For purposes of this paragraph, non-cash working capital shall include accounts receivable, inventory, pre-paid and deferred expenses, accounts payable and accrued and withheld

Sec. 2. Delivery of Stock and Payment of Purchase Price

(a) The delivery to Buyers of certificates for the shares of capital stock sold hereunder by Sellers, and the payment of the initial installment of the purchase price therefore by Buyers to Sellers, shall take place at 1:00 p.m., on <Date> (hereinafter called the "closing date") at the Office of <Name>, <Address>.

(b) On the closing date, Sellers shall deliver to Buyer the certificate or certificates evidencing the XXX shares of the capital stock of Company agreed to be sold hereunder duly endorsed for transfer, and Buyers shall pay Sellers the sum of $XXXXXXXX representing the initial installment of the purchase price to be paid for said shares by Buyers.

(c) Subject to the provisions of Section 3 hereof, the balance of the purchase price will be paid by Buyers to the Seller(s) by promissory note(s) as in the amounts indicated below:

the price per share calculated according to
Sec. 1, multiplied by XXX, minus $XXXXXXX

All unpaid balances due from Buyer to Sellers upon the purchase price hereunder shall bear interest at the rate of 8% per annum. Attached hereto and marked Exhibit "A" and made a part hereof are copies of the promissory notes and mortgages to be executed by Buyers and delivered to Sellers on the closing date.

Attached hereto and marked Exhibit "B" and made a part hereof are copies of the documents to be executed by the Sellers and delivered to the Buyers on the closing date. The Seller agrees to execute such additional documents as may be reasonably required by the attorney for the Buyers on the closing date.

Sec. 3. Notices of Breach of Warranty

There shall be deducted from the promissory notes given for the portion of the purchase price remaining unpaid such amounts as may be specified in any written notices of breach of warranty given by Buyers to Sellers and approved by Sellers in writing. Such notices of breach of warranty must specify the breach of one or more of the warranties or representations set forth in this Agreement and the amount estimated by Buyers as the damage resulting or which may result from the breach thereof.

In the event that Sellers shall not approve in writing the amounts specified in such notices of breach of warranty, the respective rights of the parties hereunder shall be determined by arbitration, each party to choose one arbitrator, the two arbitrators so chosen to select an umpire, and the decision of any two of said three persons to be final and binding upon both Buyers and Sellers. Buyers shall pay Sellers the remainder, if any, so determined to be due Sellers on account of the purchase price herein specified and the payment provisions of said promissory notes shall be revised accordingly. In the event the amount so determined to be due from Sellers to Buyers shall exceed the then unpaid balance of the purchase price due from Buyers hereunder, the Sellers shall pay (and they hereby jointly and severally agree promptly to pay) Buyers the full amount of such excess in lawful money of the United States.

Sec. 4. Warranties and Representations of Sellers

Sellers jointly and severally hereby warrant, represent, and agree to and with Buyers as follows: (a) Sellers each have full, complete, and absolute title to the following number of shares of capital stock of <Company>:

Name	No. of Shares
<Shareholder>.	<Number of shares owned>
<Shareholder>.	<Number of shares owned

(b) The title of each of Sellers to said shares is free and clear of any lien, charge, or encumbrance, and said shares aggregating XXX shares, constitute 100% of the outstanding capital stock of <Company> and by sale of said shares of stock hereunder, Buyers will receive good and absolute title thereto, free from any liens, charges, or encumbrances thereon;

(c) <Company> is a Corporation duly organized and existing under and by virtue of the Laws of <Your State>, and is in good standing under the laws of that state; said outstanding XXX shares of the capital stock of said Corporation have heretofore duly been issued; all of said issued and outstanding shares are valid, fully paid and nonassessable, and no assessment is outstanding against the same or any part thereof; before the closing of the sale of stock hereunder, Sellers will deliver to Buyers the opinion of _____ _____, Sellers' counsel, addressed to Buyers, stating that the XXX shares of capital stock of <Company> now issued and outstanding have been lawfully issued under the laws of <Your State> and are valid, and that all stock transfer restrictions affecting the transfer of said shares of capital stock to Buyers hereunder have been duly complied with or effectively waived, and that upon the closing hereunder Buyers will have full and absolute title to said shares free and clear of all liens, charges, or encumbrances; the actual stock certificates representing said XXX shares of capital stock are not in the Sellers possession and are believed to be lost or destroyed;

(d) The present Directors and Officers of <Company> are the following:

Directors: <Names>.

Officers: President: <Name>

Treasurer: <Name>

Clerk: <Name>

and the written resignations of said <Named Above> as officers and directors to be effective upon acceptance will be delivered to Buyers concurrently with the delivery of certificates representing the capital stock sold hereunder;

(e) Attached hereto and marked Exhibit "C" and made a part hereof is a balance sheet of <Company> as of <Date>; said balance sheet truly, correctly, and completely sets forth the financial condition of <Company> as of said date; title to all assets referred to and shown on said balance sheet was vested in <Company> as of said date, free of any liens, charges, or encumbrances; and its books of account, records, and files correctly reflect all operations and transactions and all assets and liabilities;

(f) Between the date hereof and the closing date hereunder, <Company> has not and will not (1) transfer, sell, or otherwise dispose of any corporate property or assets material to the operation of its business other than in the ordinary and usual course of its business as heretofore conducted, save and except such items as shall have become no longer useful, obsolete, or worn out, or rendered of no further use and, if theretofore useful in the conduct of its business and operations, as may have been replaced with other items of substantially the same value and utility as the items transferred, sold, exchanged, or otherwise disposed of; (2) create, participate in, or agree to the creation of, any liens or encumbrances on its corporate property, save and except liens for current taxes and liens created in the ordinary and usual course of its business as heretofore conducted in connection with normal purchases of materials; (3) enter into any leases, contracts, or agreements of any kind or character or incur any liabilities, save and except those to which it is presently committed and which are disclosed herein or in the exhibits hereto and purchase orders placed for raw materials and supplies and agreements to sell products to customers arising in the ordinary and usual course of business as heretofore conducted; (4) make any payments or distributions to any of its Officers, Stockholders, or employees, save and except wages and salaries made to employees in the ordinary and usual course of the business as heretofore conducted including therein contributions pursuant to health, insurance, and pension plans presently in effect; (5) amend or repeal its Articles of Incorporation or By-laws nor issue any shares of capital stock in addition to, and other than, the shares heretofore issued, or reissue any treasury stock;

(g) Attached hereto, marked Exhibit "D" and made a part hereof, is a schedule of all accounts and notes receivable shown on said balance sheet; said accounts and notes receivable and all other accounts and notes receivable accruing in the ordinary and usual course of business as heretofore conducted from the date hereof to the closing date are valid and collectible obligations and will be paid to <Company> ithin one year from the closing date; provided, however, that any liability of Sellers or each of them under this subparagraph shall be limited to the excess over the reserve for bad debts account in the amount of $_____ as shown in Exhibit "B" hereto; provided further that upon payment of any sums to Buyers pursuant to this subparagraph Buyers will assign to Sellers the notes or accounts receivable with respect to which such payment is made; and provided further that the first sums received by Buyers from the obligors of said notes or accounts receivable will be applied to the extent necessary to payment of the balance due upon said notes or accounts;

(h) Attached hereto, marked Exhibit "E" and made a part hereof, is a schedule of all the notes and accounts payable, accrued taxes, and other liabilities of <Company> shown on said balance sheet; there are no undisclosed or contingent liabilities of <Company> (except those referred to in subparagraph (f) of this Section), and in the event that any such undisclosed or contingent liability shall hereafter arise applicable in whole or in part to a period prior to the closing date, Buyers shall give Sellers written notice thereof and Sellers will thereupon within 30 days following receipt of such notice discharge such liability or liabilities or undertake to defend and hold Buyers free and harmless therefrom and shall so notify Buyers. Upon failure of Sellers to discharge or undertake to defend against said liability within the time specified, Buyers may settle said liability, and the joint and several liability of Sellers under this subparagraph shall be conclusively established by such settlement;

(i) Attached hereto, marked Exhibit "F" and made a part hereof, is the duly executed original Lease agreement between <Landlord> as lessor and <Company> as lessee, under which<Company> occupies those certain premises shown as Exhibit "A" on said Lease. Said Exhibit "F" has not been amended or modified orally or in writing and constitutes the entire agreement between <Company> and said lessor;

(j) Attached hereto, marked Exhibit "G" and made a part hereof, is a list of the fixtures

254

and equipment located on the plant premises of <Company>; said fixtures and equipment are the property of said Corporation and upon the expiration of the term of the lease of said plant premises, each of said fixtures and equipment may be removed without liability to the lessor of said plant premises except for the liability incident to the obligation to restore any damage caused by such removal;

(k) Attached hereto, marked Exhibit "H" and made a part hereof, is a list of the insurance policies presently in effect with respect to the corporate property and business of <Company>; said policies or policies procured in lieu thereof providing at least equal coverage and issued by a carrier having at least equal financial responsibility with that of the prior carrier shall be in effect on the closing date and will be delivered to Buyers concurrently with the delivery of certificates representing the capital stock sold hereunder;

(l) There is no litigation pending against <Company>, and none of the Sellers is aware of any threatened litigation;

(m) All tax returns required to be made by<Company> have been properly prepared, executed, and duly filed pursuant to applicable laws and regulations;

(n) <Company> has not violated any federal, state, or municipal law, statute, rule, or regulation or any executive order or presidential directive required by it to be observed or performed;

(o) All patent or patent rights, trade formulas, secret formulas, and technical information used or useful in the business of <Company>, or owned by, or known to or held in the name of any of Sellers, or anyone controlled by any of Sellers, will be transferred to and vested in <Company> and/or disclosed to Buyers before the closing date.

(p) None of the products manufactured and sold by <Company> infringe upon any patents, patented formulas, or private trademarks; <Company> has not in the past manufactured or sold any products which infringe upon such patents or trademarks, and the continued production and sale of such products in accordance with presently used formulas and technical procedures and methods of manufacture and under presently used trade names will not infringe upon existing United States patents or trademarks or state trademarks.

Sec. 5. Continuing Warranties

The warranties, representations, and agreements set forth herein shall be continuous and shall survive the delivery by Sellers and the receipt by Buyers of the capital stock to be sold hereunder and shall also survive the deduction of amounts claimed to be due from the purchase price as provided in section 3 hereof, and Buyers right of recourse against said installments of the purchase price is not intended to be Buyers exclusive remedy for the breach of any such warranties, representations, or agreements.

Sec. 6. Indemnity

Without in any way limiting or diminishing the warranties, representations, or agreements herein contained or the rights or remedies available to the Buyers for the breach thereof, Sellers hereby jointly and severally agree to hold Buyers harmless from and against all loss, liability, damage, or expense arising out of any claims, demands, penalties, fines, taxes, or other loss resulting directly or indirectly from the assertion against <Company> of claims by the federal government, any corporation, partnership, or any person or persons arising before the closing date and not fully disclosed herein or not expressly excepted by the provisions hereof.

Sec. 7. Due Diligence

Between the date hereof and the closing hereunder, Buyers may, conduct such due diligence as Buyers deem necessary, including but not limited to inspection of the corporate records, legal records and/or financial records of <Company> and/or its premises, permits, assets and/or liabilities. If Buyers shall not be satisfied with the results of such due diligence, then at Buyers option, Buyers may terminate this agreement by giving notice to Sellers on or before September 16, 1999, and all obligations of the parties hereto shall cease and this agreement shall be void and without recourse to the parties hereto.

Sec. 8. Waiver of Stock Transfer Restrictions

Sellers hereby waive all preemptive rights and restrictions on the sale and transfer of the capital stock sold hereunder and agree to hold Buyer harmless from and against all liability, loss, damage, or claims arising directly or indirectly from Buyer's failure to obtain hereunder absolute, entire, and unconditional ownership of the entire outstanding capital stock of <Company>, free and clear of all restrictions, liens, charges, or encumbrances.

Sec. 9. Agreement Binding on Heirs and Assigns

The provisions of this Agreement shall inure to the benefit of and bind the successors and assigns of Seller and Buyers and the executors, administrators, heirs, successors and assigns of Stockholders.

Sec. 10. Notices

All notices required or permitted to be given hereunder shall be in writing and shall be sent by first-class mail postage prepaid, deposited in the United States mail, and if intended for Stockholders or Seller shall be addressed to <Name and address of Shareholders>, and, if intended for Buyer shall be addressed to <Name and address of Buyers>. Such notices shall be addressed to each party at the address set forth herein. Any party may by written notice to the others change the address for notices to be sent to it.

Sec. 11. Entire Agreement

This Agreement (including the schedules and annexes hereto) and the documents delivered pursuant hereto constitute the entire agreement and understanding between the parties hereto and supersede any prior agreement and understanding relating to the subject matter of this Agreement. This Agreement may be modified or amended only by a duly authorized written instrument executed by the parties thereto.

Sec. 12. Counterparts

This Agreement may be executed simultaneously in two or more counterparts, each of which shall be deemed an original and all of which together shall constitute but one and the same instrument. It shall not be necessary that any single counterpart hereof be executed by all parties hereto so long as at least one counterpart is executed by each party.

Sec. 13. Law

This Agreement shall be construed in accordance with the laws of the <Your State>.

In Witness Whereof, the parties have executed this Agreement as of the day and year first above written.

_____

<Name>., Seller

<Address>

_____

<Name>., Seller

<Address>

_____

<Name>., Buyer

<Address>

_____

<Name>., Buyer

<Address>

Purchase and Sale Agreement

THIS AGREEMENT made and entered into this ____ day of _____, 200__ (the "Agreement), by and between <Seller>, of the <Full address>, D/B/A <Business Name>, <Business Address>, (the "Seller") and <Buyer>, of <Complete Address> (the "Buyer")

WITNESSETH:

WHEREAS, the Seller is the owner and operator of a business D/B/A <Business Name>, <Business Address>; and

WHEREAS, the Seller desires to sell, and the Buyer desires to purchase, those assets of said Business listed on <u>Schedule</u> <Equipment List> annexed hereto and made a part hereof, the name <Business Name>, the telephone number <Telephone Number> and good will, as more particularly set forth below; and

WHEREAS, Buyer further desires to lease certain machinery and equipment listed on <u>Schedule</u> <Schedule of Equipment to be leased> annexed hereto and made a part hereof, and

WHEREAS, the Buyer further desires to lease the real estate located at <Complete Address.,

NOW, THEREFORE, in consideration of the purchase price hereinafter set forth, and other good and valuable consideration, the sufficiency of which is hereby acknowledged by each of the parties hereto, it is agreed as follows:

1 <u>Sale and Purchase of Business</u>. The Seller agrees to sell, and the Buyer agrees to purchase those assets of the Seller and the Business, as set forth in Schedule <X> attached hereto and incorporated herein, the exclusive right to the name <Business Name>, and the telephone number <Telephone Number>, and any and all customers' and suppliers' lists, trade names, technical information and all other intangible property of Seller necessary to enable Buyer to continue and carry on the Business (collectively, the "Assets"). The sale of said Assets shall be free and clear from all liens and encumbrances.

2. <u>Purchase Price</u>. The purchase price for the Assets shall be $XXX,XXX. The total purchase price shall be payable in the following manner:

(i) Buyers' promissory note m the original principal amount of $XX,XXX with the terms and in the form set forth in <u>Schedule <X></u> attached hereto and incorporated herein secured by a duly executed and acknowledged Security Agreement substantially in the form set forth in <u>Schedule <X></u> attached hereto and incorporated herein and a UCC-1 Financing

Statement; and

(ii) The balance of $XXX,XXX by cash, bank check or certified check payable to Seller's attorney, as escrow agent.

3. <u>Accounts Payable. Accounts Receivable and Inventory</u>. All accounts receivable and inventory existing as of the closing shall belong to Buyers, and Buyers shall assume and pay all obligations of the business due as of the date of closing. The difference, estimated to be $_____ shall be paid by the Buyers' note for said sum due ninety (90) days from closing, with interest at the rate of ___ % per annum.

4 <u>Allocation of Purchase Price</u>. The parties agree that the purchase price shall be allocated

as follows:

a. To goodwill, including the name "Quick Print-Rainbow Press", and the telephone number <Telephone Number>8, the sum of $ XXXXX,

b. To fixtures and equipment as set forth on <u>Schedule B</u>, the sum of $XXXXX.

5. <u>Bulk Sale</u>. The Seller agree to indemnify and hold the Buyer harmless from and against any and all claims, debts, liabilities or obligations, whether matured or unmatured, liquidated or unliquidated, direct or contingent, or joint or several, arising out of or related to the Seller or the Business at any time prior to closing or incurred by the Seller or the Business prior to closing, excepting trade debts assumed by the Buyer pursuant to the terms of Paragraph 3 hereof. The foregoing indemnification and hold harmless shall be construed to cover all costs and expenses incurred by the Seller or the Business, including reasonable attorney's fees, arising out of or relating to any and all such claims, debts and obligations. The terms of this paragraph will survive the closing.

6. <u>Sellers' Representations</u>. The Seller warrants and represents that:

a. It owns the marketable title to all the Assets subject to this Agreement free and clear of any and all liens or encumbrances. The Seller agrees to provide complete releases at closing for any liens or encumbrances on the Assets.

b. All federal and state income tax returns which the Seller is required to prepare and file have been duly prepared and filed in good faith, and all taxes shown thereon have been paid. All state sales and use tax returns, except for the current calendar quarter, have been duly prepared and filed in good faith, and all taxes shown thereon have been paid. All other taxes which the Seller is required by law to collect or withhold have been duly collected and withheld and have been paid over to the proper governmental authorities.

c. The Seller is not a party to any pending or threatened litigation, nor, to the knowledge of the Seller is there any. pending or threatened governmental investigation involving the

Seller or any of the Assets or the Business, including, but not limited to, inquiries, citations, or complaints by any federal, state or local government or agency, and there are no outstanding government orders, decrees or stipulations affecting the Seller or any of the Assets or the Business.

d. The Seller is not in default in the payment or performance of any of its obligations, including the obligations of filing reports or returns to any federal, state or municipal authority.

e. The Seller has no liabilities, whether matured or unmatured, liquidated or unliquidated, direct or contingent, or joint or several, except accounts payable incurred in the ordinary course of business and credit card debt incurred for boiler replacement.

f. The Seller's financial statements as of December 31,<Year>, prepared by <Name Accountant>, CPA, prepared from Seller's books and records and in accordance with generally accepted accounting principles, previously furnished to Buyers, are true, accurate, complete and correct in every material respect, there ha snot been any material adverse change in the financial condition of Seller since December 31, <Year>, and Seller has no liabilities, fixed or contingent, which are not fully shown or provided for in the financial statements referred to above.

g. Seller shall execute and deliver to Buyer at closing a certificate certifying that all the representations and warranties contained herein are true, accurate and complete as of the date of closing.

h. Seller is not in default or violation of any trust, decree, statute, law, indenture, agreement, order, covenant, lease, license, permit, obligation or regulation to which it and/or any of the Assets are bound, and neither the execution and performance of this Agreement nor the consummation of the transactions contemplated by this Agreement will result in such a default.

1. When executed and delivered, this Agreement will b& effective as valid and binding agreement and obligation of Seller and enforceable in accordance with its terms.

j. Seller has no contractual commitments (including, without limitation, any pension, profit sharing or bonus plan or other employee benefit agreement), and is not a party to any executory agreements, whether written or oral, that now are, or may hereafter become, binding upon Buyer, which relate to the Business.

k The operation of the Business at <Address> is in full compliance with all zoning, building codes and other regulations, statutes and ordinances, including without limitation all environmental regulations, statutes and ordinances of the United States of America, the State of Connecticut and the Town of Torrington; and the operation of the Business by Buyer, as contemplated in this Agreement, is permitted by all applicable statutes, regulations and ordinances.

l.   There are no employment contracts in existence affecting any present employee of Seller; and there are no collective bargaining agreements in force relating to such employees; and there is no organizing campaign being conducted relating to such employees.

m.   No representation or warranty by or information supplied by Seller contained in this Agreement or in any statement, certificate, schedule, or other written document furnished (i) to Buyers pursuant to the terms of this Agreement or to any person or firm acting for Buyers or (ii) to Buyer or such person or firm in connection with the transactions contemplated by this Agreement, contains or will contain any untrue statement or misstatement of a material fact or omits or will omit any statement of a material fact necessary to make the statement of facts contained herein or therein not misleading.

7. Adjustments. The Seller and the Buyers agree to apportion personal property and other similar taxes due local authorities, rent and insurance premiums (if the Buyer elects to continue existing coverage) in accordance with the custom prevailing in <County/State>. Seller shall be responsible for paying any local, state or federal sales or transfer tax due on account of the transfer contemplated by this Agreement.

8.   Taxes. All federal, state and local taxes, owed by the Seller as of the date of closing, whether or not due and payable, shall remain the liability of the Seller. The Seller agrees to indemnify and hold the Buyers harmless from and against any and all such taxes. It is hereby intended that this indemnification and hold harmless shall be a part of and included in the indemnification and hold harmless referred to in Paragraph 5 above.

9.   Closing. The closing and transfer of possession of the Assets to be conveyed hereunder shall take place on _____, 1999 at 10:00 a.m. at the offices of <Escrow Agent/Attorney>, <Complete Address>, or at such other time and place as may be mutually agreed upon by the parties. The Buyers and Seller agree that in the event that all the contingencies of this Agreement have been satisfied prior to <Date>, the Buyers and Seller will consummate the closing hereunder immediately upon the satisfaction of said contingencies. Time is of the essence with respect to the closing hereunder.

The Seller agrees to execute and deliver at the closing all instruments reasonably required to carry out the terms and intent of this Agreement including, but not limited to, a Bill of Sale conveying good and marketable title to said Assets free and clear from any and all liens and encumbrances, a corporate resolution and incumbency certificate satisfactory to Buyers' counsel authorizing Seller to enter into and consummate the transaction contemplated by this Agreement.

Exclusive possession of the Assets shall be delivered to the Buyer at closing.

10.   Broker. The Buyers represent to the Seller that they have had no contact with any broker except <Broker> with respect to the transaction which is the subject of this Agreement, and agree to indemnify and hold Seller harmless against the claims of any

other brokers claiming a commission based on contact with the Buyers. Seller agrees to pay the commission of <$ Amount>.

11. Contingencies. It is understood and agreed that the Buyers' obligations under this Agreement are expressly contingent upon the satisfaction of the following matters on or before <Date>

a. <Enter Contingency>

In the event that Buyers fail to satisfy any one or more of the above contingencies, Buyers may give written notice of such failure to Seller whereupon Seller shall return to Buyers all deposits paid pursuant to this Agreement and the parties shall be released of any and all further liabilities each to the other hereunder. The closing shall not take place until all contingencies hereunder have been satisfied or waived by Buyers.

c. Due execution by the parties hereto of lease of machinery and equipment listed on Schedule <X> hereof with the terms and in the form of Schedule D hereof.

d. Due execution by the parties hereto of a lease of the real property located <Business Address> with the terms in the form of Schedule <Premise Lease> hereof.

12. Notices. All notices, requests or other communications provided for by this Agreement shall be deemed given if in writing and sent by certified or registered mail, return receipt requested, to the parties' respective addresses first written above, or to such other addresses as any of the parties may later specify in writing. However, nothing in this Paragraph 10 shall prohibit giving written notice by any other method. Copies of all notices shall be sent to the parties' respective attorneys.

13. Entire Agreement and Modification. This is the only agreement among the parties hereto with respect to the subject matter hereof and cancels and takes the place of all previous agreements or understandings, whether written or oral, if any, heretofore made among the parties hereto. This Agreement may not be modified except by a writing executed by all parties hereto.

14. Binding Effect. This Agreement shall be binding upon and inure to the benefit of the parties hereto, their respective heirs, legal representatives, successors and assigns. The Buyer may assign this Agreement to a corporation, limited liability company or other legal entity wholly owned or controlled by Buyer, provided that Buyer shall personally guarantee the promissory note referred to in Paragraph 2 above.

15   Waiver. No omission or delay on the part of a party hereto in requiring due and punctual performance by the other party hereto of the obligations of such other party as set forth herein shall be deemed to constitute a waiver of the right to require performance of any other obligation(s) hereunder, whether similar or otherwise, or a waiver of any remedy it might have hereunder.

16. Severance. If any provision of this Agreement is held unenforceable for any reason, the remainder of the Agreement shall nevertheless remain in full force and effect. If such provision is held unenforceable due to its scope or breadth, then it shall be narrowed and enforced to the scope and breadth permitted by law.

17.   Gender. Any reference to the masculine gender shall be deemed to include the feminine and neuter genders and vice versa, and any reference to the singular shall be deemed to include the plural and vice versa, unless the context otherwise requires.

18.   Governing Law. This Agreement shall be construed in accordance with the laws of the State of <State> without regard to its conflict of law rules.

19.   Counterparts. This Agreement may be executed in any number of counterparts, all of which shall constitute one and the same instrument and shall for all purposes be deemed to have been made, executed and delivered as of the date first written above, irrespective of the time or times when the same or any of the counterparts may be made, executed and delivered.

20.   Headings. The headings are intended only for convenience and do not constitute part of the text of this Agreement and shall not be used in the interpretation of this Agreement or any of its provisions.

IN WITNESS WHEREOF, the parties hereto have executed or caused to be executed this

Agreement as of the day and year first above stated.

Signed, sealed and delivered in the presence of:

Seller

Buyer

Witness

Date

Security Agreement

Security AGREEMENT dated this _____ day of <Month>, <Year>, by and between <Buyer(s))>, of <Address> (The "Debtors") and <Seller(s)> of <Address> (the "Secured Party").

In consideration of the promises contained herein and the mutual benefits to be derived by the parties, it is hereby agreed as follows:

1.   Indebtedness Secured.   The indebtedness of Debtors to Secured Party (the "Indebtedness"), payment of which is saecured hereby, is set forth in the promissory note in the principal amount of <Spell out amount> ($000,000) made by Debtors in favor of Secured Party and dated <Date> (the "Note").

2.   Security Interest and Description of Collateral.   In order to secure payment of the Indebtedness to Secured Party, Debtors hereby give Secured Party a continuing and unconditional security interest (the "Security Interest") in the following property of Debtors located at <address>: all equipment, inventory, machinery, fixtures, furniture, goods, accounts, accounts receivable, leasehold improvements, contract rights, bank accounts, instruments, documents, chattel paper, insurance policies and proceeds, general intangibles, good will, the right to use the name <Business Name>, and the telephone number <telephone number>, and all other personal property, now existing or hereafter created or acquired or arising and all accessions and accessories thereto, substitutes and replacements therefore, and any interest now existing or hereafter arising with respect thereto, and proceeds and products of the foregoing (the "Collateral").

3.   Obligations of Debtors. Covenant. So long as this Agreement is in effect, Debtor shall:

a)   Promptly pay all sums due and owing Secured Party pursuant to the Note and perform its obligations thereunder and under this Agreement;

b)   Keep the Collateral, other than inventory sold in the ordinary course of business, identifiable and at Debtors place of business at <address>, unless Debtors shall obtain Secured Partys written concent to a change of location;

c)   Keep the Collateral in good repair, not use4 the Collateral in violation of this Agreement, nor any statute or ordinance or any policy of insurance respecting said Collateral and permit Secured Party or his agents to inspect the Collateral upon reasonable notice;

d)   At their own cost and expense defend any action that may affect Secured Partys interest in said Collateral;

e)   Take, at their own expense, whatever action Secured Party reasonably deems advisable to perfect the Security Interest and any additional security interests granted Secured Party in accordance with Paragraph 4(d) below, including, without limitation, the execution and delivery of a UCC-1 financing statement;

f)   Pay promptly when due all taxes and assessments levied on the Collateral; and

g)   Insure the Collateral against risks by obtaining insurance policies (none of which shall be cancelable without at least thirty (30) days prior written notice to Secured Party) in coverage, form and amount and with companies satisfactory to Secured Party, containing a loss payee provision in favor of Secured party, and at Secured Partys request shall deliver a certificate of insurance therefore to Secured Party.

h)   The Debtor agrees to furnish the Secured party with internally prepared monthly financial statements, including balance sheet, profit and loss, and cash flow statements, within ten (10) days of the end of each month, and an annual review level financial statement prepared in accordance with GAAP, by <accountants name>, or some other CPA approved by the Secured Party, within thirty (30) days of the close of each fiscal year.

i)   The Debtor agrees as additional security to carry term life insurance in the amount equal at least to the unpaid balance of the note on each of their lives, which insurance shall be pledged to the Secured Party.

Warranties.   So long as this Agreement is in effect, Debtors warrant that:

j)   Debtors are the owners of the Collateral free of all security interests or other encumbrances, except as set forth on Schedule A ~ attached hereto and incorporated herein.

k)   Debtors have full authority to enter into this Agreement.

4.   Default.   Upon the occurance of an Event of Default (as defined below), Secured Party may, without notice, declare all or any part of the Indebtedness to be immediately due and payable.   Thereupon, Secured Partys rights with respect to the Collateral shall be those of a secured party under the Uniform Commercial Code, and any other applicable law in effect from time to time. Debtors shall remain liable to Secured Party for any deficiency. Secured Party shall also have any additional rights granted herein, including the right to require Debtors to assemble the Collateral and make it available to Secured Party at a place to hbe designated by Secured Party. Debtors shall pay all costs and expenses incurred by Secured Party in enforcing this Agreement, realizing upon any Collateral and collecting any Indebtedness (including reasonable attorneys fees and other costs) whether suit is brought or not, and whether incurred in connection with collection, trial, appeal or otherwise, and shall be liable for any deficiencies in the event the proceeds of disposition of the Collateral do not satisfy the Indebtedness in full.

The occurrence of any of the following shall constitute an event of Default (hereinabove and hereinafter referred to as an "Event of Default"):

a)   Nonpayment when due on any Indebtedness.

b)   Failure by Debtors to perform any obligation under this Agreement or the Note.

c)   The entry of a decree or order for relief by a court having jurisdiction in the premises in respect of the Debtors in an involuntary case under any applicable bankruptcy, insolvency or other similar law now or hereafter in effect, or appointing a receiver, liquidator, assignee, custodian, trustee, sequestrator (or other similar official) of the Debtors or for any substantial part of its property, or ordering the winding up or liquidation of its affairs and the continuance of any such decree or order unstayed and in effect for a period of sixty (60) consecutive days.

d)   The commencement by the Debtors of a voluntary case under any applicable bankruptcy, insolvency or similar law now or hereafter in effect, or the consent by it to the entry of an order for relief in an involuntary case under such law or to the appointment of or taking possession by a receiver, liquidator, assignee, trustee, custodian, sequestrator (or other similar official) of the Debtors or of any substantial part of its property.

e)   Material falsity in any certificate, statement, representation, warranty or audit at any time furnished by or on behalf of Debtors or any endorser or guarantor or any other party liable for payment of all or part of the Indebtedness, pursuant to or in connection with this Agreement or otherwise to Secured Party, including warranties in this Agreement and including any omission to disclose any subsequent contingent or liquidated liabilities or any material adverse change in facts disclosed by any certificate, statement, warranty or audit furnished to Secured Party.

f)   Any attachment or levy against the Collateral or any other occurrence which inhibits Secured Partys free access to Collateral

g)   Default by the Debtors in the performance of any of the terms and conditions of a lease of the premises known as <Address>.

5.   In the event of default and the exercise by the Secured Party of his rights to repossess and/or sell the Collateral pursuant to this agreement and law, the Debtors agree:

a.   That they will not for a period of <spell number> (0) years from the time of such repossession, directly or indirectly, own, manage, join in, control, or participate in the ownership, management, operation or control of, or be a director, officer, employee of, or a consultant to, or otherwise be connected with, any person, or entity which is engaged in the same business as, or otherwise in competition with, the business in which the Collateral is used, within a <spell distance> (00) mile radius of the business premise at <address>.

b. That they will not, within said <spell number> <0> year period, solicit customers of the aforesaid business, or attempt in any way to persuade or entice customers to leave the business.

c. That in addition and not in lieu of any other remedies to which the Secured Party may be entitled, any violation of the provisions of this paragraph may be enjoined through proper action filed in a court of competent jurisdiction.

d. All of the provisions of this paragraph are severable and the invalidity of any provision or any portion of a provision shall not operate to invalidate the other provisions or portion thereof to the extent that a court of competent jurisdiction finds such provisions or portion thereof to be invalid because the area provided for is too large, or the time period is too long, the area or time period shall be reduced to that which the court finds to be reasonable and valid.

6. <u>Termination</u>. This Agreement is a continuing agreement which shall remain I force until all of the Indebtedness contracted for or created by Debtors and any extensions or renewals of that Indebtedness, including, without limitation, all interest thereon, shall be paid in full.

7. <u>Notices</u>. Any notice or other communication required hereunder shall be deemed to have been given or delivered to a party when deposited in the United States mail, certified, return receipt requested, and with proper postage and fees prepaid, addressed to such party at its address set forth below or to such address as any party may designate from time to time by written notice given to the other party in accordance with the terms of this paragraph:

SECURED PARTY: <Name>
<Address>

and
DEBTOR: <Name>
<Address>

8. <u>Miscellaneous</u>. The Secured Party and the Debtors hereby further agree as follows:
a. Waiver or acquiescence in any default by the Debtors or failure of the Secured Party to insist upon strict performance by the Debtors of any warrantees or agreements in this Security Agreement shall not constitute a waiver of any subsequent or other default or failure.

b.   The Debtors expressly waives all requirements of presentment, protest, notice of protest, notice of non-payment or dishonor and diligence by the Secured Party hereunder.

c.   The Secured Party may assign its interest in this Security Agreement, and if assigned, the Assignee shall be entitled upon notice to the Debtors, to performance of all of the Debtors obligations and agreements hereunder, and the Assignee shall be entitled to all of the rights and remedies of the Secured Party hereunder.

d.   This Security Agreement and all its rights and obligations hereunder, including matters of construction, validity and performance, shall be governed and interpreted under and in accordance with the laws of <State/Province>.

e.   This Security Agreement shall inure to the benefit of and shall be binding upon the respective successors, assigns, and legal representatives of the parties hereto.

f.   This Agreement may not be modified or amended, nor shall any provision of it be waived, except in writing signed by the Debtors and the Secured Party.

IN WITNESS WHEREOF, the parties, being duly authorized, have respectively signed and sealed this Security Agreement on the date and year first above written.

SECURED PARTY

<Name>

DEBTORS

<Name>

WITNESS TO ALL

Or

Personally appeared <Secured Party>, signer and sealer of the foregoing instrument, and acknowledged the same to be his free act and deed, before me

Notary Public

Personally appeared <Debtor>, signer and sealer of the foregoing instrument, and acknowledged the same to be his free act and deed, before me

Training Agreement

I, _____ owner of that

business known as _____

do hereby agree to train _____ in conjunction with the
final sale and transfer of the above mentioned business and understand the terms of
said training to be

   1) For a period of _____ days after transfer and during normal days and
hours of operation I will be present at the above referred business for the purpose of
training.

   2) In addition, I will provide full disclosure to all customers, accounts, supplies and
services as might be appropriate.

   3) I understand I am not to be compensated for this training.

   4) Additional information:

Leases and
Lease Assignments

LEASE

THIS AGREEMENT is an Indenture of Lease between the Lessor and the Lessee hereinafter named, relating to part or parts of that building complex located at (Address, City, County, State)

The parties to this Indenture of Lease hereby agree, with each the other, as follows:

DATE:

LESSOR: (Name and Address)

LESSEE: (Owner Name)

PRESENT MAILING ADDRESS OF LESSOR: (Address)

TERM OF LEASE: Six (6) months plus Additional ten 1-year options.

LOCATION OF PREMISES: The Lessor hereby demises and leases to the Lessee, and the Lessee hereby accepts the demised premises, which premises shall consist of approximately
(   ) square feet of property located at (Address, City, County, State). A said premise includes the building located on said property.

RENT: Lessee shall pay to Lessor as rent for said demised premises the sum of $_____ per month payable in advance on the 1st day of each and every month of said term commencing on _____, 20__.

COMPLIANCE: Lessor shall comply with all Federal, State, County and City Laws and ordinance, and all rules and regulations of any duly constituted authority present and future, affecting or respecting the demised premises, and Lessee shall likewise comply with all Federal, State, County and City Laws and ordinances and all rules and regulations of any respecting the use of occupancy of the demised premises by Lessee, or the business at any time thereon transacted by Lessee or any sub-Lease of Lessee.

LESSOR ACCESS: Lessor and his duly authorized agents, employees, officers and independent contractors employed by him shall have access to the demised premises at all reasonable times and hours for the purpose of examining and inspecting the same.

INSURANCE: Lessee further convenents and agrees that he will at all times during this demise, at his own expense, maintain and keep in force liability insurance in the amount of $ 100,000 total liability to indemnify Lessor and Lessee jointly as their respective interests may appear, against loss, liability or damage which may result to Lessor and Lessee, or either, from any accident or casualty whereby any person or persons whomever may be injured or killed in or about the demised premises. Lessee shall deliver to Lessor a certificate of such insurance.

STRUCTURAL REPAIRS: Lessor agrees that he will, upon written request from Lessee, during the term of this lease make any and all structural repairs to said premises including, all repairs to the roof and exterior walls, except in case of damage thereto caused by any act of the Lessee.

NOTICE: If at anytime after the execution of this lease, it shall become necessary or convenient for one of the parties hereto to serve any notice, demand or communication upon the other party, such notice, demand or communication shall be in writing signed by the party serving the same, deposited in the Registered United States Mail, return receipt requested postage prepaid and:

(a) If intended for Lessor, shall be addressed to:

Name

Street

City, State Zip

and

(b) If intended for Lessee, shall be addressed to:

Name

Street

City, State Zip

Any notice so mailed shall be deemed to have been given when the same is deposited in the United States Mail.

Lessor covenants and warrants that he has full right and lawful authority to enter into this lease for the full term hereof, and that Lessor is lawfully seized of the entire premises hereby demised and has good title thereto, free and clear of all tenancies and encumbrances.

19. It is further expressly agreed and understood that all convenents and agreements herein made, shall extend to and be binding upon the heirs, devisees, executors, administrators, successors and interest, and assigns of the Lessor and of the Lessee.

IN WITNESS WHEREOF, the parties have hereunto set their hand and seals this day and year first above written.

_____   _____

Lessee   Lessor

_____

Witness to both

LEASE

THIS LEASE made and entered this _____ day of _____, 20__ by and between _____ (hereinafter called "Lessee") and _____ (hereinafter called "Lessor").

WITNESSETH that Lessor, for and in consideration of the convenents and agreements hereinafter contained and made on the part of the Lessee, does hereby demise and lease to Lessee, the following described premised in _____, <STATE>, to wit:

That property of the Lessor located at _____, consisting of approximately _____ square feet of floor space, on the first floor and in the basement.

TO HAVE AND TO HOLD the same for and during the term commencing on the _____ day of _____, 20__ , and expiring on the _____ day of _____, 20__.

In consideration of said demise and the covenants and agreements hereinafter expressed, it is convenented and agreed as follows:

1. Lessee shall pay to Lessor as rent for said demised premises the sum of $_____ per month payable in advance on the 1st day of each and every month of said term commencing on _____, 20__. Lessee's default under the terms of the promissory note to sellers dated _____ shall constitute default under this lease.

2. Lessee shall pay to Lessor the sum of $_____ which sum represents security deposit and which sum will be returned to the Lessee at the expiration of this Lease after due inspection by the Lessor provided he is satisfied that there has been no damage done to the property beyond normal wear and tear.

3. In the event Lessee continues to occupy premises after the last day of any extension of said term, and the Lessor elects to accept rent thereafter, a tenancy from month to month only will be created and not for any longer period.

4. Lessor shall comply with all Federal, State, County and City Laws and ordinance, and all rules and regulations of any duly constituted authority present and future, affecting or respecting the demised premises, and Lessee shall likewise comply with all Federal, State, County and City Laws and ordinances and all rules and regulations of any respecting the use of occupancy of the demised premises by Lessee, or the business at any time thereon transacted by Lessee or any sub-Lease of Lessee.

5. Lessee shall at all times keep the demised premises, the buildings thereon, and all appurtenances, in a clean and healthy condition, according to the applicable statutes, Town Ordinances and the directions or regulations of the proper public authorities.

6. Lessee shall protect and repair all plumbing and heating pipes from freezing during the term hereby created. Lessor and his duly authorized agents, employees, officers and

independent contractors employed by him shall have access to the demised premises at all reasonable times and hours for the purpose of examining and inspecting the same.

7. Lessee shall keep, protect and save Lessor harmless from any loss, cost or expense of any sort or nature, and from any liability to any person, natural or artificial, on account of damage to person or property arising out of failure of Lessee in any respect to comply with and perform all the requirements and provisions hereof.

7a. Lessee agrees that he will pay his proportionate share of increases of all real estate taxes and water bills payable to the <City >during the term of this lease which exceed the fiscal 1987 real estate tax assessed against the premised herein demised beginning with the taxes for the year 20__. That sum shall be payable to the Lessor on   of each year beginning with the   day of   , 20___ .

7b. Lessee agrees to make any interior repairs to the property during this term of lease at his own expense, including plumbing and heating repairs and windows.

7c. Lessee agrees that he will not keep animals or pets on the premises during this term or any extensions thereof.

8. Lessee further convenents and agrees that he will at all times during this demise, at his own expense, maintain and keep in force liability insurance in the amount of $ total liability to indemnify Lessor and Lessee jointly as their respective interests may appear, against loss, liability or damage which may result to Lessor and Lessee, or either, from any accident or casualty whereby any person or persons whomever may be injured or killed in or about the demised premises. Lessee shall deliver to Lessor a certificate of such insurance.

9. Lessor convenents and agrees that he will, upon written request from Lessee, during the term of this lease make any and all structural repairs to said premises including, all repairs to the roof and exterior walls, except in case of damage thereto caused by any act of the Lessee.

10. If said premises shall be rendered untenantable in whole or in part by fire or other casualty, the Lessor will, within   ( ) days from date of said damage, repair or replace said building to substantially the same condition it was in immediately prior to such casualty, so that Lessee may continue in occupancy. It is further agreed, however, that the rent herein required to be paid shall abate in proportion to the nature and extent of the damage during said period of untentability. It is further agreed that if said building cannot be replaced or repaired in   ( ) days to substantially the same condition it was in immediately prior to such casualty, then Lessor will be free of the liability of replacing or repairing in said   ( ) days and the Lessee may if he so desires, terminate this lease and no liability shall attach to the Lessor for failure to complete said building for the above mentioned reasons.

11. It is further agreed that the Lessee may make alterations to said building only with

the written consent of the Lessor.

12. Lessee may not assign this lease or his rights hereunder or sublet the demised premises or any part thereof without the written consent of the Lessor. In such event Lessee shall remain liable for the payment of all rent required to be paid hereunder and for the performance of all the terms, covenants and conditions herein undertaken by Lessee. Which consent may not unduly be withheld.

13. If the demised premises, or any part thereof, shall be taken in any proceeding by the public authorities by condemnation or otherwise, or be acquired for public purposes, Lessee shall have the election of terminating this lease and the term hereby created.

In any such proceedings whereby all or part of said premised shall be taken, whether or not Lessee elects to terminate this lease, each party shall be free to make claim against the condemning parting for the amount of the actual provable damages done to each of them by such proceedings

14. If Lessee shall fail to pay any installments of rent promptly on the day when the same shall become due and payable hereunder, and shall continue in default for a period of (15) days after written notice thereof by Lessor, or if Lessee shall fail to promptly keep and perform any other affirmative covenant of this lease, strictly in accordance with the terms of this lease and shall continue in default for a period of (15) day period and proceeds to complete the correction of the default with due diligence thereafter), then and in any such event, and as often as any such event shall occur, Lessor may at his sole election (and in addition to any and all other remedies provided by law or contained in this lease). This 15 day grace period is for one and only one event of default, should Lessee fail under this clause in a second event there is no grace period.

(a) Declare the said term ended, and enter into said premises demised, or any part thereof, either with or without process of law, and expel Lessee or any person occupying the same or in or about said premised, using such force as may be necessary so to do, and so to repossess and enjoy said premises as in the Lessor's forestate, or:

(b) Re-let the premises applying said rents from the new tenant on the lease and Lessee shall be responsible for no more than the balance that may be due, should a balance exist, provided however, that the Lessee's obligation to pay any such

balance is expressly conditioned upon Lessor's using his best efforts to rent the lease premises at a reasonable rental and for as much of the residue of the term as extended as is reasonably possible.

(15) If at anytime after the execution of this lease, it shall become necessary or convenient for one of the parties hereto to serve any notice, demand or communication upon the other party, such notice, demand or communication shall be in writing signed by the party serving the same, deposited in the Registered United States Mail, return receipt requested postage prepaid and:

    (a) If intended for Lessor, shall be addressed to:

        Name

        Street

        City, State Zip

and

    (b) If intended for Lessee, shall be addressed to:

        Name

        Street

        City, State Zip

Any notice so mailed shall be deemed to have been given when the same is deposited in the United States Mail.

16. Lessee agrees to pay all water, electric, heat, hot water and his fair share of snow removal expenses during the term of this lease.

17. Lessor does hereby grant to Lessee the right to extend the lease for a period of _____ ( ) years from the date of expiration hereof, upon notice in writing to the Lessor of Lessee's intention to exercise said right, given ninety (90) days prior to the expiration of the term hereof with the new rental figure to be determined as follows:

The base rent to be $_____ except that whatever increase in real estate taxes for that portion of the building occupied by the tenant shall be additionally paid to the Lessor and to be re-figured each year during any extension thereof.

18. Lessor covenants and warrants that he has full right and lawful authority to enter into this lease for the full term hereof, and that Lessor is lawfully seized of the entire premises hereby demised and has good title thereto, free and clear of all tenancies and encumbrances.

19. It is further expressly agreed and understood that all convenents and agreements herein made, shall extend to and be binding upon the heirs, devisees, executors, administrators, successors and interest, and assigns of the Lessor and of the Lessee.

20. Lessor and Lessee agree to execute a notice of lease in recordable form simultaneously herewith which shall be recorded at Lessee's expense.

21. Lessor also grants Lessee the right to first refusal on the purchase of the real estate, Book   Page   shown on the plan of land in the City of XXXXXXXXX

IN WITNESS WHEREOF, the parties have hereunto set their hand and seals this day and year first above written.

_____

Lessor

_____

Lessee

_____

Lessee

LEASE

THIS AGREEMENT is an Indenture of Lease between the Lessor and the Lessee hereinafter named, relating to part or parts of that building complex located at (Address, City, County, State)

The parties to this Indenture of Lease hereby agree, with each the other, as follows:

DATE:

LESSOR: (Name and Address)

LESSEE: (Owner Name)

PRESENT MAILING ADDRESS OF LESSOR: (Address)

TERM OF LEASE: 2 years. Additional two 3 year options after first 2 years.

LOCATION OF PREMISES: The Lessor hereby demises and leases to the Lessee, and the Lessee hereby accepts the demised premises, which premises shall consist of approximately ( ) square feet of property located at (Address, City, County, State). Said premises includes the building located on said property.

RESERVATIONS AND RESTRICTIONS: The Lessee may use and occupy the leased property for the purpose of operating a <TYPE BUSINESS> facility. The Lessee shall not use or allow the demised premises to be used for any other purpose.

(a) Except as hereinafter provided, the Lessee shall not use or occupy or permit the demised premises to be used or occupied nor do or permit anything to be done in or on the demised premises, in a manner which will in any way violate any

condition or certificate of insurance affecting the building in which the demised premises are located or any part thereof or make void any insurance thence in force with respect thereto or which will make it impossible to obtain fire or other insurance required to be furnished by either the Lessor or Lessee hereunder

at a rate no greater than the present rate, or which will make, cause, or be likely to cause, structural damage to the building or any part thereof or which will constitute a public or private nuisance, and shall not use or occupy or permit the leased property to be used or occupied in any manner which will violate any laws or regulations; the Lessee shall not erect, place or allow to be placed any sign of any nature on any part of the demised premises without the written consent of the Lessor having first been obtained, which consent shall not unreasonably be withheld.

(b) Except for the uses hereinbefore provided, the Lessee shall conduct business in such a manner, both as regards noise and other nuisances, as will not interfere with, annoy or disturb any neighboring businesses or residents.

(c) Except for the uses hereinbefore provided, the Lessee shall not keep within the leased property any article of dangerous, inflammable or explosive character which increases the danger of fire upon the leased property or which would be deemed "hazardous" or "extra-hazardous" by any responsible insurance company.

RENTAL PAYMENT: The Lessee shall pay to the Lessor at the mailing address or at such other place as Lessor shall from time to time designate by notice during the leased term, a net annual rental, (hereinafter called "Net Rent"), as follows:

(a) Rental shall be payable in equal monthly installments, in advance, commencing on the commencement date and the same sum on the first day of each and every calendar month during the term thereof. Rent shall be ($00000000.00) Dollars a month. "Net Rent" for each of the remaining ( ) years of the term of this agreement shall be determined at the commencement of each year by agreement of both parties expected increase, if any, at the beginning of each year will be ( )% over previous year.

ASSIGNMENT AND SUBLETTING: Notwithstanding any other provisions contained herein, the Lessee will not assign this lease nor sublet the whole or any part of the demised premises. In any case, the Lessee named herein shall remain fully liable for the obligations of the Lessee hereunder, including without limitations, the obligation to pay the rent and other amounts provided to be paid under this Lease.

UTILITIES AND OTHER SERVICES: Except as hereinafter otherwise specifically set forth, the Lessee shall pay all charges for gas, electricity, telephone, water and heat and shall indemnify the Lessor against any liability or damages on such account. The Lessor shall install, at its sole cost, an air conditioning unit and a heating unit on the rooftop of the leased premises. Said units shall be installed and operational on the date for commencement of this Agreement. The Lessor shall also install, at its sole cost, new pavement and markings for a new parking lot to repair and replace the parking lot currently located on the premises. Said parking lot shall be completely installed on the date for commencement of this Agreement.

MAINTENANCE AND REPAIRS: The Lessee agrees to maintain, at its sole cost, the roof, foundation, sewerage facilities and snow removal at the exterior of the demised premises.

The Lessee, shall have the right, at its sole cost, to make alterations, additions or improvements to the demised premises, subject to the prior written consent of the Lessor. Prior to making said alterations, etc. the Lessee shall submit to the Lessor written plans (i.e. blueprints, architectural diagrams) depicting the intended alterations, additions or improvements. The written consent of the Lessor shall not unreasonably be withheld. The Lessee agrees to keep and maintain the demised premises and every part thereof (except as specifically provided to be kept and maintained by the Lessor) within the demised premises, in the same condition the same are in at the time of the letting or may thereafter by put in during the continuance of the term, reasonable use and wear, damage by fire or other unavoidable casualty excepted. The Lessee further agrees to replace all glass and glass windows in the demises premises at its sole cost and expense. Lessee further agrees that the demised premises shall be kept in clean, sanitary and safe condition, reasonably free of dirt, rubbish and unlawful obstructions and in accordance with the reasonable rules and regulations of the Lessor, the laws of the (State), ordinances of the city of (City) and in accordance with all directions, rules and regulations of the Health Department, fire and police officials, building inspectors and to the governmental agencies having jurisdiction thereover. The Lessee shall not permit, suffer and commit any waste.

LESSOR'S ACCESS TO PREMISES: The Lessor shall have the right to enter upon the demised premises with reasonable frequency for the purpose of inspecting the same and at all reasonable hours for the purpose of making repairs to the demised premises (except that in an emergency, access may be made at any time). If repairs are required to be made by the Lessee pursuant to the terms hereof, Lessor may demand that the Lessee make the same within a reasonable time, and if the Lessee refuses or neglects to commence such repairs and complete the same within reasonable dispatch after such demand, the Lessor may (but shall not be required to do so) make or cause such repairs to be made and shall not be responsible to the Lessee for any loss or damage that may accrue to its stock or business by reason thereof, and if the Lessor makes or causes such repair to be made, the Lessee agrees that it will forthwith, on demand, pay to the Lessor the cost thereof, and if it shall have default in such payment, the Lessor shall have the remedies provided in Article entitled, "Lessor's/Remedies" hereof. For a period commencing ( ) months prior to the termination of Lessee's occupancy of any portion of the demised premises, Lessor may have reasonable access for the purpose of exhibiting some to prospective tenants.

The Lessee shall not be entitled to any compensation or abatement of rent as a result of the foregoing.

LIABILITY INSURANCE: Lessee agrees to maintain in full force from the date upon which Lessee first enters the premises for any reason, throughout the term of this Lease, and thereafter so long as Lessee is in occupancy of any part of the premises, a policy of public liability and property damage insurance under which Lessor (and such other persons as are in privity of estate with Lessor as may be set out in notice from time to time) and Lessee, are named as insured, and under which the insurer agrees to indemnify and hold Lessor, and those in privity of estate with Lessor, harmless from and against all cost, expense and/or liability arising out of or based upon any and all claims, accidents, injuries and damages mentioned in section entitled, "Tenant's Indemnity" in the broadest form of such coverage from time to time available in<STATE>. Each such policy shall be non-cancelable and non-amendable with respect to Lessor and Lessor's said designees without ten (10) days prior notice to Lessor. The minimum limits of liability insurance shall be (AMOUNT) ($000000.00) DOLLARS for bodily injury (or death) to any one person, and (AMOUNT) ($000,000.00) DOLLARS for bodily injury (or death) to more than one person, and (AMOUNT) ($00,000.00) DOLLARS with respect to damage property.

NON-SUBROGATION: Insofar as, and to the extent that, the following provision may be effective without invalidating or making it impossible to secure insurance coverage obtainable from responsible insurance companies doing business in the (State) (even though extra premium may result therefrom): Lessor and Lessee mutually agree that, with respect to any hazard which is covered by insurance then being carried by them, respectively, the one carrying such insurance and suffering said loss releases the other of and from any and all claims with respect to such loss; and they further mutually agree that their respective insurance companies shall have no right of subrogation against the other on account thereof. In the event that extra premium is payable by either party as a result of this provision, the other party shall reimburse the party paying such premium the amount of such extra premium. If at the request of one party, this release and non-subrogation premium is waived, then the obligation of reimbursement shall cease for such period of time as such waiver shall be effective, but nothing contained in the section shall derogate from or otherwise affect releases elsewhere herein contained of either party for claims.

EXTRA HAZARDOUS USE: Lessee covenants and agrees that it will not do so or permit anything to be done in or upon the premises, or bring in anything or keep anything therein, which shall increase the rate of insurance on the premises above the standard which Lessee has agreed to devote the premises; and Lessee further agrees that, in the event that it shall do any of the foregoing, it will promptly pay to Lessor, on demand, any cash increase resulting therefrom, which shall be due and payable as additional rent thereunder; except, however, that this paragraph is not applicable to the contemplated use as set forth hereinbefore in paragraph entitled, "Reservations and Restrictions".

FIRE: Except as herein otherwise provided, damage to or destruction of any portion of the leased premises by fire or other casualty, shall not terminate this Lease or entitle the Lessee to surrender the leased premises.

If, after commencement of the term of this Lease and prior to the expiration of said term, the demised premises shall be damaged by fire or other casualty the risk of which is covered by the Lessor's insurance, then the Lessor shall proceed with due diligence to restore the premises so damages to substantially the same condition as existed prior to the casualty, or in lieu thereof, the Lessor shall furnish, provide or build comparable premises in the building complex, provided, however, that the Lessor shall not be obliged to expend any amounts for such restoration in excess of net amounts of insurance proceeds received by the Lessor. The Lessor shall not be responsible for any delay which may result from any cause beyond Lessor's reasonable control.

In the event there shall be damage or destruction as a result of a risk not covered by the Lessor's insurance, or in the event the damage or destruction is so substantial that the proceeds of insurance are insufficient to enable the Lessor to comply with the provisions of the above section, the Lessor or the Lessee may, at the option of either, promptly after such loss, give notice of Lessor's or Lessee's election to terminate this Lease. Thereupon, this Lease shall terminate as of the date of such notice with the same force and effect as if such date were the date originally established as the expiration date thereof.

In the event of damage or destruction by fire or other casualty, the rent herein reserved shall be abated or reduced proportionately, depending upon the nature and extent of the damage, during any period in which reason of any such damage or destruction there is substantial interference with the Lessee's business of the extent that the Lessee may have to discontinue its business in the demised premises and such abatement or reduction shall continue until the premises have been restored as heretobefore provided to substantially the same condition as existed immediately prior to this damage.

In case of damage by fire or other casualty to the entire premises and buildings leased to the Lessee herein, if the damage is so extensive as to amount practically to the total destruction of the leased property and the buildings herein, this Lease shall cease and the rent shall be apportioned to the time of the damage.

In the event damage or destruction is so substantial that the proceeds of insurance are insufficient to enable the Lessor to comply with the provisions of the second paragraph titled, "Fire", the Lessee may at its option, promptly after such loss, give notice of Lessee's election to terminate as of the date of such notice, with the same force and effect as if such date were the date originally established as the expiration date thereof.

ASSIGNMENT OF RENT: The Lessee acknowledges and agrees that any assignment by the Lessor of the Lessor's interests in this Lease or in the rent payable under the provisions of this Lease, whether conditional or otherwise, make to the holder of a mortgage which includes the demised premises shall not be treated as an assumption by such mortgagee of the obligations and duties of the Lessor hereunder unless the mortgagee shall specifically agree with the Lessor hereunder, the same shall not be treated as an assumption by the said mortgagee of the Lessor's obligations hereunder except upon foreclosure, and the taking of possession of the demised premises by the said mortgagee of its assumption of the obligations of the duties to be performed and observed by the Lessor hereunder from the date of such assumption.

COVENANT OF QUIET ENJOYMENT: The Lessee, subject to the terms and provisions of this Lease on payment of the rent and observing, keeping and performing all of the terms and provisions of this Lease on its part to be observed, kept and performed, shall lawfully, peaceably and quietly, have, hold, occupy, and enjoy the demised premises during the term thereof without hindrance or ejection by any persons lawfully claiming under the hindrance or ejection by any persons lawfully claiming under the Lessor. It is understood and agreed that with respect to any repairs or services to be furnished by the one party to the other, such party shall in no event be liable for failure to furnish the same when prevented from so doing by strike, lockout, breakdown, accident, order or regulation of or by any governmental authority or failure to supply, or inability by the exercise of reasonable diligence, to obtain supplies, parts or employees necessary needed to furnish such services, or because of war or other emergency, or for any cause due to any act or neglect of the other party or its servants, agents, employees, licensees, or any person claiming by, through or under the other party, or any termination for the service being supplied by such party, or for any cause beyond the party's reasonable control, and in no event shall such party ever be liable to the other party for any indirect or consequential damages.

INVALIDITY OF PARTICULAR PROVISIONS: If any term or provision of this lease or the application thereof to any person or circumstances shall, to any extent, be invalid or unenforceable, the remainder of this lease, or the application of such term or provision to persons or circumstances other than those as to which it is held invalid or unenforceable, shall not be affected thereby, and each term and provision of this Lease shall be valid and be enforced to the fullest extent permitted by law.

PROVISION BINDING, ETC.: Except as herein otherwise expressly provided, the terms hereof shall be binding upon and shall inure to the benefit of the heirs, executors, administrators, successors and assigns, respectively, of the Lessor and the Lessee. Each term and each provision of this Lease shall be construed to be both a covenant and a condition. The reference contained to successors and assigns of Lessee is not intended to constitute a consent to assignment by Lessee, but has reference only to those instances in which the Lessor may latter give written consent to a particular assignment as required by provisions of Lease.

LESSOR'S REMEDIES: It is covenanted and agreed that if the Lessee shall neglect or fail to perform or observe any of the covenants, terms, provisions or conditions contained in these presents and/or its part to be performed or observed within fifteen (15) days after written notice of default, or if the estate hereby created shall be taken on execution or by other process of law and such process shall not be rendered inoperative within thirty (30) days after appointment, or if the Lessee shall make any general assignment of its property for the benefit of creditors, or if Lessee shall file a voluntary petition in bankruptcy or insolvency, or shall apply for reorganization or arrangement with its creditors under the bankruptcy or insolvency laws now in force or hereafter enacted, federal, state or otherwise, or if such petition shall be filed against the Lessee and shall not be dismissed within sixty (60) days after the filing, or if the Lessee shall seek a composition with its creditors by trust, mortgage or otherwise, the Lessor may, immediately, or at any time thereafter, and without demand or notice enter into and upon the said premises or any part thereof in the name of the whole and repossess the same as his former estate, and expel the Lessee and those claiming through or under it and remove its or their effect (forcibly, if necessary) without being prejudice to any remedies which might otherwise be used for arrears of rent or preceding breach of covenant, and upon entry as aforesaid this Lease shall terminate; and the Lessee covenants and agrees, notwithstanding any entry or re-entry by the Lessor whether by summary proceedings, termination or otherwise, to pay and be liable for on the days originally fixed herein for the payment thereof, amounts equal to the several installments of rent and other charges reserved as they would under the term of this Lease, become due if this Lease had not been terminated or if the Lessor had not entered or re-entered as aforesaid, and whether the demised premises be relet or remain vacant in whole or in part, for a period less than the remainder of the term by the Lessor, the Lessee shall be entitled to a credit in the net amount of rent received by the Lessor in re-letting, after deduction of all expenses incurred in connection therewith. As an alternative, the Lessee will upon such termination pay to the Lessor, as damages, such a sum as at time of such termination represents the amount of excess, if any, of the then value of the total rent and other benefits which would have accrued to the Lessor under this Lease for the remainder of the Lease term if the Lease terms had been fully complied with by Lessee over and above the then cash rent value (in advance) of the premises for the balance of the term.

Neither party shall be in default in the performance of any of his obligations hereunder unless and until such party shall have failed to perform such obligations within fifteen (15) days of such additional time as is reasonably required to correct any such default after notice by the other party properly specifying wherein such party has failed to perform any such obligation. Should the Lessee receive two (2) written notices of default within a twelve (12) month period. the Lessor, at its option, may exercise its previously described remedies without written notice upon the occurrence of any additional breaches of any covenant, term, provision or condition contained in this Agreement within said twelve (12) month period. Any failure by the Lessor to exercise these remedies without notice shall not constitute a waiver of Lessor's ability to exercise said right upon the occurrence of subsequent breaches hereinbefore described.

SUBORDINATION OF LEASE TO FUTURE MORTGAGES: The Lessee agrees that upon request of the Lessor or holder of the Lessor's interest, the Lessee will subordinate this Lease to any mortgage hereafter placed against the land and building or which the demised premises are a part with the same force and effect as if said mortgage were executed, delivered and recorded prior to the execution and delivery of the Lease, provided, however, that Lessor shall deliver to the Lessee an Agreement by the mortgage not to disturb Lessee's possession after foreclosure if the Lessee is not then in default under the provisions of the Lease and the Lessee further agrees to recognize said mortgagee as Lessor hereunder for the remainder of the term. The Lessee agrees that it will, upon request of the Lessor, execute, acknowledge, and deliver any and all instruments which the subordination requires, hereby constituting the Lessor irrevocably as the attorney in fact of the Lessee, to execute, acknowledge, and deliver such instrument in the event of failure or refusal on the part of the Lessee to do so. As used herein, the term "mortgage" shall include any modification, consolidation, extension, renewal, replacement, or substitution of any existing or subsequent mortgage upon the property.

GOVERNING LAW: This Lease shall be governed exclusively by the provisions hereof and by the laws of<STATE>, as the same may from time to time exist.

Lessors are acting as officers of a Corporation as aforesaid and not as individuals. Lessee shall look only to the Corporation and shall in no event have recourse to the individual estate of any persons named herein as Lessors or their successors or any shareholder of said Corporation for the satisfaction of any claim nor shall recourse be held to said Corporation if the officers under this Agreement and Articles of Incorporators cease to be owners of said premises for anything which shall occur thereafter.

LESSEE'S RISK: To the maximum extent this Agreement may be made effective according to law, and except as otherwise prohibited by Chapter XXX, Section XX of the General Laws of the <STATE>, Lessee agrees to use and occupy the premises and to use such other portions of the building complex as it is herein given the right to use at its own risk, and Lessor shall have no responsibility or liability for any loss or damage to fixtures or other personal property of Lessee. The provisions of this section shall be applicable, from and after the execution of this Lease and until the end of term of this Lease, and during such further period as Lessee may use or be in occupancy of any part of the premises.

To the maximum extent this Agreement may be made effective according to law, and except as otherwise prohibited by Chapter XXX, Section XX of the General Laws of the<STATE>, Lessee agrees that Lessor shall not be responsible of liable to Lessee, or to those claiming by, through or under Lessee, for any loss or damage that may be occasioned by the breaking, bursting, stopping or leaking of electrical cable and wire, and water, gas, sewer or steam pipes.

TENANT'S INDEMNITY: To the maximum extent this Agreement may be made effective according to law, and except as otherwise prohibited by Chapter XXX, Section XX of the General Laws of the<STATE>, Tenant agrees to indemnify and save harmless Landlord from and against all claims of whatever nature arising from any act, omission or negligence of Tenant or Tenant's contractors, licensees, agents, servants or employees or arising from any accident, injury or damage occurring outside of the premises but within the building complex, where such accident, damage or injury results or is claimed to have resulted from an act or omission on the part of Tenant or Tenant's agents or employees of Tenant's independent contractors.

This indemnity and hold harmless agreement shall include indemnity against all cost, expenses and liabilities incurred in or in connection with any and such claim or proceeding brought thereon, and the defense thereon.

LESSEE'S RIGHT OF TERMINATION: Notwithstanding anything hereinbefore to the contrary, and notwithstanding the provisions of the paragraphs under the heading "Fire", if, during the term of this Lease or any extension thereof, the demised premises shall be damaged by fire or other casualty and as a result thereof, the Lessee is unable to continue its operations or there is a substantial interference with the Lessee's business for a period of thirty (30) days, the Lessee may, for a period of thirty (30) days following the thirty day period, give notice to the Lessor of the Lessee's election to terminate this Lease, with termination shall take effect as of the date of said notice of termination with the same course and effect as if such date were the date original established as the expiration date of this Lease.

IN WITNESS WHEREOF, the said Lessee has duly executed this Instrument and the said Lessor has caused its corporate seal to be hereto affixed and the same to be signed by its clerk, as of this day and year first above written. This Instrument may be executed in any number of counterpart copies, each of which counterpart copies shall be deemed an original for all purposes.

(NAME)

LESSOR   LESSEE

By:_____   By: _____

Assignment of Lease as Collateral Security

The parties, hereby, agree that in the event of default under the terms, provisions and conditions of the Promissory Note, Sales and Escrow Agreement and/or Security Agreement, and in addition to the remedies provided for therein, the Buyer shall at Seller's option, transfer and/or assign to Seller all of its rights, title and interest under a Lease Agreement

with_____ dated_____, 20__.

Dated this_____ day of _____ 20__.

_____   _____

(Buyer)   (Seller)

_____

Witness to All

CONSENT TO ASSIGNMENT AS COLLATERAL SECURITY

For value received, the undersigned (Landlord), Lessor, hereby consent to the above assignment and grant to (Selling Entity) holders of said Promissory Note, Escrow Agreement, Security Agreement the right of substitution of a third party in the event of default in the terms and/or conditions of said Promissory Note or Lease. This assignment shall become null and void when all of the obligations of the said Promissory Note have been paid in full to the holder thereof. In the event a default occurs under the terms and conditions of the lease, the Lessor agrees to give said WRITTEN notice within ten (10) days thereafter by certified mail in order that the same may be cured.

Dated this _____ day of _____, 20___.

_____

Landlord

_____

Witness

ASSIGNMENT OF LEASE

Dated this _____ day of _____, 20___.

The Undersigned Lessee(s) in that certain lease covering the premises occupied by

that business known as_____

and located at _____

does hereby sell, assign, and transfer all our rights title and interest in and to the

said Lease, to _____ (Assignee(s)), upon
transfer of said business to said assignee(s).

_____   _____

Witness   Lessee

ASSUMPTION OF LEASE

In consideration of the above Assignment and written consent of the Lessor(s) thereto, I
(we) hereby assume and agree to be bound by all of the terms and conditions of the said
Lease which the Lessee(s) therein agreed to be made and performed, and to pay the rental
therein provided.

_____   _____

Witness   Assignee

CONSENT TO ASSIGNMENT

The undersigned Lessor(s) hereby consent to the above Assignment of Lease waiving none
of our (my) rights thereunder as to the Lessee(s) or Assignee(s), and with the
understanding that this Consent to Assignment is contingent upon the approval of the
above Assignee and the transfer of the above mentioned business to said Assignee.

_____   _____

Witness   Lessor

AUTHORIZATION TO SUBLEASE

This sublease made this (Date written out) Authority is hereby granted (Lessee), d/b/a (Business Name) to sublease the property located at:

(Center address)

to (Name and Address of Sub Lessee) of (Address).

It is understood and agreed that all conditions of the original lease remain unchanged and that the present use shall continue unchanged.

_____

Tenant

_____

Sub Tenant

_____

Lessor

_____

Date

Lease Extention

The undersigned Lessor(s) and Lessee(s), of that lease dated <Date> and expiring <Date> and covering property housing <Business Name> agree to amend said lease as follows:

a) It is hereby agreed that the Lessor(s) grants Lessee(s) <Number> <Number Years> options to renew said lease. Lessee(s) shall notify Lessor(s) within <#Days> of the
        expiration of each option period by registered mail to Lessor(s) notice address of his desire to exercise said option. If Lessee(s) should elect to exercise his options he will be bound by all the terms and conditions of said lease.

b) The monthly rent for the above options will be agreed to at the time and in the event of Lessee(s) exercise (ing) the options. In the event a mutually agreeable rent cannot be established, the monthly rental is to be determined by a majority of three rental agents. One appointed by Lessor(s), one appointed by Lessee(s), and the third by the appointees.

Lessee _____   Witness _____

Lessor _____   Witness _____

Date _____

Exit Strategies

Many resources address making money. Few, if any, can show you how to create value and wealth with your business. This unique book and software combination is based upon *actual in the field experience and not pedantic theory*. The book gives you scores of proven methods and tips aimed at increasing the value of and creating wealth with your business.

Buy a Business

This practical guide, written in understandable "shirt sleeve" language, simplifies a very complex subject. The book focuses upon the motivations and perceptions that drive a sale and the software "crunches the numbers." Case studies and examples are provided to illustrate every major point.

Investigate a Business

The real earnings are not found on the bottom line - they are hidden between the lines. Learn to use Actual IRS Agents Audit Methods to Expose the Real Earnings of any Private business. This Book and Software combination has been expressly created for the non-financial entrepreneur or executive engaged in buying or selling Private Companies.

Broker Businesses

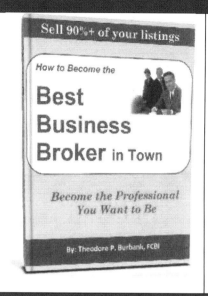

This New Book and Software Package Provides Step by Step Instructions detailing How to Become the Best Business Broker in Town or *How to sell essentially every listing you take (9+ of 10)* Created especially for Business Brokers, and others Selling Businesses

Business Transfer Documentation

Book of Samples plus CD - Transaction documentation - All the documents needed to Buy, Sell or Merge a Private company are on this easy to use CD. Find the "just right" document quickly and easily. Added Bonus - hundreds of contingency and special wording to address any situation that may arise.

Business Valuation

Reveals the previously unwritten rules for Transaction Valuations of private businesses. *The book explains and the software calculates the impact that limited or restrictive financing has on value and transaction structure.* Calculate the right price and terms for any private businesses sale.

Comprehensive Packages

Business Broker's Selling System - for business brokers

How can our *Business Selling* System methods be so superior to those employed by the majority of business brokers and essentially all Business Brokerage Franchisors? This nine part book and software package reveals the secrets to being able to sell essentially every listing you take.

Wealth Creation and Business Selling System - for business owners and their advisors

Scores of resources are available to help small businesses become more profitable but virtually none on how to make a small business more valuable. This eight part book and software combo will show you how to use Public company wealth creation techniques to build extraordinary wealth in your family businesses

Business Buying System - for business buyers

How to determine the business that's just right for you. Then, how to find it and buy it even if it's not for sale! Profit from the experience and insight gained in negotiating more than two thousand business transfers. This practical six part guide, written in understandable "shirt sleeve" language, simplifies a very complex subject. The book focuses upon the motivations and perceptions that drive a sale and the software "crunches the numbers." Case studies and examples are provided to illustrate every major point.

Sell a Business Software
Companion Software to the book
"The Complete Guide to Selling Your Business for the Most Money"

Visit
www.buySellBiz.com
for detailed information
regarding the software

Books and Software from Parker-Nelson Publishing – for more information go to

BuySellBiz.com